Social Mobility
and
Social Class in Ireland

Richard Breen
and
Christopher T. Whelan

GILL & MACMILLAN

Gill & Macmillan Ltd
Goldenbridge
Dublin 8
with associated companies throughout the world
© Richard Breen and Christopher T. Whelan 1996
0 7171 2055 4
Print origination by Typeform Repro, Dublin
Printed by ColourBooks Ltd, Dublin

A catalogue record is available for this book from the
British Library.

Contents

Acknowledgements

The account of social class and social mobility in Ireland which we provide in this volume is based on an analysis of the Survey of Income Distribution, Poverty and Usage of State Services, undertaken by The Economic and Social Research Institute in 1987, and we would like to acknowledge our debt to Brendan Whelan and the staff of the ESRI Survey Unit.

Earlier versions of some of the material presented in this volume have appeared in *Acta Sociologica,* the *European Sociological Review* and *Sociology.* We are grateful to the editors and referees of these journals for their comments and suggestions. We have also benefited from the opportunity of presenting our work at meetings organised by the European Consortium for Sociological Research and the Social Stratification Committee of the International Sociological Association. Tony Fahy and Philip O'Connell at the ESRI have been generous in the time they have taken to comment on early drafts. Furthermore, the influence of earlier work with David Rottman is obvious throughout the volume.

The support staff at both the ESRI and Queen's University have been unfailingly helpful throughout the project and we would like to acknowledge in particular Phil Browne, Pat Hopkins, Pat Hughes and Maura Rohan.

Richard Breen wishes to thank the Nuffield Foundation for financial support under Grant Soc 100(75) during the preparation of this book.

1 Perspectives on Social Mobility

INTRODUCTION

In Ireland class distinctions are thought of as a typically English phenomenon. The popular impression is that rigid social class demarcation was left behind with the ending of landlordism and the demise of the Anglo-Irish ascendancy. It is true that class boundaries in Ireland are less ritualised, or less marked by cultural difference, than in some other countries. This has encouraged the notion that we are a classless society. Our somewhat unenviable task requires us to argue that, contrary to popular belief, class barriers in Ireland are substantially more rigid than in other countries.

'Class', as we intend to use the term, does not necessarily imply either snobbishness or deference. We have something more pervasive and fundamental in mind. Individuals are located within a framework of social power of which they may, or may not, be aware. Their position of social power derives from the resources they possess to enable them to undertake particular actions and the constraints on so doing which they face (Breen and Rottman, 1995a, p. 14). Class is one such dimension of social power: other possible dimensions are race, gender and nationality. Social power based on class position derives from relationships within labour markets and production units. (Sorenson 1991, p. 72). For example, Goldthorpe (1982, 1987) develops a class schema which is based, first on the differentiation between ownership and non-ownership of the means of production, and, within the latter, between the long-term relationships of trust and commitment which are characteristic of the situation of professional and managerial employees, and labour contract arrangements defined in terms of a very specific exchange of wages for effort, which typify the situation of manual workers.

1

This manner of conceptualising class does not build income or life-style differences into the definition. However the centrality of class as an explanatory concept in sociology derives from a conviction that 'the work individuals do remains the most significant determinant of the life-fates of the majority of individuals and families in advanced industrial societies'. (Crompton, 1993, p. 120). Clearly we anticipate that class will be associated with income and wealth differences, but the impact of class normally goes well beyond these to encompass the extent to which groups are able to take advantage of available rewards and avoid deprivations. The term 'life chances' has been used to refer to 'the opportunities people have of sharing in the economic and cultural goods which exist in the society' (Giddens, 1973, pp. 103-131). Differences in economic resources are clearly fundamental but if we are to develop an appreciation of the pervasive nature of class differences it is necessary to take into account the manner in which class inequalities feed off each other. Class groups share not just economic position but a web of social relationships, attitudes and values. We are faced with not merely sets of individuals carrying out similar jobs but definite groups with a recognisable social identity. This point can be developed by looking at the consequences of inequalities in work experiences. A great deal of work is organised in a manner which minimises opportunities for the use of skills. Methods of control and/or supervision are chosen so as to eliminate the uncertainty arising from the exercise of choice by workers. The work situation has a dual significance: not only may certain kinds of labour be dehumanising, but habitual exposure to such conditions stultifies the workers' capabilities to be flexible, sensitive and creative in other areas of their lives. Thus research in Ireland has shown that unskilled manual workers are least likely to develop the kind of leisure activities and relationships between work and home life, which allow for the full enjoyment of retirement (Whelan and Whelan, 1988). Deprivations at work are not compensated for by life outside the work situation. Instead they spill over into the relations between workers and their families.

It is not only work experience which contributes to the creation of social classes characterised by distinctive life-styles. The emergence of such groups is mainly due to restricted ties of kinship, friendship and neighbourhood that cross the lines of class division. The infrequency of such ties is, in large part, a consequence of barriers to class mobility, both across generations and within an individual's lifetime. While, in one important sense, classes must be conceived of as sets of structural positions rather than the individuals who occupy these positions, the translation of such 'economic relationships' into 'non-economic' social structures is mediated by the distribution of mobility chances. The significance of social class for the distribution of life chances is crucially influenced by the extent to which institutional arrangements exist which produce a fairly high degree of continuity in the position of family units across generations (Giddens, 1973). What matters is not so much the degree of equality or inequality in chances of access to a particular class *per se* but the outcome of those activities in terms of the composition of classes. In other words what is crucial is 'the extent to which classes acquire a demographic identify — that is become identifiable as collectivities through the continuity with which individuals and families retain their class position over time'(Goldthorpe, 1982, pp. 171–2). In order to move from the structure of class positions in societies to an understanding of class norms, values and behaviour, it is necessary to take into account the process of class formation. Inequalities of mobility opportunities are not just one additional inequality but are a central mechanism through which classes 'acquire a socio-cultural identity — that is become identifiable through the shared and distinctive life-styles of their members and their pattern of preferred association' (Goldthorpe, 1982, pp. 171–2).

It is important to be clear that the emergence of groups with distinct life-styles is not dependent on the class and status evaluations of the members of such groups. Giddens (1973, p. 165) makes the useful distinction between class 'awareness' and 'class consciousness'. Class awareness involves a shared awareness and acceptance of a common style of life among the members of a class; it does not imply recognition that the attitude, beliefs and styles of life which members of this class have in common signify a particular class affiliation, that there are other classes with different attitudes, beliefs and patterns of behaviour. Class consciousness, on the other hand, implies both of these. Indeed, as Giddens notes, class awareness in the case of the middle-class might involve the 'denial of the existence of reality of classes' (Giddens, 1973, p. 111).

The importance of differences in life-styles which cannot simply be 'read off' from material inequalities is evident in relation to basic life chances. In the most literal sense of life chances the relatively favourable health situation enjoyed by professional and managerial workers, in comparison with those in the unskilled working class, cannot be explained solely by income and work environment influences. Life-style factors relating to, amongst other things, diet and cigarette smoking play a significant part (Blaxter, 1990; Nolan, 1990, 1991). Similarly, the superior educational performance of their children is, at least in part, due to parental aspirations and support. An adequate explanation of the manner in which objective conditions are translated into action requires that we take into account the mediating role of forms of consciousness. However the precise role of constraint and choice remains one of the central issues in sociology. For those who continue to adhere to an approach which stresses the rational choice of actors, the necessary reservation that must be entered seems to be that 'what counts as "rational" depends upon the social relationships in which actions are embedded (see Granovetter, 1985) and on the values and preferences which actors hold' (Breen and Rottman, 1995b). For our present purposes the crucial point which we wish to make is the role which social closure associated with restrictions on social mobility plays in shaping such relationships, values and preferences, and consequently, in producing the reality of distinctive life-styles which make class distinctions as valuable to the marketing practitioner as to the sociological theorist.

INDUSTRIALISATION AND SOCIAL MOBILITY

If many people are uncomfortable in thinking about the Republic of Ireland as a class society it may in part be due to their sense that economic change over the past thirty years has involved what Hout (1989, p. 315) refers to as a process of 'creative destruction' in which the old order is crushed and the creation of a new one brings an historic enlargement of opportunity. It is true that 'few societies have changed so rapidly and radically as has the Republic of Ireland since 1960. Success in the form of state initiatives to promote industrialisation brought a more general promise than that the fruits of independence would finally be realised. The associated expectations and excitement were captured in the catch phrase of the 1960s "the rising tide that would raise all boats" ' (Breen *et al.*, 1990, p. 1).

Such a sanguine view of the relationship between economic growth and social mobility was until recently shared by the majority of sociologists. High levels of mobility in industrial societies were considered to be a consequence of a 'fundamental trend' in all such societies towards universalism — that is towards the application in all aspects of social life of standards of judgment or decision making which derive from considerations of rationality and efficiency and which are detached from the particular values or interests of different membership grounds (Blau and Duncan, 1967). Industrial societies generate the drive towards technological and economic advancement, creating a demand for an increasing number of higher-level workers. Furthermore the family enterprise gives way to the bureaucratic organisation with its formal methods of selection, with education becoming a more significant determinant of occupational position than occupational inheritance. The central question for American researchers, operating from the perspective of 'status attainment', concerned the relative importance of ascription and achievement. A stable industrial society was seen to require that greater emphasis be placed on *what* one is rather than *who* one is or who one knows. Furthermore one is to be judged by 'universalistic' criteria such as educational attainment. Ascription is replaced by achievement. 'Nepotism and the "old school tie" must give way to publicly demonstrable merit' (Heath, 1981, p. 44).

Despite the confident nature of such conclusions regarding the relationship between economic growth, industrialisation and social mobility, Goldthorpe (1985, p. 554) concludes that the evidence on which they are based is 'confused and uncertain'. In the literature of the late 1950s and 1960s the discussion of mobility in industrial societies was linked to the question of whether American society was distinctive in the amount of mobility it displayed. The conclusion reached by Lipset and Bendix (1959) and Blau and Duncan (1967) was that economically advanced societies had *in common* a level of mobility which was, by any reckoning, high. The explanation of these strikingly similar 'total vertical mobility rates' was sought by Lipset and Bendix in factors universal to industrial societies. Of particular importance was the change in the number of available positions and the trend towards universalism. However, as Goldthorpe notes, these two processes direct attention to two rather different aspects of mobility. Emphasis on shifts in occupational structure directs attention to overall or absolute rates of mobility. On the other hand highlighting the trend towards universalism leads to a focus on relative rates, i.e. the comparison of absolute rates across different groups. The accumulation of evidence from the Comparative Analysis of Social Mobility (CASMIN) project (see Erikson and Goldthorpe, 1992a), which overcame many of the problems associated with previous work on comparative mobility, demonstrates that relative rates of mobility show only modest variation across time. Consequently substantial increases in absolute mobility associated with economic development are most likely to arise from structural effects. However as Goldthorpe (1985, pp. 558–9) stresses, such effects are exerted in different ways. One basic distinction is between 'shift' and 'compositional' effects. Shift effects refer to consequences of change in the 'shape' of the structure within which mobility is being observed. A decline in the number of farmers and an increase in the number of professional workers pushes people out of the former class and into the latter. Compositional effects arise from the fact that different classes have different inherent propensities for immobility. For example, people are much less likely to remain intergenerationally stable in the routine non-manual class than in the skilled manual class. Three main conclusions arise from the CASMIN analysis:

- absolute rates are a good deal more variable than relative rates;
- while shift effects are often generated by economic development, the importance of shift effects can vary enormously;
- there is no evidence that shift effects on mobility will steadily increase with economic development or that their importance is closely correlated with prevailing rates of economic growth.

Goldthorpe (1985, p. 560) argues, that in attempting to understand the consequences for social mobility, it is necessary to pay much more attention than has been the norm to variations in the speed rhythm and phasing of such change. This, as we shall see, certainly turns out to be true in the Irish case.

A CLASS STRUCTURAL PERSPECTIVE ON SOCIAL MOBILITY

The differences between Goldthorpe and authors such as Blau and Duncan go beyond the interpretation of particular historical changes and are associated with fundamentally different perspectives on the nature of social mobility. The status attainment perspective focuses on the manner in which individuals move up and down a series of stratification ladders. For those who follow this tradition, mobility refers to the movement of individuals as between social groupings or aggregates, that are ranked according to such criteria as their members' prestige, status or economic resources, i.e. within some form of *social hierarchy*. An alternative tradition envisages mobility as occurring between social positions that are located within *class structure* positions that are identified in terms of relationships within labour markets and production units.

From a class structural perspective, one of the limitations of analysing mobility in terms of movement up or down a prestige scale is that occupations as different as skilled manual industrial workers and small proprietors, or industrial labourers and farmers, may be attributed very similar scores. Thus major shifts, such as those arising from a decline in the agricultural sector involving the movement of small farmers and their offspring into the industrial working class, cannot be captured within this approach. 'Occupational groupings that are treated as equivalent will, in fact, often be ones that are affected in quite different ways by, for example, shifts in demand, technological innovation, or the policies of national governments and may thus be following, within the overall course of national development, quite divergent trajectories of expansion or decline' (Erikson and Goldthorpe, 1992a, p. 310). While it remains possible to address questions relating to individual attainment within a class perspective, other issues relating to the effects on mobility of patterns of economic development and political intervention, and in turn, the consequences of social mobility for class formation and action are brought into account. From this perspective social inequalities display no inevitable tendency to decline. Nor, to the extent that they are resistant to change, is this understood to be an inevitable consequence of the functional requirement of motivating individuals to enter and perform effectively in positions; or simply as an outcome of hierarchical imperatives in organisations (Davis and Moore, 1990). Instead, it is necessary to allow for the capacity of dominant groups to use their resources to preserve an existing state of affairs (Erikson and Goldthorpe, 1992, pp. 393–4).

THE ANALYSIS OF SOCIAL MOBILITY IN IRELAND

In this volume we draw on data from the Survey of Poverty, Income Distribution and Usage of State Services carried out by The Economic and Social Research Institute, Dublin in 1987. Until these data became available, analysis of social mobility in Ireland had been based on data sources which do not take us beyond the early 1970s (Breen and Whelan, 1985; Erikson and Goldthorpe, 1987a, 1987b, 1992a; Hout, 1989; Hout and Jackson, 1986; Whelan and Whelan, 1984). There are obvious limitations imposed by reliance on such data in order to assess the impact of industrialisation on social mobility in Ireland.

• The changes in class structure which occurred throughout the 1970s and 1980s were just as substantial as those occurring in the 1950s and 1960s. Thus between 1971 and 1985, the proportion of males working in agriculture fell from one third to one fifth while the number at work in non-manual occupations rose from three out of ten to four out of ten.

• Employment creation in the 1970s has a particularly distinctive features. By far the largest area of employment growth was in services: the numbers in employment grew by 136,000 between 1971 and 1981. However the bulk of these (85,000) jobs was in the public sector (Sexton, 1982, p. 36). Furthermore while on the surface the relationship between economic growth and occupational change looks rather similar for the 1960s and 1970s, somewhat different causal processes were involved. In the 1960s there was a small net change in employment, the decline in agriculture being offset by the growth in manufacturing and the public sector. In the 1970s growth in manufacturing and building slackened and the government responded through measures intended to give extra impetus to economic growth through the use of the public sector as the vehicle for the creation of jobs.

• During the 1960s and 1970s the role of manpower policy was seen to be in training the labour force and generally facilitating the efficient matching of the supply of and demand for labour. In the mid 1970s employment subsidies were introduced, as were training and temporary employment schemes, to combat unemployment. In the 1980s, manpower policy had, to all intents and purposes, become employment policy.

• By the early 1970s it was not yet possible to observe the effects of the introduction of free education in 1967. In 1970, 70 per cent of all fifteen-year-old children were remaining in school. By 1985 this had risen to over 94 per cent.

• A further important difference between the early 1970s and the 1980s relates to the substantially higher rate of female labour-force participation, particularly of young married women. The treatment of women in mobility studies and class analysis more generally has become the subject of considerable debate in recent years. The ESRI survey conducted in 1987 allows us not only to deal comprehensively with this issue in relation to the situation of Irish women but also to contribute to a number of debates which have dominated international literature.

• Finally while in 1971, 6 per cent of males were unemployed, by 1985 this had risen to 20 per cent. Given that much of this unemployment involved long-term detachment from the labour-market, the issue of whether such change undermines the relevance of class analysis and requires us to start thinking in terms of the emergence of some kind of 'underclass' is one which has been the subject of much debate.

Overall then, in addition to providing an up-to-date treatment of a range of issues which have been raised in previous work on class mobility in Ireland, we will deal explicitly with the degree of stability and change in recent decades, the impact of occupational change and the increased participation of women in the labour force, and the challenge which large-scale and long-term unemployment presents for class analysis.

OUTLINE OF THE VOLUME

In Chapter 2 we deal with the context of class mobility including emigration and the changing occupational structure. Having provided an account of the conceptual basis of the class schema we employ and the procedures involved in implementing them, we will document the extent of social mobility in Ireland. At this point the analysis is extended to deal with class inflow and the associated issues of social closure and elite self-recruitment.

Chapter 3 focuses on class mobility chances. Here we turn away from *inflow* rates and their consequence for the composition of classes, and instead focus on *outflow* rates from origin classes and an assessment of the nature and strength of barriers to class mobility. In pursuing this we elaborate on the crucial distinction between absolute probability and relative mobility (or social fluidity) and spell out its relationship to the traditional distinction between structural and exchange mobility. In explaining patterns of social fluidity we adopt a rational choice approach which views social actors as utilising the resources available to them in order to make choices between differentially preferred alternatives. At this point, we provide a relatively informal account of a model which explains social fluidity in terms of the effects of firstly, the barriers to entry to agricultural classes; secondly, the effect of resources, desirability and barriers of a hierarchical nature; and thirdly, the effect of property ownership. From this perspective we provide an informal review of the nature of class competition in Ireland and an initial assessment of the extent of inequality of opportunity.

In Chapter 4 we discuss what is involved in formally testing models of the underlying mobility process. The term 'underlying' is used in an attempt to capture the fact that two or more mobility tables might involve identical patterns of inequalities of opportunities while, at the same time, involving different absolute levels of mobility because of different origin and destination class distributions. In order to allow for this we make use of log-linear models of mobility tables which allow us to distinguish between absolute and relative mobility and to test how well our models of the underlying process of social fluidity reproduce the observed pattern of results. Some recent criticism of developments in the analysis of social mobility has involved an implicit distaste for the use of sophisticated statistical methods, such as log-linear modelling. This criticism frequently presents itself in the guise of the 'plain man' who cuts through the distracting detail in order to deal with the central issues. Here we find ourselves in agreement with Goldthorpe's (1990, p. 414) unequivocal response.

'This position . . . is both mistaken and, so far as the future of the social sciences is concerned, a dangerous one. It is not in truth that of the "plain man" but rather and, even if unintentionally, the academic Luddite. The fact is that in regard to the analysis of mobility rates, log-linear modelling is not now something that one can simply take or leave . . . it is quite integral to any worthwhile understanding of what certain major *substantive* issues are.'

Where it is possible to present substantive findings without reference to statistical procedures, we will do so. In those cases where the nature of the argument makes it imperative to provide a statistical treatment of the material, we will attempt to do this in as non-technical a fashion as is possible, and in a way in which those who have followed the account of the underlying principles of such analysis set out in Chapter 4 should have no great difficulty in following. The main substantive issues covered in this chapter relate to the relative importance of property, hierarchy and agriculture in explaining the Irish pattern of social fluidity, the extent to which the importance of such factors change over time, and finally, the degree to which the Irish profile is distinctive and the possible explanations of any such distinctiveness.

Chapter 5 deals with, perhaps, the most controversial issue in present-day class analysis — the role of gender. The analysis confronts feminist critiques of the exclusion of women from mobility studies and the more general question of whether the appropriate unit of class analysis should be the family, the couple or the individual. These issues are analysed in light of the dramatic changes in women's participation in the labour force. The analysis deals with the relative importance of husbands' and wives' class positions for life-style and poverty outcomes. It goes on to address women's employment mobility, their mobility through marriage, and the analysis of 'complete' mobility tables where the decision as to which member of married couples should be included in the analysis is made on the basis of which one has the 'dominant' relationship to the labour-market. Finally, we provide an assessment of the extent to which the disadvantages suffered by women in the labour-market can be accounted for in class terms.

In Chapter 6 we look at the relationship between class origins, educational qualification and class position. The liberal theory of industrialisation (Kerr *et al.*, 1960; Parsons 1960, 1964, 1970; Treiman, 1970) predicted a weakening of the relationship between origin class and entry class and a strengthening of that between the latter and educational qualifications with a consequent weakening in the origin class/final class relationship. Society becomes increasingly meritocratic as a consequence of the functional necessities of industrial development. The class perspective on the other hand, while it accepts the increasing role of education in allocating people to positions, argues that education is far from being the only factor that plays this role, and further, that there may be at most only a very modest change in the origin class/class of entry/destination class relationships, and that the direction of such change is indeterminate. In contrast to the liberal theory of industrial development, this approach draws attention to the ability of those in positions of power and privilege to maintain their position against encroachment by outsiders even in the face of the functional requirements of industrial society and specific state policies that threaten them (Goldthorpe, 1985). The Irish case provides a particularly useful test of the liberal theory of industrialisation because industrialisation has been both recent and rapid. Because the data available to us spans the period of industrialisation, and the accompanying changes such as free education, they allow hypotheses about the changes consequent on industrialisation to be subjected to empirical test. It is to this end that our analysis in Chapter 6 is directed.

In Chapter 7 we deal with work — life mobility. In recent years a critique of standard mobility analysis in terms of 'parent to child relationships' has emerged. In this chapter we address the issues raised by this critique and look at the relationship between class origins and first job before going on to examine mobility from this point to class destination. Of particular interest is the degree to which work — life mobility continues to be shaped by class of origin. The analysis we present includes a comparison between Ireland and England which illustrates the need to understand work — life mobility in the context of its contribution to the overall pattern of social closure in the society.

A great deal of our interest in issues relating to class mobility is motivated by our belief that life chances are significantly related to class position. In recent years this assumption has been increasingly challenged and the argument has been advanced that class is an increasingly outmoded concept. In Chapter 8 we examine the relationship between class situation and a range of life chances which include access to economic resources, ability to avoid extreme economic strain, poverty, and ability to avoid physical and psychological ill-health. In addition we examine the challenge which the emergence of large-scale unemployment poses for proponents of class analysis. Increasingly the question has been raised of the extent to which these developments undermine the ability of class models to adequately portray and explain structured inequality. One response has been an increasing tendency by both the left and right to resort to 'underclass' explanations. Once again Ireland provides a particularly good testing ground for the ideas which have driven this debate. Our analysis in this chapter seeks to demonstrate the manner in which arguments that the unemployed fall *outside* the class structure undermine our ability not only to understand the dynamic of labour-market marginalisation, but also to develop an adequate appreciation of the consequences of such marginalisation for Irish society. Pursuing further the issue of long-term dynamics we show that the specific causal processes in generating class outcomes display a good deal of diversity.

Finally, in Chapter 9 we draw together our findings and provide an overview of the current state of knowledge on the cause, pattern and consequences of class mobility in Ireland.

2 The Changing Class Structure and the Scale of Social Mobility

THE CONTEXT OF SOCIAL MOBILITY

Emigration

Trends in social mobility are undoubtedly influenced by social and demographic patterns. In Ireland emigration has been a crucial factor. From the nineteenth century until the 1960s Irish society was characterised by high levels of emigration, late age at marriage, high rates of non-marriage and overall population decline. Emigration had a striking effect on the population's age structure. Overall about one-fifth of the persons born after the founding of the State and living in Ireland in 1951 had emigrated by 1961. However since emigration primarily occurred in the late teens and early twenties these age-groups experienced a particularly dramatic decline. Thus, of persons aged ten to nineteen in 1950, only about three-fifths remained in Ireland by 1961.

Emigration was selective not only of particular age-groups but also of particular social classes. O'Connell and Rottman (1992) estimate that 82 per cent of the Irish-born living in Britain had left school at the age of fifteen or earlier. The bulk of emigrants were from agricultural backgrounds — farm labourers, children of small farmers and the owners of small farms. Many had never had a job before emigrating and many others were unemployed. Against this background, the reversal which occurred in the 1960s was dramatic. The annual emigration rate fell from 2 per cent of the population in the 1950s to 0.6 per cent between 1961 and 1966. In the 1970s migration was in the opposite direction and the country experienced an inflow of 0.4 per cent per annum. Marriage rates began to rise in the 1960s and marital fertility to fall. As the National Economic and Social Council (1991) report on *The Economic and Social Implications of*

Emigration notes, the traditional stereotype of the Irish emigrant as a person who is largely unskilled, or at best, possesses rudimentary manual skills is supported by data contained in the 1954 *Commission on Emigration Report* relating to overseas emigration in the 1920s and 1940s, and it is unlikely that the occupational profile of emigrants changed during the 1950s. However from the 1960s onwards, when economic conditions began to improve, the nature of emigration changed. This was reflected in the changing sex composition of migration with a majority of females now being involved. By the mid 1980s the migratory flow appeared to be broadly representative of the structure of Irish society with less indication than in earlier periods of any marked predominance by any one particular social group (Sexton, 1991, pp. 82–4). Any slight imbalance which now exists appears to involve above average flows by those from higher social groups with the outflow rate among those with third level qualifications being significantly greater than the national average (Sexton, 1991, p. 255). The bulk of the recent emigrants have been young persons in transition from education who cannot secure a foothold in the labour force. Different factors are at work depending upon level of education. '. . . economic "push" factors appear to dominate the migration decisions of the more poorly-educated, while occupational status and "pull factors" appear to be more important in the decisions of the better-educated middle-class' (Sexton, 1991, p. 160).

Hout and Jackson (1986, p. 115) note that while there are many general discussions of the role of immigrants in the process of social mobility by contrast emigrants have received almost no attention. Emigration may affect not only the distribution of occupations, but also the dissimilarity between origins over time, and the associations between origins and destinations. The impact of emigration is likely to occur over relatively long periods of time and to operate through a variety of relatively complicated processes. In the absence of adequate information on the background of emigrants and returned emigrants, and of any means of offering definitive assessments of the impact of emigration on long-run economic development and levels of inequality in the society, it is impossible to measure the extent of such effects.

It is clear though that the return of large-scale emigration,together with the emergence of large-scale and long-term unemployment,in the 1980s took place in the context of an international labour-market which, unlike the 1950s, offered few opportunities for those without skills and qualifications. The consequences of recent mobility for working-class marginalisation in Ireland appear to be rather different from the past. The Sexton report showed that among school leavers the upwardly mobile middle-class had the greatest tendency to emigrate with the stable working-class being only half as likely to do so. Such mobility appears to be associated with achieving, or aiming for, quite elevated positions. One of the problems in estimating the impact of such emigration is that we lack sufficient evidence regarding the likelihood that such emigrants will return to professional and managerial positions. At the bottom of the class hierarchy the picture is somewhat clearer. The scale of emigration among the poorly-educated working-class is no longer sufficient to enable us to export our marginalised working-class. This group displays particularly low propensities to emigrate because the probability of their finding employment abroad is no greater than if they were to remain at home. The implications of this will be pursued later.

The Changing Class Structure

As we have stressed in earlier work, while the core processes which contributed to Ireland's changing class structure are typical, their sequencing was not (Breen *et al.*, 1990). Perhaps the most crucial processes inherent in all modern social structures that have a direct effect on the rate of social mobility are (i) changes in the number of available vacancies and (ii) changes in the number of inheritable status positions. The former focuses our attention on the fact that industrial societies are those which need increasing numbers of high-level workers in professional, managerial and administrative positions. The latter directs attention to the manner in which the family firm gives way to the bureaucratic enterprise, with its formal methods of selection, where education becomes a more significant determinant of occupational position than occupational inheritance. For Blau and Duncan (1967) the prevalence of high mobility in industrial societies stems from a 'fundamental trend' in such societies towards universalism — that is towards the application, in all aspects of social life, of standards of judgment and decision-making which derive from considerations of rationality and efficiency which are detached from the particular values or interests of different groups.

In Table 2.1, which draws on O'Connell and Rottman (1992) and O'Connell (1995), the pattern of class transformation for males over a period of forty years from the early 1950s is set out. Issues relating to women's mobility are dealt with separately in Chapter 5. In the early 1950s almost half of the male labour force worked in class categories which depended on property ownership. Professionals, managers and administrators numbered under 50,000 and represented a mere 5 per cent of the labour force. Only 10 per cent were skilled manual workers and a quarter were engaged in semi-skilled or unskilled manual work. O'Connell and Rottman (1992, p. 69), referring to the 46 per cent of the labour force who derived their income from property, concluded that: 'for the children of these individuals life chances centred on the prospects of inheriting the family business and the accompanying house and household goods. Realistically, education or training could secure a livelihood within Ireland for only a minority of those aspiring to the workforce'.

Not only emigration but marriage rates were determined by these social and economic realities. Farm-inheritors had quite high rates of marriage, non-inheritors had negligible rates and farm labourers had low rates. Those born into the lower portions of the class structure had quite rational expectations of impoverishment given the high fertility that would result from marriage. Given the dominance of small-scale family property in the economy, marriage decisions were largely determined by the timing and process of inheritance (Breen *et al.*, pp. 104–5).

While the decline in agricultural employment is crucial in promoting structural mobility, the actual pattern of decline and its association with other structural change may be quite variable (Goldthorpe, 1985, p. 561). In Ireland late and rapid industrialisation meant that a massive decline in agricultural employment could not be compensated for by alternative opportunities. Emigration filled the gap. The class structure today reflects the selective process of emigration to Britain as much as it does growth in new opportunities. Between 1926 and 1961 the percentage of gainfully occupied males in agriculture fell from 58 per cent to 43 per cent. While there was some growth in numbers among the non-manual middle-class and the non-agricultural working-class, a broad stability in the class structure was ensured by emigration which resulted in a decline in the total of gainfully occupied males from 950,000 to 820,000 over the same period.

After 1961 rapid change replaced stability. Between 1961 and 1990 males in agriculture, as a percentage of the total at work, fell from 44 per cent to 21 per cent. The upper middle-class group represented by professionals, managers and salaried employees, more than doubled between 1961 and 1981 by which time they comprised 16 per cent of males at work. This figure continued to climb, reaching 18 per cent in 1990. The lower middle-class increased somewhat less dramatically from a base of 16 per cent in 1961 to a peak of 20 per cent in 1981. Skilled manual work followed a similar pattern going from 12 per cent in 1961 to 21 percent in 1981 before falling back to 18 per cent by 1990. Non-skilled manual work showed a steady decline from 21 per cent in 1961 to 13 per cent in 1990; this decline was particularly sharp among agricultural workers. One significant change which was confined to the 1980s was the increase in non-agricultural employers and self-employed from less than 10 per cent to 14 per cent. The increase was particularly striking among the self-employed. Finally,and perhaps most significantly, the total unemployed as a percentage of the gainfully occupied increased from 6 per cent to 16 per cent.

Table 2.1: Males at Work by Class Categories 1951–1990

Employers and Self-Employed		1951	1961	1971	1981	1990
		%	%	%	%	%
Non-Agriculture		38.4	36.0	27.5	19.2	17.6
Employees						
(i)	Upper Middle-Class	5.3	7.6	10.9	16.0	18.1
(ii)	Lower Middle-Class	13.8	15.6	18.0	20.3	19.6
(iii)	Skilled Manual	10.1	12.0	16.5	20.3	17.9
(iv)	Semi-/Unskilled Manual					
	(a) Agricultural	10.6	8.4	5.2	3.2	3.3
	(b) Non-Agricultural	13.9	12.5	13.6	11.2	9.3
Toal at Work		100.0	100.0	100.0	100.0	100.0
Total Unemployed		3.7	5.7	6.6	10.1	15.5

Source: O'Connell and Rottman (1992; Table 1) and O'Connell (1995)

While on the surface the relationship between economic growth and change in the class structure since 1960 can be characterised in terms of the expansion of the white collar and skilled manual and *petit bourgeois* classes and the contraction of farming and non -skilled manual classes somewhat different causal influences were at work in each decade. The changes in the 1960s were associated with the response to economic stagnation involving a departure from earlier policies of protectionism and the pursuit of foreign investment and closer integration into the international economy. Late industrialisation in a peripheral economy does not transform the class structure in the manner experienced by the core group of advanced industrial societies. O'Connell and Rottman (1992, p. 213) stress, that while state industrial policies may have been instrumental in setting the class transformation in motion, state policies in other arenas proved equally, if not more influential, in reshaping the class structure. In the 1960s the decline in agricultural employment was offset by growth, particularly in manufacturing, though in the long term, the growth in manufacturing employment in Ireland proved to be modest. While manufacturing output rose almost fivefold between 1959 and 1988, employment in manufacturing increased by only one-quarter over the same period.

Over the last three decades while agricultural employment continued in its long-term decline, there was some increase in industrial employment and massive growth in employment in services. Three overarching trends accompanied these sectoral changes: an upgrading of the quality of positions in the labour-market, a marked expansion in public sector employment, and from the mid 1970s onward, a steady expansion in the ranks of the unemployed. The main underlying logic to the transformation these changes represent, however, is not the replacement of positions lost in agriculture, nor even the upgrading of skills within manufacturing. Instead the predominant shift is away from positions governed by pure market forces towards those dependent on state intervention. (O'Connell and Rottman, 1992).

The direct effect of state interventions in labour-markets was an increase in the public sector. Employment numbers in the state sector grew from 118,000 in 1961 to 235,000 in 1981 (Kennedy and McHugh, 1984). If state-sponsored bodies are included, by 1981 the public sector employed one-third of the non-agricultural labour force (Humphreys,1983, p. 88) Consistent with this is the fact that, throughout the 1960s and 1970s, the most striking expansion in opportunities for labour-market participation was observed among upper middle-class employees. Ireland's class structure is also distinctive in the degree to which it produced an expansion in the number of non-agricultural proprietors. Native entrepreneurs were encouraged by the substantial package of tax incentives, adaptation grants, advisory bodies, subsidised labour, and sectoral specific schemes. Self-employment has also been encouraged by attempts since the 1980s to reduce public sector employment which resulted in a substantial transfer of tasks to the private sector (O'Connell and Rottman, 1992, pp. 216–7)

THE EXTENT OF SOCIAL MOBILITY

Census data allow us to reconstruct the context within which the structural sources of mobility in Ireland evolved. However, there are limits to the conclusions which can be drawn on the basis of such data. Documentation of detailed patterns of mobility requires that we draw on survey data. The most recent source of such data is the Survey of Income Distribution and Usage of State Services carried out by the Economic and Social Research Institute in 1987. This survey was designed to provide a national sample from the population of the Republic of Ireland resident in private households. The data available from this survey are particularly suitable for examining the implications of the appropriate unit of analysis in mobility research: i.e. should the focus be on households or on individuals, on all individuals or on men only? The difficulties raised by these questions involve complex issues of conceptualisation and measurement to which we will devote considerable attention. For the moment though, in order to provide a broad overview of what we consider to be the defining characteristics of the class mobility process in Ireland, and to facilitate comparisons across time and across countries, we focus our attention on male mobility. We also follow the normal practice in mobility studies of restricting our attention to those aged between twenty and sixty-five. Our initial analysis will therefore be based on a weighted nationally representative sample of such men. Our comparisons across time and country will be facilitated by the availability of data from the Comparative Analysis of Social Mobility in Industrial Societies (CASMIN) project. (Erikson and Goldthorpe,1992). This data set also includes data for Ireland collected in 1973 (Hout,1989).

Classes and Classification Concepts

Up to this point the class categories we have used have involved aggregations of CSO occupational categorisations. We have acted as if the measurement of social class is relatively problem free. In fact there are a variety of approaches to the conceptualisation and measurement of social class and findings in relation to social mobility make sense only when the assumptions underlying the measurement process are understood. It is not our intention in this book, however, to provide an assessment of the varying approaches. (See Breen and Rottman, 1995a). Instead we will concentrate on spelling out the theoretical underpinnings of our preferred approach.

Our analysis of the social mobility process in Ireland draws on Goldthorpe's model of the mobility process. Goldthorpe (1980/87, p. 99) has suggested that the pattern of social fluidity is shaped by three factors. These are the relative desirability of different class destinations; the resources available to individuals within each origin class which help them to gain access to more desirable destination classes; and barriers to movement between classes. Typically we think of resources as 'economic, cultural and social resources' (Erikson and Goldthorpe, 1987a, p. 64) while barriers to mobility would include the necessity to own the means of production, educational and other qualifications needed for entry into occupations that comprise a class grouping, and so forth.

The assignment of individuals to classes in the Goldthorpe schema entails a threefold procedure. Firstly, respondents are placed in occupational groups according to the content of their jobs; secondly, they are given an employment status that reflects their social relationships at work. In both cases the categories and definitions are those adopted in Britain by the Registrar General for the analysis of official statistics. Finally, a social class position is obtained by cross-classifying the relevant occupational and employment status (Marshall, 1990, p. 55). This manner of constructing the class schema involves a departure from the common assumption that an occupation is a work role and set of work tasks which can be identified independently of the economic relationships in which its incumbents are involved. The class categories provide a degree of differentiation in terms of both occupational function and employment status. Thus, for example 'self-employed plumber', 'foreman-plumber' and 'rank and file plumber' are treated as distinct. Since we lacked the resources to conduct a full assignment of occupations according to the British procedures, we mapped the Irish occupational codes on to the British 1970 Office of Population Censuses and Surveys scheme. Where we felt that an occupational code according to the Irish Census classification could not be unambiguously coded into the OPCS classification and that this could affect the respondents' ultimate allocation to a class category, coding was carried out on the basis of the original information contained in the questionnaire.

Goldthorpe's procedures bring together within a class category those positions whose incumbents are typically comparable in terms of their sources and levels of income, their degree of economic security, their chances of economic advancement and their degree of autonomy in performing work tasks. The classification is based on an understanding of the importance of the development of class relations within capitalist organisations and the nature of control in such organisations (Goldthorpe, 1982, Kurz and Mueller, 1987, pp. 421–2, Marshall, 1990).

Underlying the differences in conditions of employment is a more basic distinction in the nature of the employment relationship between different types of employee and their employer. Goldthorpe distinguishes between a service relationship, characteristically enjoyed by higher white-collar workers, and a labour contract, typical of working-class employees. As Breen and Rottman (1995b) put it — 'The greater rewards that accrue to the former are associated with the need for employers to engender long term relationships of trust and commitment with employees who, by virtue of their specialised knowledge or exercise of delegated authority, cannot be directly supervised (Erikson and Goldthorpe 1992, p. 42). By contrast, a

Table 2.2: *The Class Schema*

	Full Version		Seven-Class
I	Higher-grade professionals, administrators and officials; managers in large industrial establishments; large proprietors.	I + II	Service class; professionals, administrators and managers; higher-grade technicians; supervisors of non-manual workers.
II	Lower-grade professionals, administrators and officials; higher-grade technicians; managers in small industrial establishments; supervisors of non-manual employees.		
IIIa	Routine non-manual employees, higher grade (administration and commerce).	III	Routine non-manual workers; routine non-manual employees in administration and commerce; sales personnel; other rank-and-file service workers.
IIIb	Routine non-manual employees, lower grade (sales and services).		
IVa	Small proprietors, artisans, etc. with employees.	IV a + b	*Petit bourgeoisie:* small proprietors and artisans, etc. with and without employees.
IVb	Small proprietors, artisans, etc. without employees.		
IVc	Farmers and smallholders; other self-employed workers in primary production. (i) owning 100 acres or more (ii) owning 50–99 acres (iii) owning less than 50 acres.	IVc	Farmers: farmers and small-holders and other self-employed workers in primary production.
V	Lower-grade technicians, supervisors of manual workers.	V + VI	Skilled workers; lower-grade technicians; supervisors of manual workers; skilled manual workers.
VI	Skilled manual workers		
VIIa	(i) Semi-skilled manual workers (not in agriculture, etc.).	VIIa	Non-skilled workers; semi- and unskilled manual workers (not in agriculture, etc.).
VIIb	Agricultural and other workers in primary production.	VIIb	Agricultural labourers: agricultural and other workers in primary production.

directly supervised (Erikson and Goldthorpe 1992, p. 42). By contrast, a labour contract involves a very specific exchange of wages for effort.'

Thus the organising principle of the Goldthorpe schema is the nature of employment relationships rather than the content of the work tasks or work roles and the key feature of this employment relationship is the way in which commitment is obtained from the work force. 'In simple terms one could say that the service class employees are controlled by the "carrot" of long-term benefits and workers by the "stick" of close regulation and the labour contract' (Evans, 1992, p. 214)

The range of classes distinguished in the CASMIN class schema is set out in Table 2.2 The most detailed classification distinguishes eleven classes. Frequent use is also made of the seven class schema which is also reproduced in Table 2.2. At various points in the analysis that follows a few further distinctions are made: the first involves separating the semi-skilled manual group from the unskilled manual, while the second involves breaking down farmer groups into three categories on the basis of farm size.

MOVEMENT AND STABILITY

The degree of mobility that is observed in any society depends on the number, size and character of the class categories distinguished. A comparison of the Irish situation in 1973 and 1987 leads to the conclusion (which holds across different versions of the class schema) that there has been a significant increase in the level of absolute social mobility in Ireland — that is to say, in the proportion of men who have moved out of the social class into which they were born. In the case of the seven class schema the rise is from 58 per cent to 63 per cent; or in other words the percentage remaining immobile in their class of origin declined from 42 per cent in the 1973 data to 37 per cent in the 1987 data. Of other western societies in the 1970s, only Sweden displays a decisively higher level.

These figures clearly demonstrate that class societies are quite different from caste societies. Class is most certainly not fixed at birth. However, for a good deal of the movement involved in the seven class schema it is difficult to characterise it as 'upward' or 'downward'. Therefore in order to pursue the issue of the extent of such movement we aggregate the seven classes into three classes in the following manner.

Professional and Managerial Class: Classes I + II

The Intermediate Class: Classes III + IV + V

The Working-Class: Classes VI + VII

In Table 2.3 we show both the overall level of mobility in the 1987 data using this schema and a range of indicators of upward and downward mobility. In each case the comparable outcome for England and Wales in the 1970s is reported.

Employing this classification it emerges that 43 per cent of Irish men had been mobile across these boundaries compared with slightly less than 50 per cent of the English respondents. This difference is almost entirely due to the higher probability of upward mobility into the professional and managerial class in England where over 17 per cent had managed this transition — almost 5 per cent more than in Ireland. In both countries the percentage mobile out of the working-class is almost double that into it. There is little difference in the percentage of those with professional and managerial origins found in the working-class — 1 per cent in Ireland and 2 per cent in England. Ireland thus shares with other industrial societies a high level of social mobility but appears to be characterised by relatively strong barriers to mobility into the service class. The nature of these barriers will be explored further in the chapter that follows. At this point, however, we turn to a discussion of social closure.

Table 2.3: Absolute Mobility: Three Class Classification
(figures in parentheses relate to England and Wales, 1972)

%			
%	Mobile	43.3	(49.3)
%	Mobile into the Professional and Managerial Class	12.5	(17.3)
%	Mobile from the Working-Class to the Professional and Managerial Class	6.5	(8.3)
%	Mobile from the Professional and Managerial Class into the Working-Class	1.1	(2.1)
%	Mobile in to and out of the Working-Class	34.9	(36.8)
%	Mobile out of the Working-Class	22.5	(23.0)
%	Mobile into the Working-Class	12.3	(13.8)

CLASS COMPOSITION: SOCIAL CLOSURE AND ELITE SELF-RECRUITMENT

By social closure we mean the extent to which the highest classes are based on self-recruitment. The primary focus of social closure theorists has been on the effect of strategies of exclusion on the composition of elite groups.

Here the basic thesis is that since self-recruitment plays such a major role, and external recruitment involves mobility of a predominantly short-range kind, elite groups will contain no more than a negligible proportion of working-class men. Elite groups will be particularly homogeneous in the social origins of their members. This argument is one which must be settled in terms of the absolute number of individuals who have been mobile into the elite category rather than in terms of the extent of inequality of opportunity. This is so because the composition of a class is affected not just by how open a society is, when viewed in terms of relative mobility opportunities, but also by changing structural conditions which affect the size of the elite group. To summarise, what matters is not so much the degree of inequality in class mobility chances but the outcome of those chances in terms of class composition. The relevant data relate to the 'inflow' to the elite category from the various origin categories.

Table 2.4: Comparative Inflow Rates: Percentage in Selected Classes from Different Class Origins

% of the Professional, Administrative and Managerial Class (I + II) originating in				% of the Industrial Class (V/VI + VIIa) originating in			
Industrial Working Class (V/VI + VIIa)		*Agricultural Classes (IVc + VIIb)*		*Industrial-Working Class (V/VI + VIIa)*		*Agricultural Classes (IVc + VIIb)*	
England	45	Poland	34	England	74	Hungary	46
FRG	41	Hungary	25	FRG	65	Poland	46
Sweden	40	Ireland 1973	23	Ireland 1987	63	Sweden	32
Poland	35	Ireland 1987	18	Ireland 1973	57	France	29
Hungary	32	Sweden	17	Sweden	51	Ireland 1973	27
Ireland 1987	32	France	10	France	47	Ireland 1987	24
Ireland 1973	28	FRG	8	Poland	42	FRG	16
France	28	England	4	Hungary	39	England	7

Source: Whelan, Breen and Whelan (1992: p. 14).

In Table 2.4 we present selected inflow rates for Ireland for 1973 and 1987 and provide cross-national comparisons using the CASMIN seven-class schema. The results show that in relation to the professional and managerial class in Ireland, the most striking feature is not the extent of social closure but the degree of heterogeneity of the origins from which the groups are drawn. If we define the industrial working-class as comprising lower-grade technicians and supervisors of manual workers and all grades of non-agricultural manual workers we find that almost one in three of the service class is drawn from this class. This figure is slightly higher than that for 1973 and is similar to other countries, such as Poland and Hungary which possess large agricultural sectors. Ireland is distinctive among western European countries in having a relatively high inflow to the service class of men from the agricultural classes. These account for just less than one in five of that class in 1987 compared to just less than one in four in 1973. Self-recruitment in the service class accounts for only just over one in four of the service class or, put another way, over three-quarters of the class are recruited from outside. Given the class schema we have employed the notion of elite social closure does not appear to be one which is applicable to the Irish case.

Of course the conclusions that one draws regarding the extent of social closure will depend upon one's definition of elite. Just over one in six men are located in the service class and this may well be seen to constitute too large a group to provide a reasonable basis for testing the elite self-recruitment hypothesis. The higher professional, managerial and administrative component of the service class contains just over 6 per cent of the total group. Can our conclusions regarding heterogeneity be sustained when we focus on this group? Some slight modification of our position is indeed required. While self-recruitment accounts for just over one in five of the lower professional, managerial and administrative group this figure rises to just over one in three of the upper stratum. While the degree of exclusivity has increased, notions of elite closure cannot be sustained. Undoubtedly, with a sufficiently large sample, further differentiation within the upper reaches of the service class would reveal groups displaying higher levels of self-recruitment. However at this point it would seem likely that we would be dealing with occupational rather than class recruitment, and one suspects that a great deal of such detailed social closure involves not just elite occupations but the creation of elites within occupations. The evidence we have presented demonstrates clearly that, notwithstanding the inequalities in opportunity which we will document later, structural change has created room at the top for many who have their origins outside the upper reaches of the service class, with one in four of this group coming from the industrial working-class. Paradoxically, a preoccupation with the degree of closure at the peak of the class structure tends to lead to a neglect of the far greater homogeneity of origins which is evident among the working-class.

When we focus on the industrial working-class, an interesting point of comparison is the situation in England where this class forms a self-recruiting bloc in which three-quarters of its members may be reckoned as at least second generation. By 1987 in Ireland almost two-thirds were second generation even though almost one-quarter came from agricultural classes. Only in England is self-recruitment substantially higher — 80 per cent of the industrial working-class in Ireland are drawn either from that class or from the agricultural classes. Between 1973 and 1987 a significant increase in self-recruitment occurred, matched by a corresponding drop in recruitment from the *petit bourgeoisie*. Within the industrial working-class the percentage of skilled manual workers coming from farm backgrounds almost doubled — increasing from 10 per cent to 18 per cent. This change was particularly significant because the skilled manual group increased by close to 50 per cent during this period. In contrast the inflow from farm origins to the non-skilled manual group fell from 24 per cent to 16 per cent. The degree of homogeneity within the working-class is directly related to skill level; the figure for recruitment from the industrial working-class rises from 68 per cent for the skilled manual group to 77 per cent for the unskilled manual class. Within this overall categorisation further processes of segregation occur. While less than one in four skilled manual workers come from unskilled manual origins this rises to almost one in two for the current unskilled manual group. The extent of homogeneity at the bottom of the class structure is reflected in the fact that a mere 7 per cent of this group are drawn from outside the industrial working-class or the class of small farmers.

Farmers are also a critical group in relation to the *petit bourgeoisie* in Ireland with one-third of their members originating in this group. In this respect Ireland comes closest to Sweden and can be distinguished from England, which has a particularly large inflow from the industrial working-class, and France, where very high levels of self-recruitment are observed. Between 1973 and 1987 in Ireland a substantial decline was observed in the level of self-recruitment to the *petit bourgeoisie* accompanied by a corresponding increase in recruitment from the industrial working-class. In 1973 almost one in three men currently in *petit bourgeois* positions had been born into that class, compared to just less than one in six by 1987; the corresponding figures for inflow from the industrial working-class were one in five in 1973 and just less than two in five in 1987. Important differences, however, are observed between those members of the *petit bourgeoisie* who employ others and those without employees. Professional, managerial and *petit bourgeois* origins account for 28 per cent of the former but only 13 per cent of the latter; the corresponding figures for inflows from the unskilled manual working-class are 10 per cent and 17 per cent. It is important to note, however, that the distinction based on the existence of employees has little relevance for those from farming or skilled manual backgrounds.

The extremes in terms of class composition for men are provided by the farming class and the routine non-manual class. The former displays almost complete self-recruitment. The latter has a distribution in terms of composition which is extremely heterogeneous — 13 per cent can be described as experiencing self-recruitment but relatively similar numbers are drawn from the professional managerial class and the working-class.

CONCLUSIONS

The nature of the changes that took place in Ireland during the 1970s and the 1980s were such as to produce a convergence of the marginal distribution of the Irish class mobility table to a pattern not untypical of modern industrial societies. By 1987 the overall level of mobility in Ireland came close to the norm for western European societies. Class societies are far from being caste societies and, in 1987, and using the seven-class schema we find that almost two-thirds of men aged between twenty and sixty-four had been intergenerationally mobile.

In terms of class composition the Irish professional, managerial and administrative class had, in common with those in other countries, inflows of men from a heterogeneous set of origins. Even when attention is restricted to the higher stratum there is no support for the thesis of elite self-closure. The *petit bourgeoisie* in Ireland had, by 1987, also become a rather heterogeneous group in terms of origins with a significant decline in self-recruitment taking place accompanied by a substantial inflow from the industrial working class. The search for social closure at the peak of the class hierarchy has rather obscured the fact that it is among the working-class that striking levels of intergenerational stability can be observed.

3 Class Mobility Chances and Equality of Opportunity

CLASS MOBILITY AND OUTFLOW RATES: INTERNATIONAL
COMPARISONS AND TRENDS OVER TIME

When we focus on class mobility chances we must direct our attention away from *inflow* rates and their consequences in terms of class composition and, instead, focus our attention to *outflow* rates and the information they provide about the probability of men of given class origins being found in particular class destinations.

Once again the particular outflow rates we observe will depend on the number and type of classes we distinguish. In Table 3.1, in order to facilitate cross-national comparisons, we operate with the seven-class schema already employed in Chapter 2. The figures displayed in the table relate to selected outflow rates for a number of European countries including Ireland; and in the Irish case allow for comparisons of changes over time between 1973 and 1987. A remarkable degree of stability is shown across time in Ireland in the outflows from the professional, managerial and administrative class and in the extent of movement out of the industrial working-class. At both points in time just over one-half of those from service class origins had held their position in that class, with just above a fifth displaying downward mobility into the industrial working-class. These figures are quite typical of those for other western European countries in the early 1970s. When we focus on men from the industrial working-class we find that one in nine are located in the service class while seven out of ten have remained stable across generations. The Irish figures for immobility are comparatively high with only the FRG, of the western European countries reaching this level, and with Sweden coming eight percentage points lower. It is, however, the extremely low levels of long-range inter-generational upward mobility which gives the

28

Irish pattern a quite distinctive character. All of the other countries have outflows from the industrial working-class which are at least five percentage points higher and the corresponding figures for the FRG and Sweden are double that for Ireland. However, since the industrial working-class increased in Ireland from 40 per cent to 50 per cent of the total between 1973 and 1987 the absolute percentage experiencing such mobility has risen.

Table 3.1: Comparative Outflow Rates: Percentage of Those of Selected Class Origins Found in Different Classes

% of those of Professional, Administrative and Managerial Origins (I + II) found in				% of those of industrial working-class origins (V/VI + VIIa) found in			
Professional, Administrative and Managerial Class (I + II)		*Industrial Working-Class (V/VI + VIIa)*		*Professional, Administrative and Managerial Class (I + II)*		*Industrial Working-Class (V/VI + VIIa)*	
Poland	67	Hungary	34	FRG	22	Hungary	73
FRG	61	FRG	26	Sweden	22	Poland	71
France	60	Poland	25	Poland	21	FRG	69
England	59	Sweden	25	England	18	Ireland 1987	69
Sweden	56	England	22	France	17	Ireland 1973	68
Ireland 1987	56	Ireland 1987	22	Hungary	16	England	66
Ireland 1973	55	Ireland 1973	21	Ireland 1987	11	France	63
Hungary	52	France	21	Ireland 1973	11	Sweden	61

Source: Whelan, Breen and Whelan (1992, p. 116).

The picture of stability at the top and the bottom contrasts with the substantial changes observed in the mobility chances of those from *petit bourgeois* and farming origins. A major improvement took place in the chances of mobility to the service class for the sons of small employers: particularly so for those without employees. The percentage succeeding in making this transition rose from 30 per cent to 36 per cent for the former group and from 13 per cent to 36 per cent for the latter. The percentage remaining immobile in these classes dropped sharply and the flows to the non-skilled manual classes were halved ; in the case of the self-employed from one in four to one in eight. The outflows of sons of small employers is now broadly similar to that for France in the early 1970s. Those from self-employed origins, on the other hand, enjoy distinctively higher rates of upward mobility.

In the case of farmers, the most obvious shift over time is the decline in immobility, where the relevant figure drops from one-half to just over one-third. The percentage becoming agricultural labourers almost halved. This change was accompanied by a significant increase in the flows to the service class, but more particularly to the skilled manual class where the figure rose from 4 per cent to 14 per cent. Apart from sharing with France a relatively high level of immobility, those from farming origins also have a particularly low outflow to the non-skilled manual class. The Irish pattern of class mobility chances displays the following distinctive features.

- Opportunities for long-range upward mobility from the industrial working-class to the professional and managerial class are substantially lower than in other European countries.

- The advantages enjoyed by property-owning groups are significantly greater than is the case in other European countries.

ABSOLUTE AND RELATIVE MOBILITY

Absolute mobility rates refer to the proportion of individuals in some base category who are mobile. Such rates are easily expressed in the sort of percentage terms we have employed thus far. By contrast, relative rates are produced by comparisons of absolute rates. Such comparisons, may be across countries, time or socio-demographic groups.

The distinction between absolute and relative mobility rates arose originally from attempts to understand what were considered to be two rather different sorts of mobility, which have frequently been labelled **structural** and **exchange** mobility. Structural mobility relates to that share of inter-generational mobility that arises because of change over time in the class structure. Those originating in classes that are declining in number over time, such as farming, will be 'pushed' out of their class of origin. Similarly, as the professional managerial class expands dramatically many people from other class origins are 'pulled' into this class. The difference between origin class and destination class distributions has sometimes been taken as an indicator of the extent of such structural mobility. On the other hand, exchange mobility is considered to arise as a consequence of the differential advantages associated with different class origins that might be used to obtain access to desirable destinations i.e. inequalities of opportunity. Different origins are understood to confer varying chances of mobility because they provide people with differential resources for mobility. So people born into more advantaged classes are likely to benefit from access to higher levels of economic resources, to be more successful in acquiring educational qualifications, and in addition, are likely to be relatively favoured in terms of other resources (such as kinship or friendship networks) which facilitate access to desirable class positions. In the absence of structural mobility, changes in the pattern of exchange mobility would necessarily require both winners and losers, with increased upward mobility for those from lower classes being compensated for by greater downward mobility for others.

Attempts to disaggregate mobility in this fashion, however, involve assumptions about what the extent and pattern of social mobility might have been in the absence of structural change. In practice, it is implausible to assume that the factors which transform the class structure, such as the rate of economic growth, are unrelated to those which influence the pattern of exchange mobility, such as the nature of the educational system. It thus seems better to avoid the notion that mobility in any particular table can be divided into structural and exchange components. Instead it seems preferable to analyse both absolute mobility (that is the flows from one class to another) and relative mobility (how the chances of acquiring a position in a given destination class depend upon one's origin class).

Table 3.2:   Class Mobility Chances: A Comparison of the Service Class and Non-Skilled Manual Class

Class Origins	Service Class	Present Class Non-skilled Manual
	Per Cent	
Service Class	56.6	10.6
Non-skilled Manual	11.7	47.7

In order to develop the concept of relative mobility, it is necessary to deal with the notions of disparity and odds ratios. In Table 3.2 we display a section of the overall outflow or class mobility chances table showing the movement between the service class and the non-skilled manual class. A useful indicator of the advantage enjoyed by those from service class backgrounds over those with non-skilled manual origins in gaining access to the service class is provided by dividing 56.6 (the percentage of men from service class origins who are currently in the service class) by 11.7, (the percentage of men from the non-skilled manual class who are currently in the service class). This yields a ***disparity ratio*** of 4.85, meaning that those from service class backgrounds have that much greater chance of ending up in the service class than those from non-skilled manual backgrounds. Similarly, an index of the disadvantages experienced by the non-skilled manual class relative to the service class, with regard to current location in the former class, is given by the *disparity ratio* 47.7/10.6, i.e. 4.50; meaning that those from non-skilled manual backgrounds have a 4.5 times greater chance of remaining in that class than those from service class backgrounds have of being downwardly mobile into it. Multiplying these disparity ratios gives us an *odds-ratio* of 21.8.

An odds-ratio can be calculated for every pair of origin and destination classes in a mobility table. The notion of odds is a familiar one to anyone with an interest in gambling; rather than saying that the probability of one team winning is 0.2, we say that the odds are four to one against them winning. Our odds-ratio is constructed by comparing the odds of entering one destination rather than another for two classes of origin: in other words we compute the ratio of the two odds. The set of odds-ratio associated with a mobility table can be interpreted sociologically as showing the outcome of a series of 'competitions' between individuals of different class origins to achieve — or avoid — one rather than another location within the class structure. The closer is the value of the odds-ratio to unity the more equal or 'perfect' is the particular competition to which it refers.

Odds-ratios are usually set up so that they measure the odds of getting into a 'higher' or more desirable destination class relative to entering a lower or less desirable class. If the odds-ratio is more than one, this reflects greater advantage to the class whose odds form the numerator of the ratio, while an odds-ratio less than one indicates that the advantage accrues to the origin class whose odds form the denominator. So, in the example we have been using, the odds of a man from service class origins being found in the service class rather than the non-skilled manual class is 21.8 times greater than the odds of a man from non-skilled manual origins being found in the service class rather than the non-skilled manual class.

Odds-ratios can be interpreted as expressing the pattern of association between origins and destinations *net* of the marginal distributions of origins and destinations. In other words, they measure how strongly class origins influence class destinations independently of any change in the total sizes of each class, and hence provide a measure of how 'open' a given class structure is. So, two mobility tables could have quite different origin and destination distributions and still display the same pattern of relative mobility rates or, as Erikson and Goldthorpe (1992a, p. 56) express it, the same pattern of *social fluidity*.

Recently, a number of British authors have argued that an emphasis on relative rates by sociologists such as Goldthorpe, grossly overstates the extent to which Britain is a closed society (Payne, 1990; Saunders, 1990). Does the application of procedures based on odds-ratios leave us vulnerable to a similar accusation with regard to Irish society? In fact, as Goldthorpe (1990, p. 421) emphasises, such critiques require that 'social fluidity' be equated with social mobility. It is clear, however, from Goldthorpe's writings that he understands increased openness as involving a reduction in the degree of inequality of relative rates; in other words, an enhancement of the *ability to compete* of those for whom the dice were unfavourably loaded (Gagliani, 1990, p. 90).

In answer to the question of whether relative or absolute mobility is more important, the only sensible response is that it depends on the particular issue with which one is trying to grapple. Social mobility is a complex phenomenon and it is desirable that we should avoid one 'true' number approaches. If the focus is on class formation and elite closure, then what is crucial is the *de facto* patterns of mobility as reflected in the current composition of each class. In this case we should focus on absolute mobility. If, on the other hand, concern is with equality of opportunity, then mobility must be assessed in relative terms.

A RATIONAL CHOICE APPROACH TO THE ANALYSIS OF SOCIAL MOBILITY

We adopt a rational choice perspective in attempting to explain patterns of social fluidity. This approach which 'views actors as utilising resources in order to make choices between differentially preferred alternatives each of which carries a cost, is widespread in the social sciences' (Breen and Rottman 1995a, p. 2). Even when the term 'rational choice' is not explicitly used, this perspective may be found to underlie a particular explanatory model; for example in Goldthorpe's (1980/87, p. 99) model which incorporates the relative desirability of different class destinations, the economic, social and cultural resources associated with different class origins and barriers to mobility. (See also Breen and Rottman 1995a, p. 3.)

What might be the important aspects of desirability, resources and barriers in shaping social fluidity? One important element here concerns the hierarchical ordering of classes, in terms of the resources they confer, their desirability as destinations and in terms of the barriers that exist to entry into them. Clearly, one would expect that the service class would be harder to get into than, say, the non-skilled manual class but that, by and large, it would be the more highly desired destination. Equally, those who originate in the former class will usually possess better resources for mobility than those who originate in the latter. But hierarchical differences are only one such element. Other important effects relate to inheritance and sector. Inheritance effects cover all those that increase the likelihood of individuals being found in the class from which they originated. A tendency towards such inheritance, in excess of that which we might expect on the basis of the impact of hierarchical influences, could be expected to arise as a result of the particular attractiveness to individuals of positions within their own class of origin or as a consequence of opportunities and barriers being of a somewhat different sort for 'insiders' and 'outsiders'. Over and above this, we should expect some degree of immobility to result from inheritance in the direct sense of the transfer of ownership of a business. Finally, with regard to sectoral effects, tendencies towards movement within the agricultural and non- agricultural sectors are likely to be stronger than movement between the sectors, even when we allow for the influence of hierarchy and inheritance.

Breen and Whelan (1992; 1994), taking Goldthorpe's theoretical model as a base, provide details of a model which is intended to account for the pattern of social fluidity or inequalities in competition which characterises male mobility in the Republic of Ireland. The model, which they refer to as the Agriculture, Hierarchy and Property (AHP) model, involves the following three main dimensions:

Agriculture: the existence of a barrier to movement into agricultural destinations;

Hierarchy: the effect of generalised resources, desirability and barriers, of a hierarchical kind;

Property: the effects arising from the existence of classes based on ownership of the means of production.

In the remainder of this paper we will give account of social fluidity in Ireland from this perspective. For the moment though our use of this model will remain at an informal level. In Chapter 4 we will proceed to give an account of the outcome of the formal statistical application of such models.

OUTFLOW RATES:COMPARISONS ACROSS CLASSES

At this point we want to move from the seven-class schema employed so far for comparative purposes to an eleven-class schema. This more detailed

Table 3.3:   Class Mobility Chances for Men aged twenty to sixty-four in 1987 (Outflow Percentages by Column)

Class Origins

Current Class	Higher Professional and Managerial	Lower Professional and Managerial	Higher Routine Non-Manual	Lower Routine Non-Manual	Higher Petit Bourgeoisie	Lower Petit Bourgeoisie	Farmers	Technicians and Supervisors of Manual Workers	Manual Skilled	Unskilled Semi-Skilled Manual	Non-Manual	Total
Higher Professional and Managerial (I)	41.6	21.6	27.4	3.1	10.7	9.6	3.8	2.6	6.3	3.3	1.3	6.4
Lower Professional and Managerial (II)	18.4	33.4	13.2	15.7	25.1	26.8	7.4	9.2	6.9	9.8	6.3	10.7
Higher Routine Non-Manual (IIIa)	8.5	9.7	3.1	8.4	2.1	3.8	1.7	6.9	6.3	5.5	1.0	6.3
Lower Routine Non-Manual (IIIb)	7.5	5.8	6.8	17.8	9.6	2.5	2.6	7.6	6.7	7.5	7.4	7.4
Higher Petit Bourgeoisie (IVa)	7.3	2.2	2.2	1.1	18.6	5.6	4.2	0.0	3.3	1.4	1.5	3.2
Lower Petit Bourgeoisie (IVb)	4.4	1.2	6.9	4.7	12.6	4.0	4.7	3.1	4.1	2.2	3.7	4.1
Farmers (IVc)	0.0	0.2	0.0	0.0	3.3	0.0	36.2	1.3	0.4	1.1	0.9	10.1
Technicians and Supervisors of Manual Workers (V)	10.1	7.3	7.9	4.4	4.3	14.3	4.7	13.3	11.9	7.0	9.1	8.1
Skilled Manual (VI)	1.7	12.6	14.0	18.4	7.0	19.4	13.4	24.1	32.5	24.1	20.9	19.5
Semi-Skilled Manual (VIIa (i))	0.0	5.8	12.7	20.5	5.9	11.6	6.7	21.6	11.6	24.5	19.6	13.6
Unskilled Manual (VIIa (ii) and VIIb)	3.4	0.3	5.8	5.9	1.0	2.0	14.5	10.4	10.2	13.7	28.4	14.1
Total	2.8	5.4	2.5	4.4	2.8	3.0	26.3	5.0	15.2	10.7	22.0	

classification distinguishes between a higher and lower professional and managerial class and between higher and lower routine non-manual classes. It also distinguishes between members of the *petit-bourgeoisie* with and without employees; and between semi-skilled and unskilled manual workers. The eleven by eleven outflow pattern is set out in Table 3.3.

We direct our attention first to the higher professional and managerial class. This class includes all higher grade professionals, self-employed or salaried, higher grade public service administrators and managers in large establishments.In the private sector employment status tends to be rather ambiguous in this category as in the case of company directors, 'working' proprietors or managers with ownership interest. The occupations within this class generally offer their incumbents incomes which are high, secure and likely to rise steadily over their lifetimes. They are also positions which typically involve the exercise of authority ,within a wide range of discretion, or at least offer considerable autonomy and freedom from control by others. This class, together with the lower professional and managerial group, may be taken as very largely corresponding to the higher and intermediate levels of what has been referred to as 'the service class' of modern capitalist society — the class position of those who exercise power and expertise on behalf of corporate bodies — plus elements of the classic *bourgeoisie* (independent businessmen and 'free professionals') who are not as yet assimilated into this new formation (Goldthorpe, 1980/1987, pp. 40–1). Over 40 per cent of this group originated in this class, the highest degree of immobility observed for any of the eleven classes. In addition one in five are found in the lower professional and managerial class giving a total outflow rate to the service class of 60 per cent. The influence of ownership is reflected in the fact that almost 12 per cent are found in the ranks of the *petit bourgeoisie*; with almost two-thirds of these falling into the employer rather than the self-employed category. The remaining respondents originating in this class are fairly evenly spread across the routine white-collar classes and the higher grade technician class. Long-range downward mobility is almost entirely avoided with only 2 per cent being found in manual work. The upper professional and managerial group are quite distinctive not only in the extent to which they succeed in maintaining their class positions but also in the manner in which they limit the degree of downward mobility experienced.

The lower professional and managerial class comprises lower rank professionals and higher grade technicians, lower grade administrators and officials, managers in small businesses and industrial establishments, and in services, as well as supervisors of non-manual employees. Typically, such positions guarantee incomes that rank just below the previous group and carry 'staff status' and favourable conditions of employment in terms of such matters as sick leave and pension entitlements. These occupational roles tend to be located in the middle and lower ranges of bureaucratic hierarchies of one type or another, so that they exercise some degree of authority and discretion in the performance of their work tasks while at the same time being subject to more or less systematic, if not particularly close supervision. The patterns of mobility of the upper and lower professional and managerial group differ in a number of important respects. While the degree of inheritance observed is slightly lower in the case of the latter, nevertheless one in three are inter-generationally stable. Partly as a consequence of this, those from the lower professional managerial group are one and a half times as likely as those from the upper portion to be found in the lower region of the service class, and only one-half as likely to occupy the higher region; in total 55 per cent were found in both segments. The groups differ little in their tendency to be located in the routine non-manual class but the lower professional and managerial class are much less likely to be currently members of the *petit bourgeoisie*. Finally, those from lower service class origins are substantially more likely to be found in manual work; with the relevant figure reaching 18 per cent as compared to 2 per cent. The majority of those experiencing downward mobility are, however, located in the skilled manual class and almost none are found in the unskilled manual class.

The routine non-manual class may be considered an intermediate one in that it comprises positions with associated employment relationships that take a very mixed form. Erikson and Goldthorpe (1992, pp. 42–3) note that for these occupations employing organisations appear to display considerable uncertainty over whether the roles performed by such personnel are ones that would justify 'staff' status or, alternatively, ought to be treated essentially as labour. The position is somewhat clearer if we distinguish between the non-manual employees in administration and commerce on the one hand (clerical workers, cashiers, commercial travellers) and service workers (hairdressers, shop salesmen and assistants, telephone operators and barmen) on the other . The level of income of the former group is lower than that of the professional and managerial classes, but such occupations nevertheless provide relatively high security of employment and are, to some extent, integrated into the base of bureaucratic structures offering at least some features of 'staff' status. In contrast the routine non-manual service workers tend to be more or less undifferentiated in their conditions of employment from those of non-skilled manual workers. Not surprisingly these two parts of the routine non-manual class display strikingly different patterns of mobility. The higher routine non-manual group appear to occupy a position in the hierarchy just below the professional managerial class. This is reflected in the fact that 40 per cent of those from such origins were found in the professional and managerial class. It is interesting to note that they were twice as likely to be found in the higher than in the lower professional and managerial class. This may be associated with a tendency to achieve mobility by advancement through the level of bureaucratic hierarchies, or setting up one's own business, rather than directly through educational qualifications and entry to the minor professions. It is certainly true that they are a good deal more likely than the lower professional and managerial group to be found in the lower *petit bourgeoisie*: the respective percentages being 7 and 1. The only other factor differentiating these groups is that the routine non-manual group have a substantially greater probability of being found in the semi-skilled and unskilled manual groups; in fact, almost one in five of this class are found there. The final distinguishing characteristic of this group is that they have the lowest tendency of all classes to inherit their class of origin.

The lower routine non-manual class, as we would have hypothesised, display a pattern of mobility, which, as we shall see, falls between those of the classes discussed so far and that characterising skilled and semi-killed manual workers. They are as unlikely as non-skilled manual workers to be found in the service class but are somewhat more likely to achieve lower professional and managerial positions. In total, just less than one in five are found in the professional and managerial class. A further one in four hold routine non-manual positions; with over two out of three of this group being located in the lower stratum. Men originating in this class display relatively weak tendencies to be found in either of the *petit bourgeoisie* groups. Strong outflows into manual work, however, are observed with 45 per cent of this group following such routes; the number entering unskilled manual work, however, remains a modest 6 per cent. In summary, those from lower routine non-manual backgrounds have a relatively low likelihood of being found at the top or the bottom of the class hierarchy, or in the *petit bourgeoisie*, but are spread relatively evenly across the remaining classes.

The *petit bourgeois* categories include small proprietors, self-employed artisans and all other 'own account workers' apart from professionals. The market situation of its members is distinctive by virtue of their employment status, although income levels show considerable variability. Economic security and prospects must also be regarded as generally less predictable than in the case of salaried employees. The upper stratum is distinguished from the lower on the basis of being small employers rather than self-employed per se. Men from these origins display almost identical levels of upward mobility into the professional and managerial classes with over one in three being found in these classes. In each case the predominant flow is into the lower professional and managerial class with one in four, overall, following this route. The major factor differentiating the sections of the *petit bourgeoisie* is their relative probability of remaining in that class versus being downwardly mobile into the industrial working-class. The upper *petit bourgeoisie* display a strong tendency to remain within the class as a whole, with over 30 per cent falling into this category while for the lower *petit bourgeoisie* the figure drops to 10 per cent. The latter group are characterised by a strong flow into the industrial working-class with almost one in two making this transition: the comparable figure for the upper segment is less than one in five. It is noticeable that movement from self-employment origins is predominantly into the lower grade technicians and skilled manual classes. Such moves account for one in three men from this background. These, of course, are just the kind of locations which we would anticipate would facilitate movement back into the *petit-bourgeoisie.*

The category of lower grade technicians, whose work is to some extent of a manual character, tends to offer relatively high income levels and reasonable security of employment. On the other hand it is probably the case that their incumbents have less favourable economic prospects than do staff in positions that are more completely integrated into administrative and managerial bureaucracies. The skilled manual class includes such employees in all branches of industry, including all those who have served apprenticeships and also all those who have acquired a relatively high degree of skill through other forms of training. Evidence, which we will present later, suggests that the technicians category and the skilled manual class differ more as destinations than as origins. The similarity in their outflow patterns is consistent with this view: 70 per cent of those originating in the former class are found in the industrial working-class compared to two-thirds of the latter. The level of outflow to the professional and managerial classes is weaker than for any of the classes examined so far — at 12/13 per cent. The only factors distinguishing the two classes are a substantially stronger tendency toward immobility in the skilled manual class (with almost one in three remaining in their class of origin) and a stronger outflow from this class to the *petit bourgeoisie.* Conversely, there is a significantly greater probability of men from technician background being found in semi-skilled manual work; the respective percentages being 22 and 12. While the lower routine non-manual group may be considered to occupy a slightly ambiguous position, technicians and skilled manual workers display class mobility chances which mark them off quite decisively from the middle-class.

The outflow pattern of the semi-skilled manual group differs very little from that of the previous two groups. It is when we turn to the unskilled manual class that a further clear degree of differentiation is observed. The factor which distinguishes this class as an origin is the likelihood of those originating in it currently being located in this class. They are more than twice as likely to be found in this class than men from any other class origin. Correspondingly, they are less likely to appear in any of the remaining class categories. Thus in terms of mobility chances the important division is between the unskilled manual group and all others.

Finally, not surprisingly, farmers display a distinctive mobility profile. Just over one-third have inherited farming positions. The other major flows observed are into skilled manual and unskilled manual work — which in each case accounts for, approximately, one-seventh of the total. Those from farming origins are similar to the self-employed in their tendency to enter the *petit-bourgeoisie* and the skilled working-class and in their probability of achieving professional and managerial positions.

Previous studies of social mobility in Ireland have been unable to distinguish between farmers by farm size. In Table 3.4 we compare the class mobility chances of farmers with (i) less than 50 acres, (ii) 50–99 acres and (iii) 100 or more acres. The first point to be made is that the percentage remaining in farming shows little variation by farm size. The bulk of inheritance is within the same size category. As we might expect access to the professional and managerial class is closely associated with farm size. One in five of those from large farm backgrounds are found there compared with 12 per cent of the medium sized group and 8 per cent of the small farm group. The other significant variation by size is at the opposite end of the class hierarchy where the risk of being in the unskilled manual class is halved as one moves from the smallest to the largest farm category. Elsewhere variation by farm size is relatively modest. Although those from medium sized farms are most likely to be found in routine non-manual positions, the figure still reaches only 7 per cent. The sole other variation of note is a slightly stronger tendency for those from small farm origins to be found in skilled manual work.

Earlier we noted that in comparing the outflow patterns for 1973 and 1987 there had been a decline in immobility among farmers and corresponding increases in the flow to the professional and managerial classes, but more particularly into skilled manual work. In Chapter 4 we

Table 3.4: Class Mobility Chances for Men of Farming Origins by Farm Size (Percentage by Column)

Class of Origin

Current Class	Less than 50 Acres	50–99 Acres	100 + Acres
Higher Professional and Managerial (I)	1.9	6.2	5.4
Lower Professional and Managerial (II)	5.7	5.7	14.9
Higher Routine Non-Manual (IIIa)	0.7	3.5	1.6
Lower Routine Non-Manual (IIIb)	2.1	3.8	2.4
Higher *Petit Bourgeoisie* (IVa)	4.2	3.8	4.9
Lower *Petit Bourgeoisie* (IVb)	5.4	4.1	3.3
Farmers (IVc)	34.5	39.2	35.9
Technicians and Supervisors of Manual Workers (V)	4.6	4.8	5.1
Skilled Manual (VI)	16.3	10.2	10.3
Semi-Skilled Manual (VIIa [i])	7.0	6.4	6.5
Unskilled Manual (VIIa [i] and VIIb)	17.5	12.3	9.5

pursue the issue of whether the advantages enjoyed by property-owning groups in Ireland are best thought of as accruing to propertied classes in general or whether specific classes, such as farmers, are particularly favoured; and whether the relative advantages enjoyed by propertied groups are related to changes in the underlying pattern of advantages between 1973 and 1987, or simply involve the exercise of constant advantages in a changing structural situation. In either event the success of those 'displaced' from farming in achieving service class and skilled manual positions, while almost three in ten of those from unskilled manual origins remain trapped in that class, provides support for Hannan and Commins' (1992, p. 103) claim in relation to the small-scale holding sector that:

'The communities of that class have disproportionately benefited from industrial expansion policy, and its members have adapted with relative success to the educational demands of the labour-market. In an economic and demographic context in which labour supply has outstripped demand, the Irish smallholding class has consistently won the competition with the working class for industrial jobs, as well as for upward educational and social mobility for its children'.

The small-scale farming group, Hannan and Commins argue, have enjoyed a number of advantages over the working-class, including well-developed dispersion strategies, strong kin networks, higher and more varied mobility aspirations, and perceived social and geographic barriers to their attainment that have been less constraining than those found among the working-class.

CLASS COMPETITION AND ODDS-RATIOS: AN INFORMAL OVERVIEW

The outflow table provides us with a means of examining class differences in mobility chances. Thus we can readily compare the percentages from two different class origins entering the higher professional and managerial class. However as a step towards formal modelling of the underlying patterns of social fluidity we will make such comparison not in terms of probabilities (or percentages flowing into a particular destination class from a given origin class) but rather in terms of odds. The notion, as we have already mentioned, is familiar to anyone with an interest in gambling. Instead of looking at the probability that a man from the unskilled manual class ends up in the higher professional and managerial class, we can look at the odds that he ends up in that class *rather* than in the unskilled class. From Table 3.3 we can see that the respective probabilities are 0.013 and 0.284. So the odds on being in the higher rather than the lower class are 0.013/0.284 which is equal to 0.04577, i.e. less than one in twenty. The corresponding probabilities for the higher professional and managerial class are 0.416 and 0.004 and the odds ratio is thus 0.416/0.004 which is equal to 104. We can compare these two odds simply by taking their ratio thus yielding an odds-ratio 104/0.04577 which is equal to 2,272. The odds-ratio is the conventional measure of inequality in access to particular class destinations from different class origins. Equality of access to a more desirable, rather than a less desirable, destination class as between different origin classes would give rise to an odds-ratio of one. In Table 3.5 we show the odds-ratio summarising the competition between the unskilled manual class and all other classes in turn, to gain entry to the upper professional and managerial class and avoid being located in the unskilled manual class. The results we report do not allow for sampling error and ideally the odds-ratios should be estimated from the type of model fitting exercise which we conduct in Chapter 4. They do, however, allow one to gain an intuitive grasp of the broad scale of inequalities of opportunity. The higher professional and managerial class, as we have already seen, enjoy a competitive advantage over the unskilled manual in excess of 2,000:1. This derives from their almost complete success in avoiding entry to the unskilled manual class and their 32:1 advantage in gaining access to their own class of origin. This also allows the lower professional and managerial class to maintain an advantage of greater than 1500:1 over the unskilled manual class. The competitive advantage is reduced dramatically but remains in excess of 200:1 for the higher *petit-bourgeoisie*. For the higher routine non-manual and the lower *petit-bourgeoisie* the advantage still remains above 100:1. For the remaining classes the advantages enjoyed are a good deal more modest but the unskilled manual class still emerges as a particularly disadvantaged group.

Table 3.5: Odds-Ratio Summarising the Outcomes of Selected Competitions to Enter the Upper Professional and Managerial Class and Avoid Entry to the Unskilled Manual Class

Classes in Competition with the Unskilled Manual Class	Odds-Ratio
Higher Professional and Managerial	2,272.7
Lower Professional and Managerial	1,557.6
Higher *Petit Bourgeoisie*	233.7
Lower *Petit Bourgeoisie*	104.8
Higher Routine Non-Manual	103.2
Lower Routine Non-Manual	11.5
Skilled Manual	13.5
Farmers	5.7
Semi-Skilled Manual	5.3
Technicians	5.5

It might seem that there is a plethora of possible odds-ratios that we could calculate for any table. However, not all odds-ratios are independent of each other. For example, we can calculate the relevant odds-ratios for the competition between the upper and lower professional managerial classes in relation to entry to the upper professional rather than the unskilled manual class simply by dividing the odds-ratios reported for these groups in Table 3.4 (i.e 2,272.7/1,557.6) which gives us an odds-ratio of 1.46. In a mobility table using N classes there are $(N-1)^2$ independent odds-ratios which, for an eleven-class schema, gives 100 odds-ratios and 36 for a seven-class table. This 'basic set' of odds-ratios can be seen as determining the remainder (Goodman, 1979). In the chapter that follows we turn our attention explicitly to developing models whose implied odds-ratios provide a satisfactory explanation of the observed patterns of mobility. In other words, we seek to account for the outcomes of the series of competitions which are reflected in the odds-ratios through a rational choice type explanation which involves factors such as hierarchy, ownership of property and sectoral barriers.

Inequality of Opportunity: An Initial Assessment

Class composition and class mobility chances provide very different perspectives on Irish society. We have seen that structural change in Ireland has been associated with large-scale class mobility and as a consequence even the upper reaches of the service class do not constitute a closed *elite*. However, such openness in terms of absolute mobility is entirely compatible with very substantial inequalities of opportunity. The creation of increased room at the top and a contraction of places at the bottom can lead to a general shift upward without, necessarily, reducing the relative advantages enjoyed by those families which experienced privileges in the old class structure. Economic change, no matter how deep, may not produce a change in the underlying pattern of relative advantages. Our analysis so far suggest that this is what has happened in Ireland, with the strength of hierarchical and property influences, or inequality of opportunity, remaining apparently undiminished over time. The available evidence points to a remarkable stability in class mobility chances at the extremes of the class hierarchy.

The importance of hierarchical factors is illustrated by the extent of the inequalities in the outcomes of competitions to again access to the peak of the class hierarchy and to avoid assignment to the base. The higher professional and managerial class are strikingly successful in remaining in their class of origin, gaining access to the *petit bourgeoisie* and almost entirely avoiding entry to manual work. The lower stratum of the professional and managerial class are almost as successful in achieving access to the service class, and at this level, these classes are distinguished only by their distribution *within* the service class. The lesser role played by property in the latter case is, however, reflected in their much lower tendency to be currently located in the *petit bourgeoisie*. Their less advantageous position in terms of access to resources also appears to be reflected in their substantially higher probability of experiencing downward mobility into manual work, albeit primarily skilled manual work.

Outside the service class the groups displaying the most favourable patterns of mobility chances are the higher routine non-manual and *petit bourgeoisie* groups. They have broadly similar probabilities of entering the service class but the former are concentrated in the higher echelons while the latter are, predominantly, found in the lower segment. The higher *petit bourgeoisie* groups display a striking tendency towards immobility in that class as a whole and a significantly lower likelihood than the routine non-manual group being characterised by downward mobility into manual work. The lower *petit bourgeoisie* come next in the hierarchy of mobility chances with access to the service class which equals that of small employers; but with a low probability of 'inheritance' and a much stronger tendency towards downward mobility into the industrial working-class.

If the lower routine non-manual class is thought of as comparable as a destination to the industrial working-class, then their class mobility chances are distinguished from those originating in that class only by a somewhat higher tendency for mobility into the service class and a significantly lower likelihood of being located in the unskilled manual class.

Within the industrial working-class the major contrast is between the unskilled manual group and all others. The logic of Irish industrial development involving the dispersal of industrial location to rural areas in the 1960s imposed particular costs on the urban working-class. The main beneficiaries though were not those from the rural working-class but the offspring of farmers and the *petit bourgeoisie*. An appreciation of the extent to which the unskilled manual class was marginalised must await our discussion of the relationship between class, class origins and unemployment in Chapter 8.

4 Modelling Social Mobility Regimes

INTRODUCTION

As we have already seen, the basic source of data for mobility analyses comprises a table or cross-classification relating the class position of a sample of people at two different points in time. In very many analyses these points in time would be the person's class at the adolescent stage (the so-called origin class) and the person's current class, but there are other possibilities. For example, we might consider the crosstabulation of a person's origin class with the class first occupied on entering the labour force. Another much-used table is the class of first job by current class crosstabulation. In this chapter we begin by discussing how we formulate models that account for the particular pattern of social mobility as between two such points in a given society. We write about tables of origin and destination (or current) class position using these terms in a generic sense. It should be understood that what we have to say applies to tables that crosstabulate any pair of class positions.

Since the data that we use in mobility analyses usually come from sample surveys, such crosstabulations tell us the exact nature of the relationship between, for instance, class origin and current class, among the members of the sample. However, in mobility analyses we usually seek to go beyond an examination of the table as it is given, in order to *model* mobility. We do this for three main reasons. First, although the data that we use come from a sample, we are not usually interested in the sample *per se*. Rather, we are interested in saying something about the larger population from which this sample is drawn. Thus, if our sample is drawn from the population of all men aged between eighteen and seventy in a particular country, then it is all men aged between eighteen and seventy that we would like to be able to talk about and not merely the particular sample of

46

2,000 (or however many it may be) men that we have actually interviewed. We can use methods of statistical modelling and statistical inference to do this. But once we recognise the distinction between the sample and the population we must acknowledge that the sample may not reflect the population exactly. Although the sample may have been drawn so as to be representative of the population in question (for example by random sampling) there is still the possibility that some of the features we observe in our data will be idiosyncratic to the particular sample in question. This means that these features may well not be found in other samples from the same population and that they may not, therefore, be characteristics that are shared by the whole population. By modelling the mobility table we seek to separate such features from those that are genuine reflections of the situation in the population as a whole.

The second reason for trying to model mobility tables has to do with parsimony. A mobility table will normally be quite complex to understand and interpret: for example, a 7 by 7 table will have 49 cells, each containing a particular frequency, and interpreting them all is quite a daunting undertaking. When we fit a model to a mobility table we are seeking to provide a simpler account, in the sense of one that requires that we interpret not the 49 values in the cells of the table but, rather, a much smaller number of parameters. These parameters in turn are believed to be characteristics of, and to summarise, the underlying social processes that generate the observed mobility patterns in a given society. So in modelling mobility tables we use the information that is present in the table (together with other information that we may have) to generate a reasonably simple explanation of what we observe. And finally, the third reason for modelling mobility tables is that this allows us to test alternative hypotheses about these social processes. In almost all cases there will be rival explanations about why the mobility regime is the way that it is. For example, data on the Republic of Ireland have been interpreted by Erikson and Goldthorpe (1992a) on the basis of their own preferred model of mobility, which they call the Core Model of Social Fluidity (CmSF). But the same data have also been interpreted in the light of the model we referred to in the previous chapter — our own Agriculture, Hierarchy and Property (AHP) model. Each of these models explains the Irish mobility pattern in a different way: each postulates a slightly different set of social processes to explain it. In this sort of circumstance, how can we decide which model is better?

One important consideration in modelling mobility concerns 'goodness of fit'. A mobility model is essentially a mathematical or statistical encapsulation of a particular account of the factors that shape the pattern of social mobility. In fact, mobility models are almost always formulated as 'log-linear models' which are a set of techniques for analysing data that is presented in the form of a contingency table or crosstabulation (see, e.g. Bishop, Fienberg and Holland 1975 or Fienberg 1977). Because this model is simpler than the observed table itself, one way of testing whether or not it is a good model is to compute the frequencies in the cells of the table that would be observed if the model were true and compare these with the actual or observed frequencies in the cells of the table. The former set of frequencies are sometimes called the 'fitted values' or the 'expected frequencies' under the given model. The two sets of frequencies will seldom be identical, but if the model provides a good account of the data the two should not be very different. But we should also expect a more complicated model — one that uses a lot of parameters relating to an underlying social process — to be a better fit to the data than one that uses fewer. However, from the point of view of parsimony, models that use fewer parameters are often considered preferable. The distinction here — taken to extremes — is between a very complicated model that fits the observed data very well and a much simpler model that captures the main features of the mobility process without picking up every detail.

So when we come to judge how closely the frequencies computed under the assumptions of a particular model correspond to the observed frequencies (how well, in short, the model fits the data) two quantities are used. The first of these is called G^2 and this measures the magnitude of the difference between the observed frequencies and those that follow from a given model. Thus we should like G^2 to be as small as possible, indicating that the model fits the data closely. (This is the opposite situation to the case with which people tend to be most familiar where the model being fitted is that of independence and we are normally seeking to observe a large value of the chi-square statistic). But we also compute another statistic called the 'degrees of freedom' or df, for short, which relates to the complexity of the model. Here the idea is that any mobility table has a certain number of observed frequencies — 49 in a 7 by 7 table for example. If we hypothesise a model that has 49 parameters we could fit the data exactly (so G^2 would be zero). This model would not be a very parsimonious model but it would fit the data very well. Suppose that, as an alternative, we fitted a model that had only 12 parameters. We should expect this not to fit the data as closely as the model with 49 parameters, but it would clearly be much more parsimonious. This greater parsimony would be reflected in the model's degrees of freedom, which are calculated as the number of cells or frequencies in the table (in this case 49) minus the number of parameters in the model. So in this example the model would have 37 (49-12) df. The model that fitted 49 parameters would have zero df. Any model that uses up all the available degrees of freedom, as this one does, is called the 'saturated model' for obvious reasons.

To judge how well a given model fits the data we need to look at both the G^2 and df values. We hope to find a model whose G^2 is not too much greater than its df. The exact balance between these two measures need not detain us here, except to say that if the model's G^2 falls within a certain distance of its df (the G^2 normally — but not always — being at least as large as the df) we say that the model provides a statistically significant fit to the data at the 0.05 or 5 per cent level. All that this means is that any differences that exist between the frequencies implied by this model and the observed frequencies themselves can reasonably be supposed to have arisen as a result of idiosyncrasies of the sample and not because of some feature in the population as a whole that our model has omitted to take into account.

SOME MOBILITY MODELS

What almost all mobility models have in common is that they take the distribution of class origins and class destinations to be exogenous to the mobility process. That is to say, they take the distribution of individuals across the classes in which they started out and the current class distribution, as reflected in the class destination distribution, as given. These things set the context in which social mobility occurs. The factors that shape them are accepted to be largely outside the domain of mobility table analysis as it is usually pursued. The emphasis is then placed on modelling the pattern of frequencies that appear in the body of the table, taking these marginal origin and destination distributions as fixed.

Because of this, it follows that mobility models are essentially concerned with patterns of social fluidity — in other words with relative, rather than absolute, mobility. Another way of putting this is to say that they deal with the question of how the class of origin from which someone starts influences the class in which he/she is found. So perhaps the simplest mobility model of all is the model of 'perfect mobility' which postulates that there is no relationship between class origins and class destinations. In the competition for any destination class being born into any origin class is no more advantageous than having been born into any other. Needless to say this model has never been found to fit any mobility table but it will be worthwhile persisting with it for a moment in order to illustrate some of our earlier points. First, how many degrees of freedom has the perfect mobility model? The answer will depend on the size of the mobility table being analysed, but in the 7 by 7 case the answer is 36. How do we arrive at this number? We have already said that mobility models take the origin and destination distributions as given, but doing this carries a price. This is because, in order to take these things as given, we have to fit them exactly in the model. So, to fit the two marginal distributions of a 7 by 7 table requires 13 parameters. More generally we always lose 2N-1 because of this (where N is the number of classes in our table). In a 14 by 14 table fitting the margins would take up 27 parameters. In a real sense, when we are modelling mobility tables we actually have not N x N degrees of freedom but rather N x N minus 2N plus 1 degrees of freedom, which amounts to (N – 1) x (N – 1). In a 7 by 7 table we have (7 – 1) x (7 – 1) degrees of freedom — 36 as we saw earlier.

These 36 degrees of freedom are available to us to model the way in which origins and destinations are linked, or as it is usually put, the pattern of association between origins and destinations. But in the perfect mobility model we are assuming that there is no association between the class position people start from and the one they are found in: rather, current class position is independent of origin class. In this case we do not use up any further degrees of freedom: the association between origins and destinations is left unspecified, which means that the distribution of people over current class positions is random with respect to the origin class distribution.

It follows that any of the maximum possible (N – 1) x (N – 1) parameters that we use in other models will involve some assumption of non-randomness in the relationship between origins and destinations. However we have already seen one measure of how origins and destinations are related, namely the odds-ratio. Recall that an odds-ratio tells us how unequal is the competition between people of different origin classes in the competition for one rather than another destination class position. It will perhaps not be surprising that the association between origins and destinations in a mobility model is measured in exactly the same way. So, in the perfect mobility model, when we do not model this association explicitly we are in effect setting all odds-ratios in the data to be equal to one. An odds-ratio of one means that the competition to which we referred a few lines ago is completely equal. Class origins convey no advantages. As we noted earlier, mobility models are operationalised as log-linear models for contingency tables, and in such models the association parameters are functions of odds-ratios. Put another way, in the table of frequencies expected under the model, the odds-ratios that we could compute are all functions of the association parameters, and, conversely, the association parameters are all functions of the odds-ratios in the table of expected frequencies. Since the odds-ratios are independent of the origin and destination marginal distributions so too are the association parameters of the model.

The perfect mobility model stands at the opposite end of the spectrum to the saturated model which fits, in the 7 by 7 case, 13 parameters to fit the margins and all 36 association parameters, and so reproduces the observed data exactly. Both models have been used as baselines against which to compare other models — the saturated model because it fits the data exactly, the perfect mobility model because it hypothesises a sociologically interesting (but empirically non-existent) state of affairs.

One common elaboration of the perfect mobility model is the model of quasi-perfect mobility or QPM for short. This modifies the perfect mobility assumption, that all odds-ratios are equal to one, by saying that being born into a given class confers an advantage in the competition for entry to that class over those born into another class. However it does not confer any advantage for access to any other destination. This model encapsulates the idea of 'class inheritance': through direct inheritance or by other means, people born into a given class have a better chance than anyone else of being found in that class later in life.

While this model usually fits mobility table data better than the perfect mobility model it is unusual to find that it provides an acceptable fit. There are two reasons for this. First the process that it models — class inheritance — is not found to exist with anything like the same intensity among all classes. It is mainly (though not exclusively) in those classes that own the means of production that class inheritance is most likely to occur. Second, this model, although it postulates that, say, men of *petit bourgeoisie* origins have a better chance of entering the *petit bourgeoisie* than men of skilled manual origins, also hypothesises that both have the same chance of entering the higher professional and managerial class. But this assumption that differential advantage is confined to class inheritance, is clearly at variance with what we observe in most modern economies. To take these factors into account we need to move to some rather more complex models.

NON-MEASURED VARIABLE APPROACHES TO MODELLING MOBILITY

Broadly speaking, two kinds of approach have hitherto been used in modelling social fluidity. In the first kind, the sociologist hypothesises that a particular social process or factor accounts for a certain part of the pattern of social fluidity observed in the mobility table. For example, the belief that a particular pair of classes share a certain 'affinity' that leads to a markedly higher flow of people between origins in the one class to a destination in the other than is true of other pairs of classes. The reasons for this might be historical, cultural, economic and so forth. Another example is the opposite of this — the existence of a barrier to mobility such that the flow between certain origins and certain destinations is reduced. This is exemplified by the movement into the class of farmers among those born into other classes. This is something that rarely happens, particularly in Ireland. By and large people who are not born into the agricultural sector can either not afford or do not wish to move into farming. A third example is the one we have already seen in the QPM model, namely class inheritance.

What is characteristic of this first kind of model is that the sociologist does not have any exogenous measure of the processes that he/she is putting forward to account for these patterns. This is not to say that the patterns are hypothesised *because* they occur in the data: rather the patterns are hypothesised and explained by an essentially verbal account for which purpose explicit measures are not available. Technically speaking these various 'effects' are then entered into the log-linear model as what are termed 'dummy variables'.

Entering the various hypothesised effects into the model in the form of dummy variables has the result that the cells of the mobility table are each allocated to one or more mutually exhaustive sets of cells. So, for example, in the simple case of a barrier to mobility, the cells in question might be allocated to one of two sets — a set on each side of the supposed barrier. In Erikson and Goldthorpe's (1992a) 'core model of social fluidity' (CmSF) four sets of effects are used. First there are hierarchy effects that distinguish three levels of hierarchy among the classes. Second àre inheritance effects. Here an overall tendency for class inheritance, common to all classes, is modelled, together with specific parameters for those classes containing employers and self-employed men and for farmers. The purpose of these additional parameters is to capture the even greater propensity towards class inheritance in these cases. Third is the sectoral distinction between agricultural and non-agricultural classes. The rate of movement between these groups of classes is considered to be diminished because of a barrier to mobility between these sectors. And lastly there are affinity effects. These are of two kinds. The first is a parameter relating to the flow between the service class and the class of agricultural workers. Since this flow is assumed to be particularly *un*likely this parameter might better be termed one of disaffinity. The second is applied to those classes in which the level of mobility is higher than would be expected given only the other terms in the model. This model was developed to analyse the mobility data from the CASMIN project. As its name suggests the core model is advanced as

> an attempt to express the common, or core, fluidity that the FJH [Featherman *et al.*, 1975] hypothesis postulates; but at the same time the model is intended to serve as a means of presenting the hypothesis so that it may receive more systematic testing than hitherto. By applying the model to comparable mobility tables for a range of industrial societies, it should be possible . . . to assess the extent to which national deviations from the core pattern occur, and further to establish the nature of these deviations. (Erikson and Goldthorpe 1987b, p. 145)

MEASURED VARIABLE MODELS OF MOBILITY

What is perhaps most striking about the CmSF model is that there is no attempt to measure the hypothesised dimensions other than through the dummy variable procedure. That such effects are operative is argued at some length by Erikson and Goldthorpe but there is nowhere any attempt to include a set of corresponding measured variables in the model. For example, there is no attempt to directly measure dimensions such as hierarchy or property ownership. Rather, the strength of these effects can only be gauged *ex post* from the estimated parameters attaching to the dummy variables. Given the difficulty in obtaining comparable measures across a range of societies, this is not entirely surprising.

An alternative approach seeks, so far as possible, to provide exogenous measures of the factors that are held to shape the mobility process. We therefore refer to it as the measured variable approach. For example, if we believe that patterns of social fluidity are partially determined by the differential distribution of resources across origin classes then we should seek to measure this distribution and enter it into our model so as to see whether it has the effect we expect and how strong this effect proves to be. Among log-linear models that sought to do this, the earliest were Hope's (1982) models and Hout's (1984) 'status, autonomy and training' (SAT) model. The AHP (agriculture, hierarchy, property) model is a further example (Breen and Whelan, 1992).

An approach that underlies the AHP model derives from the 'rational choice' perspective on mobility captured in the quotation from Goldthorpe, cited earlier, to the effect that the important factors shaping patterns of social fluidity are the resources attached to different origins and the desirability of, and barriers to entry to, different destination classes. The AHP model seeks, so far as is possible, to measure these factors. So, the desirability of different class destinations and also the barriers to entry to these classes, are captured in a single measure, Y. This is made up of the average values for each class on four measures drawn from the sample of men interviewed in 1987. These are

Y1: the gross mean household income in each destination class;

Y2: the mean score in each destination class on a 20-item consumption scale;

Y3: the percentage of men in each destination class unemployed or permanently unable to work due to illness or disability at the time of the survey;

Y4: the percentage of men in each destination class having more than primary education.

We have two similar measures relating to origin classes:

X1: the percentage of fathers in each origin class having only primary education;

X2: the mean score in each origin class on a scale measuring the respondent's perception of his family's relative financial deprivation when he was growing up.

We obtain a composite measure of destination class desirability and barriers by taking the first principal component of Y1, Y2, Y3 and Y4. Similarly we construct a composite measure of origin class resources (called X) by taking the principal component of X1 and X2. For technical reasons (see Breen and Whelan 1994, p. 266) these two measures, X and Y, cannot be included separately in the model: rather they are multiplied together to form a variable XY that models the effect of generalised resources, desirability and barriers conceptualised in a hierarchical fashion.

The ownership of the means of production is a further resource for mobility among men born into those classes that own the means of production. At the same time this is also a barrier to mobility into these classes, since the means of production are not easily acquired. We model this resource/ barrier as the proportion of fathers in each origin class who are self-employed or own a business (we call this variable P1) multiplied by the proportion of men in each destination class who are self-employed or who own a business (P2). The product of these two is the variable P.

Table 4.1 shows the scores of the four measures, X, Y, P1 and P2 in respect of the sample of men in the 1987 survey, using the seven-class categorisation.

Table 4.1 Scorings of origin and destination classes, 1987 data

	Score			
Class	X	Y	P1	P2
Service	1.73	1.71	0.07	0.07
Routine non-manual	0.42	0.43	0	0
petit bourgeoisie	0.39	0.73	1	1
Farmers	-0.24	-0.47	1	1
Skilled manual	0.10	-0.17	0	0
Non-skilled manual	-0.37	-1.05	0	0
Agricultural workers	-0.75	-1.10	0	0

Source: Breen and Whelan 1994, p. 265

In addition to these directly measured variables, however, the model also contains three other effects that, while not measured directly, relate to the theoretical formulation underlying the model. First we have class inheritance over and above that which would be implied by the variables XY and P. We model this inheritance as a single effect, common to all classes, augmented by an extra inheritance parameter for farmers. This allows for a higher level of self-recruitment among the farming class than elsewhere. The necessity for this extra term arises because, in practice, almost the only way of becoming a farmer is through inheritance — something which is not true to the same extent for the other classes. Second we also draw a sectoral distinction between the agricultural (farmers and farm workers) and non-agricultural classes. We posit a barrier to mobility from the latter into the former, though we do not assume a barrier to movement in the opposite direction. This amounts to saying that it is very unlikely that someone born outside the agricultural classes will move into them, but that there are no particular obstacles to men born in the agricultural classes moving outside them. Finally we also add a parameter that captures a certain sort of advantage associated with being born into the farming or *petit bourgeoisie* classes. This is the increased likelihood for such men to be found in the service class, net of all other effects already in the model.

All three of these additional non-measured effects can be seen as representing specific resources (for inheritance of class position or for access to the service class) or barriers (the sectoral division) to mobility.

IRELAND 1987

How well does this model fit the data? Applied to the 7 by 7 table of class origins by class destination for men, the AHP model fits 6 parameters in addition to the 13 necessary to fix the origin and destination distributions. These 6 parameters are labelled β, which measures the effect of the resources/desirability/barriers measure XY; α which measures the effect of the resources/barriers measure, P; plus the two inheritance terms — INH1 representing overall class inheritance and INH2, the additional inheritance term for farmers; the barrier to entry into agricultural classes, AGB; and the term capturing the advantages associated with origins in the *petit bourgeoisie* or farming classes for entry to the service class, SLP. When we fit the model to the data we obtain a G^2 of 40.19 with 30 df. This model provides a statistically significant fit to the data at the 0.05 or five per cent level. In other words, we can be confident that it captures the main features of the Irish mobility regime and does not omit any important aspects of it.

Table 5.2 shows the parameter estimates for the six effects that capture the manner in which class origins and class destinations are associated. These are all individually statistically significant and have the size and signs that we should expect. There is a significant tendency for all men to be found in their class of origin (INH1 = 0.2586) but this is particularly pronounced among farmers, as the very large value of INH2 shows. We can also give all these parameters an interpretation in terms of partial odds-ratios. These are the odds-ratios that arise from a particular effect in the model, holding all other effects constant. So, the odds of a man born into class A being found in class A rather than class B divided by the odds of a man born into class B being found in class A rather than class B defines an odds-ratio. This ratio is increased by exp $(0.2586) = 1.3$ due to the overall class inheritance effect. In other words the inequality is 1.3 times greater than it would be given the other effects in the model, because of the tendency for class inheritance. But if class A is the farmer class this inequality is much greater, because we must add, to INH1, the value for INH2 also. In this case the partial odds-ratio is 4.97, showing that the inequality in access to the farmer class between those who are born into it and those born outside it is increased by a factor of almost five because inheritance proves to be virtually the only way to enter this class.

Table 4.2   Parameter estimates for AHP model applied to 7x7 table for Irish men, 1987.

	Scores	
Parameter	Estimate	Standard error
INH1	0.2586	0.063
INH2	1.344	0.366
AGB	-1.796	0.234
SLP	0.7602	0.133
β	1.259	0.172
α	0.6058	0.049

Source: Breen and Whelan 1992, p. 136

The parameter representing the barrier to entry to the agricultural sector is very large and negative, showing that movement from the non-agricultural to the agricultural sector is much lower than would be expected on the basis of the other components of the model. Here the partial odds-ratio is 0.17, showing that men born into the non-agricultural sector have, all else constant, only about one-sixth the chance of being found in the agricultural sector (rather than elsewhere) of men born into that sector. The parameter representing the advantages for access to the service class among the *petit bourgeoisie* and farmers is large and positive suggesting that, when we control for other factors, such men have roughly twice the odds of being found in the service class of men originating in the other classes.

The parameter β tells us how strongly the measure XY influences social fluidity. It is large and positive indicating that differences between classes in their origin scores (the X variable) and/or in their destination scores (the Y variable) are magnified so as to lead to large inequalities between men of different class origins in the competition for different destination classes. These measures constitute a hierarchy of classes in terms both of origins and destinations. The higher the destination score, Y, the more desirable and the more difficult to enter is a given class. The higher the X score, the greater the resources attached to origins in a given class. So, given any pair of destination classes, the greater the difference in the resources score, X, between two origin classes the more unequal will be the competition for one rather than another of the destination classes. Similarly, this inequality will increase the greater is the difference in the Y score between the destination classes in question. Greater resources will make it relatively easier to enter classes with a high desirability/ barriers score. The magnitude of this effect is given by the β parameter. Finally, α plays a similar role in relation to the measure P. Access to the classes in which the self-employed are found is easier the higher the value of P.

More generally, the fact that this model fits the data strongly suggests that three main components shape the pattern of social fluidity in Ireland. These three components are the barrier to entry to the agricultural sector; the hierarchical ordering of classes given by X and Y; and the advantages associated with the ownership of the means of production encapsulated in the inheritance effect among farmers, the resources/ barriers measure P, and the specific advantages linked to origins in the farming and *petit bourgeoisie* classes captured in SLP. In its ability to explain the Irish pattern of social fluidity the AHP model contrasts with Erikson and Goldthorpe's 'core model' which falls considerably short of fitting the data (G^2 = 81.1 with 28 df which is not a statistically significantly adequate fit).

One test of the ability of the AHP to account for the Irish data is to fit it to a more disaggregated table. Accordingly we fitted it to a 14 by 14 table, in which several finer class distinctions were drawn (for details see Breen and Whelan 1992, p. 137). In this case the model returned a G^2 of 247.8 with 162 df. Because this means that the model does not fit the data it suggests that there may be some factor missing from the account of Irish fluidity. However, this factor is likely to be very minor. In addition, the parameter estimates from this model proved almost identical to those found when the model was fitted to the smaller 7 by 7 table. This is reassuring, since it suggests that these effects are invariant to the level of class disaggregation that might be adopted.

CHANGE BETWEEN 1973 AND 1987

Given these three main sources of influence on the pattern of social fluidity we can now address the question of how that pattern may have changed between the 1973 mobility survey and the 1987 survey. Specifically we are interested in whether the same three factors also shape the earlier pattern of social fluidity and, if so, how any change in that pattern between 1973 and 1987 might be explained in terms of changes in the effects of one or more of them.

Part of the difficulty in doing this, however, stems from the fact that some of our measured variables are not available in the 1973 data. One solution to this problem is to use the 1987 hierarchy measures and estimates of self-employment for the 1973 data (the details of the subsequent analysis are given in Breen and Whelan, 1994). Minor modifications have to be made to the model in order for it to fit the 1973 data, some of which appear to arise from the use of proxy measures. However, the six parameters of the AHP model in fact remain completely identical over the two data sets. The only substantive differences between 1973 and 1987 relate to some changes in the pattern of inheritance. The 1973 data shows a high level of class inheritance among skilled manual workers and a degree of class *dis*inheritance among unskilled manual workers, neither of which patterns are evident in the 1987 data. In addition there is also a somewhat higher rate of movement from the service class into farming and a lower rate of movement from the non-skilled manual class into the white-collar classes in the earlier data. Beyond this, however, nothing changes in the pattern of association between class origins and class destinations. The major differences between the 1973 and 1987 tables are in their marginal distributions and hardly at all in the way in which class origins influence class destinations.

Using the AHP model we can capture the changes in the Irish mobility regime in a very concise fashion. The pattern of inheritance effects for the 1973 data differs not only from that found in the 1987 data but also from what is typically found in mobility tables. It is difficult to see what the appropriate substantive explanation might be. In particular, it does appear plausible that it could be a consequence of unmeasured heterogeneity in the hierarchy or property variables, arising from the use of 1987 scores; or the failure of the AHP model to capture some important explanatory factor. The pattern of inheritance effects in the 1973 data does appear to be *sui generis*. The departures from expectation in the remaining two cells, on the other hand, are clearly ones which might be accounted for by unmeasured differences over time in the hierarchy or property terms.

All the change between 1973 and 1987 relates to two additional inheritance parameters and the extra pair of affinity terms. Particularly in view of the necessity of applying the 1987 measures to the 1973 data, these findings provide substantial support for the value of the AHP model when applied to data for which it was not originally formulated. In substantive terms, they also provide support for the argument that changes in the pattern of social fluidity between 1973 and 1987 have been of a highly restricted nature, involving little in the way of significant change in the manner in which the underlying factors shaping mobility patterns operate.

Cohort Analysis of the 1987 Data

One possibility that exists is that changes over time in the mobility regime have occurred but the extent of the overlap of cohorts in the 1973 and 1987 samples conceals such change. In order to test this proposition we fit the AHP model to the thirty to forty-four-year-old and forty-five to sixty-four-year-old cohorts; in the 1987 data we once again retained the same exogenously given measures of resources and desirability/barriers, this time across both cohorts. When we came to fit the unmodified AHP model to these cohorts, we found one substantial residual, in that the flow between farm origins and non-farm unskilled work is significantly overestimated in the younger cohort and underestimated in the older. If we fit this cell exactly (using an affinity term which we label AF) in each table, then the model yields the goodness-of-fit statistics shown in Table 4.3. The model which constrains the fluidity parameters to be constant across cohort (line 1 of panel A) fails to fit the data, but the model which allows those parameters to vary by cohort provides a statistically adequate

Table 4.3:   AHP Model Applied to 30–44 and 45–64 Year-Old Cohorts in 1987 Data

A. *Goodness of Fit*	G^2	df
Common social fluidity	92.7	65
Heterogeneous social fluidity	72.9	58
Common social fluidity except for β and affinity term, AF	74.3	63

B. *Social Fluidity Parameter Estimates (Standard Errors in parentheses) from model 3*

Common parameters		
INH1	0.335 (0.08)	
INH2	1.700 (0.37)	
SLP	0.123 (0.18)	
AGB	- 1.263 (0.28)	
α	0.739 (0.06)	

Heterogeneous Parameters		
	30–44 cohort	45–64 cohort
β	0.695 (0.23)	1.486 (0.27)
Affinity term	- 0.599 (0.23)	0.700 (0.22)

fit. However, as good a fit can be obtained from a model which keeps all the fluidity parameters constant across the cohorts, with the exception of the affinity term, AF, and ß, the property parameter. This is shown on line 3, panel A of Table 4.3. The parameter estimates of this model are given in panel B of Table 4.3. Once again they show the importance of the inheritance effects, the barrier to access to agricultural destinations, and the hierarchical mobility effect arising from the distribution of resources and of desirability and barriers. In this case, however, the SLP parameter which captures the additional advantage associated with being born into the farming or *petit bourgeoisie* class in terms of access to the service class, does not reach significance; probably because of the pronounced role played by the property parameter, ß, in the older cohort. The heterogeneous parameters reveal the magnitude of difference in the two mobility regimes. So, the property effect is stronger in the older than the younger cohort, and the flow from farming origins to unskilled non-farm work is much stronger among the older than the younger cohort. The declining importance across cohorts in the size of the property parameter is open to interpretation as involving a substantive change in the underlying pattern of social fluidity or as simply reflecting the fact that the full advantages associated with a propertied background are not yet fully reflected in the mobility patterns of the younger cohort. The failure to observe any significant change in the size of the property parameter between 1973 and 1987 suggests that the latter interpretation may be nearer to the truth. The change in flows from farming origins to unskilled non-farm work is consistent with the account given by Hannan and Commins (1992) of the manner in which the children of farmers have benefited disproportionately from Irish industrial and educational policies since the 1950s.

THE AHP MODEL AND ERIKSON AND GOLDTHORPE'S CORE MODEL COMPARED

Both the CmSF and the AHP models are class-structural models, and thus share a good deal in common, not least their derivation as attempts to operationalise Goldthorpe's (1980) formulation of social fluidity as resulting from the interplay of resources, desirability, and barriers. Nevertheless, there are also important differences between the two.

The application of the CmSF model to the 1973 Irish data is particularly interesting because it proves to fit the data very poorly. For example, using either the dissimilarity index or $G^2(S)$ (a measure which adjusts G^2 for sample size), Ireland returns the poorest goodness of fit for the CmSF of any of the nine European nations in Erikson and Goldthorpe's study (1987b, p. 148). Furthermore, Erikson and Goldthorpe (1987b, p. 160) argue that the deviations of the Irish data from the CmSF specification are not amenable to macro-sociological explanation. Thus while the Republic of Ireland provides an instance where the pattern of social fluidity does not conform at all closely to the core model, the deviations that occur seem to be fairly specific and relate mainly to the agricultural sector. Faced with the failure of the CmSF model to fit, Erikson and Goldthorpe (1987b, p. 154) then modify the model as it applies to four cells of the table. The pair of cells indicating mobility between the class of farmers and the service class are included in the AF2 (positive affinity) term, as are the cells indicating mobility from farm origins (IVc) into the class of agricultural workers (VIIb) and from unskilled non-farm origins (VIIa) into the agricultural workers class.

According to Erikson and Goldthorpe these modifications seem to be required because of certain features of Ireland's large agriculture sector. 'Of greatest importance is the wide variation in the size of farms and indeed the tendency . . . for two relatively distinct types of farmer to emerge . . . on the one hand, large farmers operating as capitalist entrepreneurs and with various affiliations, economic and socio-cultural, to urban business and professional communities; and, on the other hand small, often in fact, marginal farmers' (Erikson and Goldthorpe, 1987b, pp. 154–5). These authors also point to the distinctive nature of the rural working class which is internally undifferentiated in terms of its sectoral employment, but whose membership overlaps, to some degree, with that of the farmer class. It is these particular class linkages that yield the justification for the additional positive affinities. This modified model fits the Irish data for 1973 and provides results which are in agreement with the findings of a number of other authors that Irish society displays unusually strong tendencies towards intergenerational mobility (Breen and Whelan, 1985; Hout, 1989; Whelan and Whelan, 1984). However, while other authors stress the importance of general hierarchical effects in shaping the Irish pattern of social fluidity, the CmSF model puts the emphasis rather on specific affinities and disaffinities.

The availability of data for 1987 allows us to test the adequacy of the CmSF model in explaining data other than that which influenced its formulation. As Hout and Hauser (1992, p. 255) state 'it will probably be more useful to validate the CmSF model against fresh data than to compare any measure of its fit with that of other models of the same data'. However, such validation is not simply a question of goodness of fit. Erikson and Goldthorpe (1992, p. 286) would seem to wish to argue that, since the core model is aimed at trying to capture the commonality in national fluidity patterns implied by the FJH hypothesis, it cannot be expected to provide an accurate representation of the pattern of mobility in a specific nation. Rather, the usefulness of the model lies in its function as a yardstick against which to compare the pattern of social fluidity in different nations. In its most general form this approach is open to a response such as Sorenson's (1992, p. 309) that 'any mobility regime can be represented as *some* core model with national variants'. The position we adopt is that what is at issue is not whether the AHP model provides a better fit to the Irish data than does the core model, but whether the pattern of results suggests that the Irish deviations from the core model are a consequence of historical peculiarities or, alternatively, of the failure of the core model to capture adequately the crucial dimensions of the mobility process.

In fact, the Irish variant of the CmSF model comes nowhere near fitting the 1987 data. Furthermore, although the model suggests that significant change has taken place in the pattern of social fluidity between 1973 and 1987 none of this is captured by the model. Thus a model which constrains the parameters to be constant across time fits as well as one which allows all of them to vary over time. Furthermore when we replace the hierarchical terms of the CmSF model with that from the AHP model it produces a significant improvement in the fit (Breen and Whelan, 1994). This finding leads us to agree with Hout's (1989, p. 150) conclusion that the core model understates the importance of hierarchy in Ireland as a consequence of the fact that the hierarchy terms in the CmSF model are inadequate. Our analysis suggests that a correctly specified hierarchy term is a very important component of Irish social fluidity and one which the CmSF model does not incorporate.

Erikson and Goldthorpe (1992a, p. 29) argue that hierarchical effects derive from more than one vertical dimension. Thus the areas of both 'white-collar' and 'blue-collar' fluidity that are a feature of the core model do not result from closeness within the threefold hierarchical divisions, reflecting differences in reward and entry requirements, but are rather produced by countervailing effects which must be understood in status terms. Connected to consistent findings of differential association (Mitchell and Critchley, 1985), affinities within both white- and blue-collar classes are seen as 'lying in the evident "closeness" of the classes in question within the *status* structures of modern societies, understood *stricto sensu*, in relational rather than attributional terms' (Erikson and Goldthorpe, 1992a, p. 129). Thus, over and above any reference to the sort of hierarchical differences which we have attempted to measure in the AHP model, it is necessary to take into account sub-cultural divisions between manual and non-manual classes. As we have noted earlier, such affinities are argued to be particularly important in the Irish case. But, other than to the extent to which such factors are reflected in our overall inheritance parameter, we find no need to make specific reference to them in our model.

The fact that the CmSF model, even with the inclusion of the AHP hierarchy term, does not provide a satisfactory fit to the 1987 data indicates that the superiority of the AHP model does not derive solely from the inclusion of this term. The availability of detailed information on the proportion of self-employed in both origin and destination categories also proves crucial in facilitating a general explanation of the nature of the Irish social-mobility regime. The fact that the Irish variant of the CmSF model does such a poor job in accounting for changes in Irish social fluidity over time and across cohorts suggests that this particular model could not be made to approach an adequate fit to the data, short of accumulating a large number of *ad hoc* 'affinity terms'.

CONCLUSIONS

Has such economic change led to increases in social fluidity — as the 'liberal theory' of industrialism would seem to imply? The most obvious critique of the liberal theory is that it neglects the means by which those who occupy positions of relative privilege can maintain them (for themselves and their families) in the face of such 'functional requirements' and the legislation which may accompany them. Thus, while the liberal theory would seem to imply greater societal openness (as measured by social fluidity), such critiques suggest that an increase in fluidity is, at best, problematic (Erikson and Goldthorpe, 1992a, p. 368). The Irish data provide a means of adjudicating on this question. In our comparison of the 1973 and 1987 mobility data the liberal theory would point towards some increase in social fluidity between the two. A similar distinction should be evident in the comparison we make between the older and younger cohorts in the 1987 data. The AHP model operationalises a theoretically based account of the factors shaping the pattern of social fluidity in Ireland. It is parsimonious while providing a very good fit to the observed data. When applied to mobility data from 1973 to 1987 and the cohort data for 1987 it shows that the advantages associated with class differences in resources have shown virtually no change, despite the continued processes of economic development and significant social change.

One possible reason why we observe relatively little change is that the working through of policies that might be expected to influence the pattern of social fluidity — most notably, perhaps, the educational reforms of the late 1960s and early 1970s — is a long-term process. In the 1973 data almost none of the sample would have benefited from free secondary education, while even in the 1987 data this is confined to the younger members of the sample. Another possibility is that changes in educational participation levels have less influence on relative mobility rates than many had imagined. (We will pursue this issue in Chapter 6). However, some policies do seem to have had an impact. For example, the retention of advantage by the *petit bourgeoisie* and farmers is consistent with the marked decline in revenue shares from tax on property, inheritance tax and corporation income tax that occurred over this period. More generally, the balance of cash transfers received and tax paid also favoured the propertied classes over employees. In the 1970s all farm categories received, on average, more in cash transfers than they paid in tax, regardless of their income level. Once direct transfers and taxes are brought into the picture, small proprietors were significantly better off, gaining more than they lost in the tax and transfer systems. By contrast all employees, except unskilled manual workers, ended up worse off on average. Perhaps the single most striking index of the tax advantage enjoyed by the owners of capital is that in 1980, large proprietors and unskilled manual workers enjoyed a common effective tax rate of 16 per cent. Over the 1970s period cash transfers were allocated in a progressive fashion over this period but taxes were only weakly progressive. This meant that for employees, state actions left market-based income differences little changed, whereas for property owners such actions led to an improved financial position (Rottman and Reidy, 1988). Against such a background it is hardly surprising that the pattern of social fluidity in Ireland remained largely undisturbed.

5 The Class Mobility of Women

INTRODUCTION

Gender has frequently been identified as the most controversial issue confronting present day class analysis (Marshall *et al.* 1988, McRae, 1990). Hayes and Miller (1993) acknowledge that the debate has become increasingly acrimonious and offer a review of the evidence which is intended to promote discussion and reflection. However, their conclusion that the neglect of women 'has effectively distorted understanding of the central social process of social mobility' is itself far from uncontroversial, as anyone familiar with Erikson and Goldthorpe's (1992a, b) most recent contributions to the debate will recognise.

In this chapter we seek not only to provide an account of the class mobility experiences of Irish women but also to make use of the Irish data to examine a number of issues which have been prominent in the debate concerning gender and class mobility. The central issue relates to the appropriate unit of composition for class analysis. Those, like Erikson and Goldthorpe, who seek to defend the so-called 'conventional view' insist on continuing to regard the family as the appropriate unit of class analysis. Against this, many feminist sociologists (and others) argue that it is the individual who is the appropriate unit of class analysis (Abbot and Sapsford, 1987; Stanworth, 1984). We take advantage of the availability of data which are particularly suitable for testing hypotheses relating to this question. Our approach to the modelling of social mobility makes explicit both the theoretical assumptions underlying our analysis and the operationalisation of our key hypotheses. In what follows we will seek to show how the 'measured variable' approach, described in Chapter 4, facilitates the empirical assessment of at least some of the issues which have divided protagonists in the class-gender debate.

The 'conventional' approach to class analysis asserts that the class mobility of women and men is best understood if the family is given priority over the individual as the unit of class composition. The practice which has been most frequently adopted in empirical research of taking the class of the conjugal family as following from that of its male head, is based on the assumption that he typically has the fullest commitment to work-force participation. The expectation therefore is that it will be through his class position that the life chances of the members of the family will be crucially affected.

It is precisely on this practice of allocating married women to the same class positions as their husbands that the bulk of feminist criticism has focused. This practice, it is argued, has become increasingly indefensible as women's participation in the labour force has increased. As a consequence the practice of taking the family as the unit of class composition should be abandoned, and the class position of all adult individuals should be determined solely by reference to their employment situation including, if necessary, their previous employment situation (Abbot and Payne, 1990; Abbot and Sapsford, 1987; Acker, 1973; Stanworth, 1984).

A number of options are therefore available

- One can proceed with analysis of men only.

- One can follow the 'conventional' approach whereby married women are allocated to a class position on the basis of their husband's position in the labour-market.

- One can adopt an individual approach whereby individuals are assigned a position solely on the basis of their own participation in the labour-market. In this case a married woman who is a shop assistant and married to a teacher will be allocated the same class position as a woman in the same occupation married to an unskilled manual worker. It also becomes necessary to decide whether one wishes to modify this approach for married women who are not currently in the labour-market.

- One can assign the family unit a class position on the basis of the joint characteristics of the husband and wife members. (Britten and Heath, 1983; Heath and Britten, 1984). With this procedure single- and dual-earner families can be distinguished and situations where the situations of husband and wife are sufficiently disparate to constitute what has been termed 'cross-class' families can be identified. Their approach, however, creates a great deal of artefactual mobility since the class position of the family changes as wives withdraw from, or re-enter, the labour-market. Furthermore, the likelihood of women being in employment and in full-time rather than part-time unemployment is closely related to the presence or absence of children and their number and age. Consequently class effects are likely to be confounded with life-cycle effects and a great deal of artefactual mobility is observed as married women enter and leave employment.

● The class position of the family may be determined by reference to the spouse with the 'dominant' employment position. Erikson (1984) defines dominance in terms of two criteria: those of 'work time' and 'work position'. The first criterion dictates that full-time employment dominates part-time employment, the second that higher-level employment dominates lower-level employment.

Many of the controversies in this area have their roots in fundamental conceptual differences (Goldthorpe, 1983, 1984, 1990; Stanworth, 1984). We nevertheless believe that a review of the full range of empirical consequences arising from the different positions will allow their evaluation, one relative to another (Goldthorpe, 1990, pp. 407–9). In order that the empirical material we present can be subjected to such an evaluation it is necessary to make clear the position we have taken on a number of crucial issues. *Firstly,* we are concerned with *class* rather than occupational mobility. Many legitimate questions relating to individual occupational attainment are not part of our brief. One example of such issues is the influence of mothers' occupation or labour-market status on the corresponding outcomes for daughters and the potential impact of role models and socialisation (Hayes, 1990).

Secondly, class analysis focuses on processes occurring within a given context. In this sense the occupational order may be seen to form 'the backbone of the class structure' (Parkin, 1972, p. 18). Thus, a class categorisation such as the Goldthorpe class schema (which we use in our analyses) is intended to apply to occupational positions but this does not involve a commitment to the view that 'the class of all individuals alike will be most validly determined by reference to their own employment' (Erikson and Goldthorpe, 1992a, p. 37). It is not correct therefore to argue that studies of class mobility are in fact studies of occupational mobility simply because class is operationalised in terms of occupations (Abbot and Payne, 1990, p. 16).

The rationale of class analysis requires that members of a class are associated with particular sets of positions over time and would be undermined if classes were to appear as highly unstable aggregates of such positions. The existence of such stability provides the basis for the key role of the family as a unit of strategic action in terms of consumption and production.

Thirdly, the employment relationship of the family member with the 'dominant' job extends beyond the work place in terms of its consequences for '. . . experiences of affluence or hardship, of economic security or insecurity, of prospects of continuing material advance, or of unyielding materials constraints (Erikson and Goldthorpe, 1992a, p. 236).

In so far as members of family constitute a household they may be expected to experience similar material conditions not just at a point at which they are observed but also in a range of future life chances. Furthermore, economic decision-making, in regard to both consumption and labour force participation is typically of a joint kind. The family is, as Erikson and Goldthorpe (1992a, p. 233) put it, the unit of class 'fate' and a key unit of strategic action.

The extent of class-related socio-cultural variation is an empirical issue, which we will pursue in Chapter 8, as is the scale of such differences in comparison to those arising from other sources of differentiation within and between families. It is because class is defined solely in terms of employment relationship that issues such as the relative importance of class *vis-à-vis* other influences, such as life-cycle, become matters of legitimate empirical enquiry. This approach may be contrasted with that of Dale *et al.* (1985) where class is viewed as comprising two distinct dimensions, one defined at the individual level in terms of relationship to the labour-market and a second represented by family patterns of consumption.

This position does not involve a neglect of differences in resources and power among family members (Arber, 1993; Pahl, 1989, 1990). On the contrary, it is precisely the existence of such differences which typically sees the class position of other family members being 'derived' from the male 'head' in virtue of their degree of economic dependence on him. It does not deny the possibility of inequality in standards of living between men and women within households, nor that some family members exert greater influence over decision-making than others. The implication is rather that such inequalities should be viewed as being ones of gender rather than class (Erikson and Goldthorpe, 1992b, p. 233). There is no evidence that intrafamilial inequalities in standards of living are comparable to those existing between families occupying different class positions.

Fourthly, one of the criticisms directed at Goldthorpe is that he is inconsistent in treating absolute mobility as crucial to class formation among men but inconsequential from the point of view of the class analysis of women (Marshall *et al.* 1988, p. 139). Goldthorpe's point, however, would seem to be, not that the absolute mobility of women is of no interest but that, to the extent to which gender differences in such patterns are a consequence of occupational gender segregation, it is far from obvious that they are capable of explanation in class terms. In any event, gender differences in absolute mobility *per se* and, in particular, their intragenerational patterning, can hardly be held to undermine the argument for the family as the unit of analysis. The existence of such differences, arising from the disproportionate extent to which women bear the burden of family and domestic commitments, provides the major justification for this approach and, in particular, the need to identify the member of the household with the dominant relationship to the labour-market.

This approach does not require that we ignore the extent to which the structure of men's employment and, consequently, men's mobility chances, is affected by the structure of women's employment (Goldthorpe, 1990, p. 437). Indeed it is entirely consistent with the position taken by Crompton (1989, p. 577). '. . . that the division of labour in the public sphere should be viewed as an outcome of a number of processes including those of class, rather than as representing a class structure as such.' The issue of the level of explanation appropriate to absolute and relative mobility rates does not arise solely in the case of gender differences. The assessment of the impact of factors such as public sector job creation, or expenditure on training, on mobility patterns raises complex questions relating to the probable outcomes that would have arisen in the absence of such interventions. In turn these questions are aspects of the more general issue of whether a useful sociological theory of class structural change can be advanced.

Fifthly, the issue of the appropriate unit of analysis has most frequently been discussed in terms of the implications of husband's and wife's 'class position' with regard to class identification and party preference i.e. is a woman's voting preference better predicted by her husband's occupational position than by her own (Erikson and Goldthorpe, 1992b; Hayes and Jones, 1992; Heath and Britten, 1984). The point at issue is not, simply, the empirical one of whether women's employment makes a difference, but rather the conceptual one of whether such differences as are established make it desirable to abandon the family as the unit of analysis. The crucial evidence relates to the pattern of results when both husbands and wives are incorporated in the analysis. Erikson and Goldthorpe (1992b) conclude that for male respondents it is their own class position which influences class imagery and political partisanship; while that of their wife has little or no influence. For women, husband's class position not only has an influence but one which tends to be stronger than that found for the wife's own class position (see also Baxter, 1994). Surprisingly, given the inevitably contingent relationship between class imagery, political partisanship and class situation, very little attention has been directed to the relative explanatory power of different units of analysis in relation to economic resources and deprivation (Erikson, 1984). In what follows we will seek to address this issue.

Sixthly, with regard to problems caused by applying 'male' occupational classifications to women, the implications vary depending on whether one is concerned with occupational mobility *per se* or with class mobility, where occupation is used in conjunction with employment status and information on dominance in order to determine the class position of a particular unit of analysis. It does not appear that whatever difficulties may exist are resolved by employing separate occupational classifications for men and women (Murgatroyd, 1984). Class analysis which incorporates men and women does not require that one ignores power relations in the labour-market (including for example, those which contribute to the definition of 'skilled'), nor is it necessary to assume that men and women in the same occupation have identical rewards, prospects and work conditions. However, this could be made much clearer if social mobility analysts were to make explicit the underlying dimensions which they consider to be crucial in modelling the mobility process and were willing to specify the manner in which such dimensions should be measured.

In what follows we attempt to develop such an approach. In particular by introducing our measure of hierarchy which relates to the desirability of, and barriers to entry to, particular class locations we can examine the consequence with regard to this dimension of moving from the analysis of men-only tables to complete mobility tables. Such an approach can allow for change over time in the relative hierarchical position of particular classes and for changes in the relative position of specific occupations. At the same time, by making explicit the particular variables which are considered crucial to the mobility process, it is possible to show that changes in many other features of occupations, including many relating to task content, do not undermine the analysis of class mobility (Crompton, 1980, p. 118; Pawson, 1993, p. 39).

Seventhly, the approach we adopt does not require that women be excluded from mobility analysis nor that in households with married or cohabitating couples that the male should determine the family's class position. Critics of the conventional approach have been successful in bringing about a movement away from the situation where mobility analysis was restricted to males (Dex, 1990a; Roberts, 1993). This, however, does not resolve the empirical issue of the extent to which such restrictions have distorted our understanding of the mobility process.

CHANGES IN FEMALE PARTICIPATION RATES AND THE 'CLASS' DISTRIBUTION OF WOMEN

As McRae (1990, p. 122) notes, the initial impetus for the challenge to the conventional approach to class analysis arose as a result of the marked increase in the labour force participation of married women. The widespread rise in total female participation rates is due mainly to growth in married women's labour force participation. Erikson and Goldthorpe (1992a, p. 235), however, question whether this revolution in participation has been accompanied by similarly dramatic changes in the level of women's attachment to the workforce, in the continuity of their work histories or in the contribution they are able to make through employment to family incomes. Indeed, Hakim (1992, p. 144) has recently argued that, in the case of Britain, the nature of women's part-time employment has been such that the 'increase in women's employment since World War II is revealed to be largely illusory'.

Since the labour force participation of married women in Ireland has traditionally been low, it might appear at first glance, that it is not a particularly suitable case for exploring hypotheses relating to the appropriate unit of class composition. However, since the early 1970s approximate stability in the aggregate female participation rate has been accompanied by major shifts in its composition. The most significant change has involved the increased labour force participation of married women. The vast bulk of this change occurred after 1971 with the rate trebling from 7.5 per cent in 1971 to 23.4 per cent in 1987. The increases were even more spectacular in the twenty to thirty-four age group. The Irish case thus takes on a particular interest because the conventional approach would suggest that models of mobility, which might have been adequate in Ireland in the early 1970s, will have become increasingly misleading. The Irish case also provides a rather better testing ground than the overall participation rate might suggest because in 1987 only 14 per cent of female employment was part-time compared to 45 per cent in the UK (Callan and Farrell, 1992, p. 24). The potential impact of such changes is enhanced by the fact that, as we can see from Table 5.1, the increase in female participation has been almost entirely concentrated in upper-middle-class positions. The percentage of women at work in such positions has almost doubled between 1961 and 1990 from 15 per cent to 29 per cent. Women, however, are still concentrated in the lower middle-class where almost one in two are still found. The major decline has been observed in agriculture primarily in the number classified as relatives assisting where the figures in practice relate to single women and widows only, since farmers' wives are usually treated as not being in the labour force irrespective of their contribution to farm work.

Table 5.1: Females at Work by Class Category

	1961	1971	1981	1990
Employers and Self-Employed	Per Cent			
Agriculture	15.0	8.9	3.5	3.2
Non-Agricultural	7.6	5.5	4.9	6.9
Employees:				
Upper Middle-Class	14.8	16.5	24.3	28.8
Lower Middle-Class	42.7	46.7	51.4	47.3
Skilled Manual	5.8	4.6	3.9	3.5
Semi/Unskilled Manual	14.1	15.8	11.9	10.3
Total at Work	100.0	100.0	100.0	100.0
Total Unemployed	3.0	3.3	6.1	9.9

Source: (O'Connell, 1995).

OUTLINE OF OUR ANALYSIS

Our analysis addresses a range of issues which have recently been reviewed by Erikson and Goldthorpe (1992a). In addition to examining whether the more recent data for the Irish case supports their conclusions, we also seek to establish the extent to which our measured variable approach to the analysis of social fluidity can shed further light on the nature of women's social mobility. Our analysis proceeds in three stages.

(i)   We begin by examining the implication of adopting the individual as the unit of class analysis for women who are currently in 'full-time unpaid duties in the home' and those currently in the labour force.

(ii)　Then, restricting our attention to the latter, we examine the impact of class origins on women's mobility chances through employment.

(iii)　We compare women's marital mobility, in the sense of movement from their class origins to their husband's class, to married men's class mobility.

(iv)　Finally we examine complete mobility tables employing what has been described as the 'dominance' approach to the issue of the appropriate unit of class analysis (Erikson, 1984) and compare the results with those arising from 'men only' tables.

THE PATTERN OF HUSBAND AND WIFE EFFECTS: (I) MARRIED WOMEN IN HOME DUTIES

A strict application of the individual approach would require that not only should married women who are currently in the labour force be classified on the basis of their own occupation but also that those in full-time unpaid 'home-duties' should be assigned a class position on the basis of their most recent occupation. This involves classifying many women who will have been out of the labour-market for some time according to their last occupation. Certain consequences follow for our ability to explain life chances.

The measures of lifechances used in this paper are derived from an approach to the measurement of deprivation and poverty which has been discussed in detail elsewhere (Callan *et al.* 1993; Nolan and Whelan, 1996). The approach adds to the work of Townsend (1979) and Mack and Lansley (1985) by identifying distinct dimensions of household deprivation. The dimensions included in our analysis in this paper are labelled ***basic life-style deprivation*** and ***secondary life-style deprivation***. The former involves the enforced absence of basic food, clothing, heating, etc. and the experience of persistent debt difficulties arising from dealing with routine expenses. The consumption items in the scale measuring basic deprivation all relate to current consumption and display relatively low levels of non-possession and high levels of socially defined necessity. The scale runs from zero to eight. The latter measure deals with enforced deprivation of items which are characteristic of a middle-class, or comfortable working-class, life-style. These include holidays, leisure activities and expensive consumer durables. Here we find much higher levels of non-possession and lower levels of socially defined necessity. The scale runs from zero to nine.

Following Ringen (1987, 1988), who has advocated the use of both income and deprivation criteria in measuring poverty,we make use of an income threshold and the measure of basic deprivation in order to establish a poverty line. Our measure of income is household adult equivalent disposable income. A household is considered to be in poverty if its income is less than 70 per cent of the average household income, and it experiences enforced absence of one or more primary items. In theoretical terms we conceive of poverty as involving an enforced absence of socially-defined necessities arising from inadequate resources.

In our analysis in this chapter we use the seven-class CASMIN schema in which class III (routine non-manual employees) is divided into IIIa and IIIb, with the aim of isolating in IIIb occupations which, in terms of characteristic employment relations, would seem to involve straightforward wage-labour (Erikson and Goldthorpe, 1992a, p. 241). IIIb was then placed in the same class category as VIIa (semi-skilled and unskilled manual workers outside agriculture).

In addition in our log-linear analyses concerned with predicting household poverty we aggregate the modified schema into three classes: service class (I+II); intermediate class (IIIa, IVa, b and c, V/VI); and working-class (IIIb, VIIa and b). The need for aggregation arises from the relatively low incidence of poverty; within the aggregate classes, however, there is little variation in the incidence of poverty between the original classes which comprise them.

Table 5.2:   *Percentage of Variance Explained by Individual and Conventional Class Schemas in Income and Life-Style for Households where the Wife is in Full-Time Unpaid Home Duties*

	Basic Deprivation	Secondary Deprivation	Household Income
1. Individual	0.027	0.052	0.033
2. Conventional	0.070	0.192	0.221
3. Ratio of 2:1	2.6	3.7	6.7

In Table 5.2 we show the degree of association between, on the one hand, class defined in both the individual and conventional (i.e. where the wife is allocated to the husband's class) terms, and, on the other hand, household income and two measures of household deprivation, in those households where the wife is in full-time home duties. Our results clearly show the greater explanatory power of the conventional approach in relation to household deprivation and income. For basic deprivation (that is, the enforced lack of basic items) the conventional approach explains 0.07 of the variance, as against 0.027 explained using the individual approach: thus the ratio of variance explained by the conventional over the individual approach is of the order 2.6:1. This ratio rises to 3.7 in the case of secondary deprivation and finally 6.7 for income. In all cases adopting the conventional method of classifying women results in a class categorisation which has greater power to explain differences in household life-style than has the individual method.

In Table 5.3 we look at the proportion of variance explained which is due to the woman's own class and her husband's class. We are here assigning both women and their husbands to a class on the basis of their own most recent occupation, in order to examine the extent to which each accounts for variation in our three measures of life chances. Our results show that it is the husband's class which is of overriding importance. A model which expresses the level of basic deprivation as a function of both the woman's class and that of her husband explains about 8 per cent of the variance. The woman's class taken alone explains just over 1 per cent, while her husband's class alone explains about 5 per cent. The husband/wife ratio is close to 5:1 for basic deprivation and income, while for secondary deprivation it rises to over 13:1.

*Table 5.3:   Impact of Individual Class and Spouse's Class on Household
              Income and Life-Style for Married Women in Full-Time
              Unpaid Home Duties*

	Basic Deprivation	*Secondary Deprivation*	*Household Income*
1. Total R^2	0.081	0.201	0.228
2. Unique to Individual Class	0.012	0.010	0.006
3. Unique to Spouse's Class	0.054	0.11	0.132
4. Ratio of 3:2	4.5	13.1	5.1

In Table 5.4 we look at the relative power of the woman's and her husband's class to predict whether or not the household is in poverty (once again confining the analysis to households where the wife is in full-time unpaid home duties). In this case we use the three-class aggregate version of the modified CASMIN schema and we employ log-linear models to examine this question. Once again each of these models generates a set of expected frequencies which can be compared with the observed values. The goodness of fit is indicated by the G^2 or likelihood ratio chi-square statistic. Outcomes in which the 'expected' frequencies come close to the observed frequencies and the G^2 is correspondingly low are what is required to provide support for a model. The baseline model, shown on line one of the table (and referred to as the 'no effects model') asserts that neither the woman's class nor the husband's are related to the incidence of poverty, but that there is a relationship between husband's class and wife's class. This fails to fit the data by a long way, returning to a G^2 of 138.7 on 8 df. The model on the second line of the table shows the effect of the woman's own class alone on the chances of the household being in poverty; and line three shows the effect of her husband's class alone. The results are very clear. The model on line two provides a very poor fit to the data, reducing the G^2 associated with the no effects model by only 5 per cent, (rG^2 stands for the percentage reduction in G^2) showing that the wife's own class, based on previous occupation, is a very poor predictor of whether or not a household will be in poverty. By contrast the model on line three reduces G^2 by 93 per cent and is not statistically significantly different from the saturated model, showing that, once we allow for the effect of the husband's class position on the chances of household poverty, the wife's own class position is irrelevant.

Table 5.4: *Results of Fitting 'Individual Class' and Husband's Class to Household Poverty Tables where the Wife is Currently in Full-Time Unpaid Home Duties**

	G^2	df	rG^2
No Effects Model W*H + P	138.7	8	
Wife's Class Effect Only Model W*H + W*P	131.4	6	5.2%
Husband's Class Effect Only Model W*H + H*P	9.3	6	93.3%

* W = Wife's Class; H = Husband's Class; P = Poverty.

These results, concerning households where the wife is not in the paid labour force show very clearly the extent to which the implication of class position, defined in conventional terms, extends beyond the work place to the whole of the family's economic lives. We now turn to the situation of households where both spouses are in the paid labour force.

THE PATTERN OF HUSBAND AND WIFE EFFECTS (II) MARRIED
WOMEN IN THE PAID LABOUR FORCE

In Table 5.5 we look at the unique contribution of married women's
individual class position and their husband's class position (using the
modified seven-class schema) in explaining deprivation and household
income. In contrast to Table 5.1, the overall variance explained is
considerably larger and the variance ratios are much lower. Nevertheless,
with the exception of income (where parity exists), it is again the
husband's class which is the more important explanatory factor, with a
ratio of 1.65 obtaining for primary deprivation and 1.36 for secondary
deprivation.

Table 5.5:   *Percentage of Variance Explained by Individual and
              Conventional Class Schema in Income and Life-Style for
              Households where both Husband and Wife are in the
              Labour Force*

	Basic Deprivation	Secondary Deprivation	Household Income
	R^2	R^2	R^2
1. Combined Impact of Wife's and Husband's Class	0.289	0.098	0.222
2. Unique Contribution of Wife's Class	0.063	0.025	0.073
3. Unique Contribution of Husband's Class	0.104	0.034	0.073
4. Ratio of 3:2	1.65	1.36	1.0

In Table 5.6 we again extend our analysis to the prediction of poverty
(moving once again to the three-class categorisation) and find that a model
which allows for the impact of wife's own class gives a G^2 of 155.8 with
6 df and explains 6 per cent of the 'no effects' model's deviance. In
comparison the model which substitutes the effect of husband's class gives
a G^2 of 47.0 with 6 df and explains 72 per cent of the 'no effects' model's
G^2. In this case, then (and in contrast to the results reported in Table 5.3),
when we take account of husband's class, the wife's own class position
continues to be relevant in predicting the chances of the household being in
poverty, but its effect is tiny when compared with that of the husband's
class.

Table 5.6: *Results of Fitting 'Individual Class' and Husband's Class to Household Poverty Tables Where the Husband and Wife are Currently in the Labour Force**

	G^2	df	rG^2
No Effects Model W*H + P	165.9	8	
Wife's Class Effect Only			
Model W*H + W*P	155.8	6	6.1
Husband's Class Effect Only			
Model W*H + H*P	47.0	6	71.7

* W = Wife's Class; H = Husband's Class; P = Poverty.

Drawing on survey data from a range of societies, Erikson and Goldthorpe (1992b) have examined the relationship between, on the one hand, married women's class identification, and on the other hand, women's own class and that of their husbands. They find that, when both the relationship between both spouses' classes and the effect of the wife's own class on her class identification are taken into account '. . . a further significant association still regularly occurs between a wife's own class identification and her *husband's* class position; and when both are considered separately, the latter association tends to be *stronger* than that between a wife's class identification and her own class position (Erikson and Goldthorpe, 1992a, p. 250).

The evidence presented here relating to deprivation and poverty provides support for Erikson and Goldthorpe's (1992a, pp. 251–2) argument that, once the objective economic situation is adequately represented, it can be seen as quite rational for married women to regard their class interests and affiliations as being pre-eminently determined by their husband's employment rather than by their own. In circumstances where married women are currently in full-time home duties the argument for a derived class approach is even more compelling.

WOMEN'S MOBILITY THROUGH EMPLOYMENT

In this section we continue our examination of the individual approach to the analysis of social mobility by examining the mobility of men and women from their class origins to the positions they held in the work force in 1987. Respondents who were not in the labour force at that time are excluded.

If the social fluidity patterns of men and women turn out to be rather different it would seem important to consider the nature of such differences before proceeding to analyse mobility tables which incorporate men and women. Class origin has been operationalised on the basis of the class of the person who was the 'main breadwinner in your family while you were growing up'. This might be viewed as a rather crude implementation of the dominance procedure. In most cases the individual in question is the father. Even if separate information on mothers' occupation was available, on theoretical grounds we would not wish to conceptualise mobility from such positions as *class* mobility.

One simple means of measuring the degree to which men and women differ in their distribution across origin and destination classes is to calculate the percentage of one sex — say women — who would have to be allocated to a class, other than the one in which they are found, in order to make the distributions for the two sexes identical. The measure is termed the 'index of dissimilarity' or delta. In relation to class origins, Erikson and Goldthorpe (1992b, p. 243) report results for France, the Federal Republic of Germany, Hungary, Poland and Sweden showing that between 2 and 6 per cent of women would have to 'change' class in order to make the male and female distributions the same. These results suggest that there has been little or no 'selection' of women currently in the work-force by class of origin. The somewhat higher Irish value of 9 per cent arises from a tendency for Irish women in the labour force to be disproportionately drawn from the professional and managerial and *petit bourgeoisie* classes. The sex differences in relation to origins are negligible, however, in comparison to those relating to current employment situation. The results reported by Erikson and Goldthorpe show that from a quarter to almost two-fifths of employed women would have to be reallocated in order to make their distribution the same as that of men. The Irish figure of 37 per cent is at the high end of the continuum. One explanation of this is the higher probability of women being found in the service class. Over one in four women are in this class compared to just over one in six men. This finding is consistent with the evidence of selection on class origins referred to earlier. A further breakdown of the results shows, as we might expect, that it is in the lower professional and managerial class that women are particularly concentrated. The remaining differences reflect the existence of a marked sex segregation of labour-markets in all industrial societies. Apart from the exclusion of women from the property-owning classes, the crucial element is the extremely low number of women in lower-grade technical and skilled manual work; with only 8 per cent of women found in such occupations compared to 28 per cent of men. Correspondingly, women are five times more likely to be found in the upper routine non-manual occupations.

Table 5.7: *Women's and Men's Employment Mobility Chances (Percentage by Column) (Men's Figures in Parentheses)*

Employment Position	Class of Origin							
	Professional and Managerial	Upper Non-Manual	Petit Bourgeoisie	Farmers	Technicians and Skilled Manual	Non-Skilled Manual and Lower Non-Manual	Agricultural Workers	Total in Employment Class
Professional and Managerial (I+II)	52.3 (56.5)	41.4 (40.6)	34.1 (36.1)	34.9 (11.2)	14.8 (12.7)	11.5 (11.7)	4.6 (3.8)	25.6 (17.1)
Upper Non-Manual (IIIa)	21.9 (9.3)	28.5 (3.1)	26.0 (3.0)	16.2 (1.7)	16.2 (6.4)	19.0 (3.5)	5.8 (6.1)	18.6 (3.9)
Petit Bourgeoisie (IVa+b)	5.0 (6.3)	0.0 (9.1)	8.4 (20.1)	2.8 (8.9)	3.2 (6.3)	1.2 (5.2)	2.4 (2.4)	8.1 (7.3)
Farmers (IVc)	0.0 (0.2)	0.0 (0.0)	0.0 (1.8)	1.1 (36.2)	0.0 (0.6)	0.0 (0.8)	0.0 (1.2)	0.0 (10.1)
Technicians and Skilled Manual (V/VI)	2.4 (17.2)	0.0 (21.9)	4.6 (22.8)	5.9 (18.2)	13.5 (42.6)	8.6 (29.0)	17.0 (32.2)	4.9 (27.6)
Non-Skilled Manual and Lower Non-Manual (IIIb+VIIa)	16.7 (10.6)	30.1 (21.3)	26.8 (15.3)	34.9 (17.4)	52.3 (30.7)	59.4 (47.7)	69.5 (44.3)	43.6 (30.6)
Agricultural Workers (VIIb)	1.7 (0.0)	0.0 (3.9)	0.0 (0.9)	4.2 (6.4)	0.0 (0.6)	0.2 (2.1)	0.6 (15.3)	1.3 (3.5)
Total	12.6 (8.1)	3.4 (2.5)	8.7 (5.8)	23.1 (26.3)	21.2 (20.2)	27.4 (31.7)	3.6 (35.0)	100.0(100.0)
N	122 (194)	33 (59)	84 (138)	224 (627)	206 (482)	266 (757)	36 (123)	971 (2,380)

Finally, they are also more heavily concentrated than men in lower-grade white-collar work and non-skilled manual work. The former is a category which is dominated by women.

In Table 5.7 we show the outflow mobility table for women and men corresponding to the marginal distributions we have been discussing. This can be taken as showing how the class mobility of women appears if the 'individual' approach to the class allocation of women currently in the labour force is adopted. The results show some marked differences between the destination classes occupied by women and men of similar class origins. With the exception of farming origins, women from each class have very similar patterns of outflow to the service class to their male counterparts. Women from farm origins, however, are three times more likely than comparable men to enter the service class. The remaining differences appear to be connected to the overall patterns of gender segregation in the labour-market and to affect women from all class origins. Women are consistently over-represented in the white-collar and unskilled manual categories and under-represented among the *petit bourgeoisie*, farmers and the skilled manual class. Associated with such segregation there is a significantly greater tendency for women in the service class to come from farm backgrounds than is the case for men; the respective figures being one-third and one-sixth. Correspondingly, women from non-skilled manual backgrounds make up a significantly lower percentage of the service class than do their male counterparts. A similar pattern holds for higher-level white-collar work. The advantages enjoyed by women from farming origins might have been anticipated on the basis of our discussion in Chapter 3 of the more successful adaptation strategies of small farmers in comparison with the working-class (Hannan and Commins, 1992). Finally, a significantly greater percentage of women in the non-skilled manual class come from non-working-class backgrounds than is the case for men.

As a consequence of their exclusion from those class categories in which inheritance has its greatest influence the mobility stakes are higher for women. In Table 5.8 we summarise the extent of women's mobility through employment in comparison with men and provide details of the nature of their mobility. Women experience greater mobility than men with 72 per cent of women having moved from their class of origin compared to 60 per cent of men. Women are more likely than men to experience vertical mobility i.e. upward *or* downward mobility than men — 57 per cent compared to 44 per cent. They, however, have rather similar rates of non-vertical mobility. In calculating these figures we follow Erikson and Goldthorpe (1992b, p. 45) in taking the service class and the non-skilled manual class to represent the extremes of the hierarchy while all other classes are taken as intermediate. Women have identical upward mobility rates to men but somewhat greater downward mobility, with 29 per cent of women experiencing such mobility compared to 18 per cent of men. The rate of upward mobility for Irish women is almost identical to that observed by Erikson and Goldthorpe for the five countries they studied. The level of downward mobility is at the high end of the range observed for other countries giving Irish women a relatively low rate of upward to downward mobility of 0.9. The comparable rate for men is somewhat higher at 1.5.

Table 5.8: *Total Mobility Rates, Total Vertical (TV), Total Non-Vertical(TNV), Total Upward (TU) and Total Downward (TD) Rates for Women and Men from Class Origins to Current Employment Situation*

	Men	Women
Total Mobility Rates	60	72
Total Vertical (TV)	44	57
Total Non-Vertical (TNV)	16	15
TV/TNV	2.8	3.8
Total Upward (TU)	27	27
Total Downward (TD)	18	29
TU/TD	1.5	0.9

The results we have presented are very much on the lines that we would expect from our knowledge of the extent and nature of gender segregation in the labour-market. The remaining question which we seek to answer in relation to women's employment mobility is whether, underlying the differences in absolute mobility that we have observed, there are also differences in relative mobility rates that reflect male/female variation in class-based inequality of opportunity. The alternative hypothesis is that the sole source of variation in men's and women's mobility chances is differences in the objective structure of men's and women's employment.

In order to test this hypothesis Breen and Whelan (1995) sought to establish if it was possible to explain gender differences in mobility simply by allowing for differences in origin and destination distributions while assuming that the underlying pattern of association of social fluidity was the same for women and men. This is usually termed the constant social fluidity (CnSF) model. The results shown in Table 5.9 provide strong evidence in support of this hypothesis. The CnSF model has a G^2 of 57.2 with 36 df. It reduces the conditional independence G^2 by 95.6 per cent and classifies 96.5 per cent of the cases correctly. It falls marginally short of fitting the data using the conventional criterion, but this arises solely from large residuals in two cells of the mobility table: these are IVc-I+II (farmer origin, service class destination) and V/VI-IIIa (skilled manual origin, higher routine non-manual destination). For men the numbers mobile to the service class from farm backgrounds are overestimated while for women the numbers are underestimated. Similarly, the outflow from the skilled manual class to higher routine white-collar work is underestimated for men and overestimated for women. The former is clearly explicable in terms of the differential attractiveness of the farming destination for men and women while the latter suggests additional barriers to entry for women. If these cells are fitted exactly the percentage of cases correctly classified increased to 97.25 per cent.

Table 5.9: *Results of Fitting the CnSF Model to Mobility Tables for Women's and Men's Mobility From Class Origins to Current Employment**

	G^2	df	rG2
Conditional Independence O*S D*S	1,308	72	
CnSF Model O*S D*S O*D	57.2	36	95.61

* O = Origin Class;   D = Current Employment Situation; S = Sex.

Our analysis therefore leads us to reject claims that class background and gender interact (Abbot and Sapsford, 1987, p. 72). Inequalities in relative mobility chances appear to be 'gender blind' and are independent of the social processes that generate sex segregation in employment. 'And the fact that they operate in a way that is "gender blind" would thus in turn suggest that, if an adequate account is to be provided of the social processes that generate sex segregation in employment — and hence women's restricted opportunities — this will in fact need to be one that is for the most part developed independently of class analysis' (Erikson and Goldthorpe, 1992b, p. 253).

WOMEN'S MOBILITY THROUGH MARRIAGE

The debate on the appropriate unit of class composition has led to agreement on all sides that women's mobility through marriage is an

Table 5.10: A Comparison of Women's Marital Mobility Chances and Married Men's Mobility Chances (Percentaged by Column) (Married Men's Figures in Parentheses)

Employment Position	Class of Origin							Total in Employment Class
	Professional and Managerial	Upper Non-Manual	Petit Bourgeoisie	Farmers	Technicians and Skilled Manual	Non-Skilled Manual and Lower Non-Manual	Agricultural Workers	
Professional and Managerial (I+II)	60.2 (67.3)	32.7 (30.6)	24.0 (40.0)	16.8 (14.9)	20.4 (14.5)	10.1 (11.6)	6.6 (4.3)	20.3 (20.4)
Routine Non-Manual (III)	9.6 (8.8)	10.4 (16.5)	15.5 (4.7)	5.9 (3.5)	10.5 (10.3)	7.4 (10.9)	9.3 (3.1)	8.7 (8.3)
Petit Bourgeoisie (IVa+b)	7.7 (5.3)	6.0 (7.0)	12.8 (18.6)	11.3 (12.1)	6.8 (8.2)	4.8 (4.9)	6.7 (3.4)	7.8 (8.3)
Farmers (IVc)	2.2 (0.0)	2.0 (0.0)	6.0 (2.5)	23.7 (33.3)	1.7 (0.6)	2.4 (1.1)	5.1 (2.8)	7.7 (9.2)
Technicians and Skilled Manual (V/VI)	13.6 (15.5)	23.5 (25.2)	14.4 (21.3)	24.0 (18.6)	32.8 (47.1)	38.4 (30.9)	27.1 (34.3)	29.0 (28.9)
Non-Skilled Manual (VIIa)	6.7 (3.0)	23.7 (20.2)	22.3 (12.9)	15.0 (15.1)	32.1 (19.1)	33.4 (38.5)	34.9 (39.1)	23.3 (22.9)
Agricultural Workers (VIIb)	0.0 (0.0)	1.7 (0.6)	2.4 (0.0)	3.3 (2.6)	2.3 (0.2)	3.4 (2.1)	10.3 (12.9)	3.2 (2.8)
Total	8.7 (8.5)	6.4 (2.8)	6.5 (6.0)	23.8 (25.1)	21.3 (19.8)	26.2 (28.1)	7.1 (5.4)	100.0 (100.0)
N	126 (142)	91 (117)	93 (99)	342 (421)	306 (328)	376 (467)	103 (89)	1,436 (1,664)

important and neglected topic. Thus Erikson and Goldthorpe (1992b, p. 253) recognise that if married women are to be seen as tending to derive their class position from their husbands then an understanding of their intergenerational class mobility requires that we direct our attention to the experience of women in 'marriage markets' rather than labour-markets; specifically it is necessary to examine rates and patterns of marital mobility.

A recurring hypothesis in the literature is that women experience more mobility through marriage than do men through employment and their 'class fate is more loosely linked' to social origins than is the case for men (Heath, 1981). The main argument underlying this hypothesis is that physical or personality attributes, which can make women more or less attractive as marriage partners, are less closely associated with social origins than are those that mainly influence men's achievements in their working lives. If this hypothesis is true, then focusing solely on men's mobility could lead to substantial underestimation of the extent of mobility opportunities within the society.

Table 5.11: Delta Values for Outflow Rates for Marital Mobility of Women and Intergenerational Mobility of Married Men

Class of Origin	
Professional and Managerial (I+II)	9
Routine Non-Manual (III)	7
Petit-Bourgeoisie (IVa+b)	22
Farmers (IVc)	11
Technicians and Skilled Manual (V+VI)	16
Non-Skilled Manual (VIIa)	10
Agricultural Workers (VIIb)	16

For this analysis we revert to the conventional seven-class CASMIN schema in which both types of routine non-manual work are combined in Class III in order to allow for cross-national comparisons. Employing this schema, we compare women's marital mobility to the class mobility of married men through employment. The results are set out in Table 5.10. The delta values representing the dissimilarities arising from these outflow patterns are set out in Table 5.11. As with the nine countries studied by Erikson and Goldthorpe (1992b) the differences between the two sets of outflow rates are not very large — only in the case of the *petit bourgeoisie* does the figure exceed 20. For the service class and the upper non-manual class the low values for the index of dissimilarity reflect the almost identical distributions for women's mobility through marriage and men's mobility through employment. Women from the service class are slightly less likely to remain in this class through marriage than are their male counterparts to do so through employment. They are correspondingly more likely to be downwardly mobile into the non-skilled manual class. Women from upper non-manual origins are less likely to enter the skilled manual class through marriage than are men through employment. Among the skilled manual class lower levels of inheritance are set against greater movement to the top and the bottom of the class structure; while among the unskilled manual it is compensated for by movement into the skilled manual class.

While married women are somewhat less likely to be immobile through marriage than men — the respective percentages are 37 and 29 per cent — their rates of upward and downward mobility are strikingly similar, as we can see from Table 5.12. In each case just less than one-third have been upwardly mobile and in the region of one-seventh have been downwardly mobile. Once again our results bear a remarkable resemblance to those reported by Erikson and Goldthorpe (1992a, p. 257) for nine European countries in the 1970s. The only change observed for Ireland between 1973 and 1987 was an increase in downward movement in relation to both types of mobility. Our results are therefore consistent with their conclusion that an analysis of absolute mobility rates provides little in the way of evidence that women's mobility possibilities via marriage are such as to suggest that the class structures of industrial societies are a great deal more permeable than we have previously imagined.

Table 5.12: Total Upward (TU) and Total Downward (TD) Rates for Marital Mobility of Women and Intergenerational Mobility of Married Men (Figures in Parentheses are for Ireland 1973)

	Women		Men	
TU	32	(34)	30	(31)
TD	16	(11)	13	(9)
TU/TD	2.0		2.3	

It remains possible, however, that an analysis of relative mobility rates may provide greater support for the notion of looser links to class origins in the case of women's mobility through marriage. Our attention is therefore directed to the question of whether underlying the higher rates of social mobility experienced by women, are differences in the underlying patterns of social fluidity. As a first test of this hypothesis we applied the Constant Social Fluidity model to the joint table for women's marital mobility and married men's mobility through employment. This model produces a G^2 of 74.1 with 36 df and accounts for 93.4 per cent of the conditional independence model G^2. Thus it provides strong evidence for substantial underlying similarities in social fluidity patterns but also suggests significant differences between the two types of mobility.

In order to carry out a formal analysis of the differences in mobility patterns between women's marital mobility and married men's mobility we use the Agriculture, Hierarchy and Property (AHP) model discussed earlier and follow the logic set out by Breen (1985). In this analysis the scores applied to the origins and destinations to represent resources and desirability/barriers are those derived from our analysis of men aged between twenty and sixty-four since they continue to represent our best estimate of such attributes. The results of our analysis are set out in Table 5.13. We began by fitting Model 1, a common (homogeneous) model, which assumes that the effects of hierarchy, property etc. are identical for both types of mobility. The model uses one parameter to allow for the different sample sizes of the men's and women's tables. The reason for fitting such a model is that, conditional on the AHP model being true of both tables, we can relax successive parameter constraints to determine the relative contribution of different factors to mobility differences. The common mobility model or 'no difference model' clearly fails to fit the data having a G^2 of 114.1 with 78 df. Although, compared with the model of independence, this model reduces G^2 by 89.9 per cent. At the other extreme if we fit the AHP model to each table separately (a completely heterogeneous model — shown as Model 3 in Table 5.13) — this returns a G^2 of 65.1 with 60 df and does provide a satisfactory statistical fit. This model allows all mobility effects to differ between the two tables. What we would like to explain is the difference in G^2 values of these models. This has a value of 49.0 and is associated with 18 degrees of freedom (panel B, Table 5.13). We term it the total mobility difference variance.

Out next step is to allow the origin and destination effects — but not the interaction effects which shape odds-ratios — to vary between the two tables. This is Model 2, and has a G^2 of 102.4 with 66 df. The G^2 difference between this model and Model 1 is 11.7 with 12 df and it accounts for 23.9 per cent of the mobility difference. This difference is attributable to structural mobility — defined to mean the effect of differences in the marginal distributions of the two tables. The fact that this mobility difference is not statistically significant tells us that, given the AHP

Table 5.13: Results from Fitting the AHP Model to Tables of Women's Marital Mobility and Married Men's Intergenerational Mobility

A		G^2	df
1	Common Mobility Model (Homogeneous AHP Allowing for a Difference in Sample Size Only)	114.1	78
2	Heterogeneous Absolute Mobility, Common Social Fluidity	102.4	66
3	Heterogeneous Absolute Mobility and Social Fluidity	65.1	60
4	Heterogeneous Absolute Mobility and Social Fluidity but with only INH1 and AGB Parameters Varying	68.9	64

B	*Decomposition of Deviance*		
	Total Mobility Difference (1–3)	49.0	18
	Absolute Mobility Difference (1–2)	11.7	12
	Social Fluidity Difference (2–3)	37.3	6

C	*Row and Column Scores*		
	Class	*Rows*	*Columns*
	I+II 1.73	1.71	
	III 0.42	0.43	
	IVa+b	0.39	0.73
	IVc -0.24	-0.47	
	V/VI	0.10	-0.17
	VIIa -0.37	-1.05	
	VIIb -0.75	-1.10	

D	*Parameter Estimates*			
	Common Parameters	*Estimate*	*S.E.*	*Parameter*
		0.99	(0.26)	INH3
		0.63	(0.11)	SLP
		1.24	(0.14)	α
		0.61	(0.04)	β

Heterogenous Parameters	*Men*		*Deviation for Women*		*Parameter*
	Estimate	*S.E.*	*Estimate*	*S.E.*	
	-1.52	(0.29)	0.90	(0.33)	AGB
	0.36	(0.07)	-0.37	(0.10)	INH1

specification of odds-ratios in the two tables, their marginal distributions do not differ from each other in a significant fashion. The difference between Model 2 and Model 3 is 37.3 with 6 df representing 76.1 per cent of the mobility difference variance, and it is associated with differences in social fluidity (or relative mobility) between the two tables. Thus it is differences in relative mobility which are the major factors contributing to the overall mobility difference variance.

In identifying the nature of this difference it is important to note that Model 4, which allows only two of the interaction parameters (AGB and INH1) to vary between the two tables, provides as good a fit to the data as does Model 3 which allows all of the AHP parameters to vary. The G^2 for Model 4 is 68.9 with 64 df. The row and column scores (measuring resources and desirability/barriers respectively) are given in panel C of Table 5.13, and the parameter estimates for Model 4 are given in panel D. These show that *the only significant differences in the underlying patterns of social fluidity as between women's marital mobility and men's employment mobility are that (a) the barriers to entry to agriculture are weaker for women; and, (b) among women there is no overall inheritance effect*. These results indicate that women are more likely to change class through marriage than men are to change class through employment mobility; and that it is easier (*ceteris paribus*) for women to marry farmers and farm workers than for men not born into agriculture to become farmers or farm workers themselves.

These results from the AHP model confirm the extraordinary similarity of the degree and pattern of fluidity displayed by women's marital mobility and married men's mobility through employment. 'If we know how men of a given class origin have themselves become distributed within the class structure in the course of their employment we can predict, with no great inaccuracy, how their 'sisters' will have been distributed through marriage (Erikson and Goldthorpe, 1992, p. 261). The rather modest differences that do exist relate mainly to relative rather than absolute mobility and cannot be interpreted in terms of superior mobility opportunities for women.

THE ANALYSIS OF COMPLETE MOBILITY TABLES

While rejecting the individual approach to class, Erikson and Goldthorpe have accepted that men-only mobility tables do suffer from certain disadvantages, and consequently, may be in some measure misleading if not supplemented by analysis of the marital mobility of respondents' wives. Such an approach, however, neglects the experience of unmarried women. Furthermore, as a consequence of automatically taking the husband as the head of the conjugal family, it fails to take into account those situations where, on the basis of labour-market criteria, it is the wife rather than the husband who should be regarded as occupying the dominant position, and should determine how the class allocation of the family as a unit should be made.

In order to construct mobility tables which display the experience of the male and female adult population together we employ Erikson's (1984) dominance approach. This involves classifying all unmarried people according to the 'individual' approach, and classifying all married persons according to the class position of whichever partner is considered 'dominant'. Two criteria of dominance have been proposed. The first is the 'work time' criterion: here class position is assigned according to the rule that employment dominates non-employment and full-time employment dominates part-time.

The second criterion ('work position') requires that higher level employment should dominate lower level employment. Erikson and Goldthorpe (1992a, p. 266) describe two dominance orderings of their class categories. We follow them in adopting that ordering which maximises the number of wife dominated couples. This is as follows:

1. (I+II) Professional and Managerial
2. (IVa+b) *Petit Bourgeoisie*
3. (IVc) Farmers
4. (IIIa) Upper Routine Non-Manual
5. (V+VI) Technicians and Skilled Manual
6. (IIIb+VIIa) Lower Routine Non-Manual and Non-Skilled Manual
7. (VIIb) Agricultural Workers

The composition of the complete mobility table that results is as follows:

(i)   16 per cent and 15 per cent are, respectively, single men and women;

(ii)   51 per cent are couples with the husband dominant;

(iii)   8 per cent are couples with the husband and wife equal;

(iv)   8 per cent are couples with the wife dominant.

The main sources of difference between the complete and men-only mobility tables lie in their destination distributions. The complete mobility table implies a somewhat larger white-collar class and a marginally smaller skilled manual class.

Table 5.14: *Class Mobility Chances: A Comparison of Results from the Dominance and Conventional Approaches (Percentaged by Column) (Results from Conventional Approach in Parentheses)*

Employment Position	Class of Origin							Total in Employment Class
	Professional and Managerial	Upper Non-Manual	Petit Bourgeoisie	Farmers	Technicians and Skilled Manual	Non-Skilled Manual and Lower Non-Manual	Agricultural Workers	
Professional and Managerial (I+II)	56.1 (56.5)	52.1 (40.6)	35.4 (36.1)	18.6 (11.2)	16.8 (12.7)	11.6 (11.7)	6.8 (3.8)	20.6 (17.1)
Upper Non-Manual (IIIa)	12.4 (9.3)	10.1 (3.1)	11.0 (3.0)	6.7 (1.7)	8.3 (6.4)	6.9 (3.5)	2.9 (0.7)	7.8 (3.9)
Petit Bourgeoisie (IVa+b)	5.4 (6.3)	4.6 (9.1)	13.0 (20.1)	7.4 (8.9)	5.2 (6.3)	3.8 (5.2)	3.9 (2.4)	5.7 (7.3)
Farmers (IVc)	0.5 (0.2)	0.0 (0.0)	2.3 (1.8)	24.1 (36.2)	0.4 (0.6)	0.8 (0.8)	2.1 (1.2)	6.6 (10.1)
Technicians and Skilled Manual (V+VI)	11.7 (17.2)	14.6 (21.9)	18.5 (22.8)	16.8 (18.2)	33.6 (42.6)	29.8 (29.0)	31.8 (32.2)	24.8 (27.6)
Non-Skilled Manual and Lower Non-Manual (IIIb+VIIa)	13.5 (10.6)	16.3 (21.3)	19.4 (15.3)	22.3 (17.4)	35.5 (30.7)	45.9 (47.7)	46.4 (44.2)	32.6 (30.6)
Agricultural Workers (VIIb)	0.2 (0.0)	1.9 (3.9)	0.4 (0.9)	4.0 (6.4)	0.2 (0.6)	1.2 (2.1)	6.0 (15.3)	1.9 (3.5)
Total	8.6 (8.1)	2.7 (2.5)	6.4 (5.8)	24.8 (26.3)	20.5 (20.2)	31.2 (31.7)	5.7 (5.4)	100.0 (100.0)

Our findings confirm that complete tables tend to give higher rates of mobility than the men-only tables — 67 per cent compared with 60 per cent in this case. The difference arises entirely from the greater vertical mobility (51 per cent as against 44 per cent) in the complete table. Consistent with earlier findings, the rate of upward mobility is higher (29 per cent compared with 27 per cent), but, in the Irish case so is downward mobility (22 per cent *versus* 18 per cent). There are some systematic differences between the two types of table, as we can see from Table 5.14; of which mobility into the white collar-classes is the most significant. In the complete table 15.8 per cent have been mobile into the service class and 6.7 per cent into the higher routine non-manual class, while for the men-only tables, the comparable figures are 12.3 per cent and 3.2 per cent. However, it is difficult to disagree with Erikson and Goldthorpe's (1992, p. 270) conclusion that one could well be more impressed with the similarities than the differences. The striking consistency between our results and those of Erikson and Goldthorpe is particularly significant because of the widespread assumption that what is taken to be Goldthorpe's thesis has been thoroughly refuted.

This leads us to the question of how far such differences as there are between the tables can be attributed to differences in their marginal distributions (particularly in the destination distributions) or, on the other hand, to differences in the pattern of social fluidity. Clearly, if the latter is the case, then the use of complete mobility tables would require us to revise those conclusions concerning social fluidity in Ireland which have been derived from men-only tables.

In order to deal with this issue, we again make use of the AHP model. In this case the row and column scores applied to the complete table are derived from all respondents included in the mobility table. When we fit this model to the complete table we get a G^2 of 51.5 with 30 df which compares to a G^2 of 39.8 for the men-only table. That is to say, using the conventional statistical yardstick, the model fits the men-only table but does not fit the complete table. However, in order to find a version of the model which fits it is necessary only to make a slight adjustment to the SLP term. This is the term which captures the additional advantages displayed by the propensity of men of *petit bourgeoisie* and farm origins to move into the service class. It emerges that in the complete table this advantage extends to access to the higher routine non-manual class also, undoubtedly reflecting the greater attractiveness of this class for women. When we make this change we find that the model now fits both the complete table ($G^2 = 40.7$) as well as the men-only table, as shown in panel A of Table 5.15.

Table 5.15: Results of Fitting the AHP Model to Men-Only and Complete Mobility Tables

		Complete Table		Men-Only Table	
A.	*Goodness of Fit*	G^2	*df*	G^2	*df*
	AHP Model	40.7	30.0	39.8	30.0
B.	*Estimated Origin and Destination Hierarchy Scores*				
		Origin	Destination	Origin	Destination
	I+II	1.77	1.22	1.73	1.71
	IIIa	1.39	0.50	1.22	1.15
	IVa+b	0.60	0.51	0.39	0.73
	IVc	-0.14	-0.48	-0.24	-0.47
	V/VI	0.12	-0.32	0.10	-0.17
	III+VIIa	-0.24	-0.67	-0.33	-0.85
	VIIb	-0.68	-0.65	-0.75	-1.10
C.	*Parameter Estimates*				
	Parameter	*Estimates*	*S.E.*	*Estimate*	*S.E.*
	INH1	0.12	(0.05)	0.27	(0.06)
	INH3	1.14	(0.27)	1.51	(0.37)
	AGB	-1.69	(0.21)	-1.78	(0.24)
	SLP	0.68	(0.08)	0.68	(0.13)
	BETA	0.22	(0.14)	1.22	(0.17)
	ALPHA	0.70	(0.04)	0.53	(0.04)

In panel C of Table 5.15, we compare the parameter estimates for both tables. The similarity is quite striking. Apart from the modification to the SLP term, already referred to, the only noteworthy difference relates to the inheritance parameters. Consistent with the results of our earlier analysis of women's employment mobility, the inheritance effects are much weaker in the complete table. This finding is in agreement with the results of Erikson and Goldthorpe's (1992a) analysis but offers a somewhat more general conclusion. Application of their model (the Core Model of Social Fluidity) did not produce a statistically acceptable fit to any of the complete tables they analysed. Examination of the residuals, however, suggested that a major reason for this was the lower propensity for intergenerational immobility among those from *petit bourgeoisie* and farming class origins than their model predicted. Our own results suggest that the tendency to overestimate immobility in the complete mobility table is more general and extends to all origins. The propertied classes are distinctive, however, in that in the complete table we must take into account not only their lower propensity to immobility (relative to what is found in men-only tables) but also compensatory advantages in terms of ease of access to the higher routine non-manual class.

Nevertheless, the results we have reported demonstrate that only modest differences exist in the patterns of social fluidity associated with complete and men-only tables. Similarly in an earlier analysis we have shown that for men-only tables relatively little change can be observed in the mobility regime between 1973 and 1987 (Breen and Whelan, 1992). Consequently, despite the substantial expansion of labour force participation by married women throughout the 1970s and 1980s, a model of social fluidity which provides a satisfactory fit for men in 1973 will come very close to accounting for the pattern of social fluidity in the complete table for 1987. Such a finding provides substantial support for Erikson and Goldthorpe's (1992a, p. 273) conclusion that gender and class inequality are not of a cognate kind.

CONCLUSIONS

The central issue of this chapter has been the extent to which the incorporation of women into class mobility analysis requires us to alter our understanding of the basic processes involved. To avoid any possible confusion we should make clear that we fully accept the desirability of such incorporation. At the outset we described the conceptual framework from within which we have sought to answer this question. Following Erikson and Goldthorpe (1992b, p. 231) we are convinced that nothing in the argument we have provided is inconsistent with '. . . a belief in the practical concern that women should possess a full and equal opportunity with men *de jure* and *de facto*, so far as participation in economic and public life is concerned'. Our approach is based on a recognition of the limited extent to which women's increased levels of participation have gone together with such equality of opportunities. A great deal of the debate in this area has involved people talking past each other. Despite this we have adhered to the view that evidence is crucial in the evaluation of different conceptual approaches to this issue. Accordingly, much of this chapter has been devoted to replicating and extending the analysis of Erikson and Goldthorpe (1992b) using the Irish data.

The Irish case offers a particularly useful opportunity to pursue such analysis. The changing participation rates of married women in recent years provide an interesting test case of some of the claims associated with the individual approach to class analysis. In addition, we are in the fortunate position that the data available allow us to explore the consequences of varying the unit of class composition and, additionally, permit an examination of the implications of different approaches to class analysis for our ability to explain variations in life chances. We have sought to extend the work of Erikson and Goldthorpe by making use of a mobility model (the AHP model) which allows us to pinpoint the areas of difference and similarity in mobility regimes much more clearly than was possible with the models used by Erikson and Goldthorpe.

We began our analysis by examining the individual approach to the assignment of persons to classes. This revealed the problems associated with the class position of wives, regardless of whether they are currently in the paid labour force or not. In both cases the conventional approach to class analysis (assigning married women to the class position of their husbands) provided a better account of differences in objective life chances than did the individual approach. In addition, when we employed the individual approach we found that husband's class was more important than wife's own class in accounting for the household's level of deprivation and income. We also employed the individual approach to compare the mobility of men and women who were in the Irish labour force in 1987. Here we found only minuscule differences in the pattern of social fluidity among men and women, so supporting Erikson and Goldthorpe's view that differences in mobility patterns between men and women are overwhelmingly due to differences in the objectives opportunity structures facing them. Despite the frequency with which it has been asserted there is no evidence to support the claim for class/gender interaction.

We then turned to an examination of women's marital mobility, comparing this with men's mobility through the labour-market. In this analysis we made use of the AHP mobility model which, while being based on Goldthorpe's (1980) theoretical resources/desirability/ barriers framework, uses mainly measured variables in accounting for social fluidity. Because of this (and because the model provides a statistically adequate account of the mobility process) our discussion of parameter differences allowed us to define precisely the nature of the differences between men's labour-market mobility and women's marital mobility. In fact such differences turned out to be rather modest. Women are more likely to be mobile into agriculture through marriage than are men through the labour-market; and the likelihood of women marrying someone from a different class background is greater than the likelihood of men being mobile out of their class of origin.

Lastly we examined so-called 'complete' mobility tables, constructed using Erikson's (1984) 'dominance' approach. Using the AHP model to compare this table with the men-only table revealed some significant differences. Once again these involve higher mobility into the white-collar classes. These findings are consistent with our earlier results relating to female employment mobility and on this occasion we once again find that the objective opportunity structure is the critical factor. The only differences in the underlying patterns of social fluidity for men-only and complete mobility tables relate to lower inheritance parameters, and a broadening of the affinity term (relating to the ease of mobility from *petit bourgeoisie* and farm origins to the service class) to incorporate mobility into the higher white-collar class. The fundamental similarity between the mobility regimes for these two types of tables, and the earlier evidence for relatively modest differences between 1973 and 1987 for the men-only tables, indicates that substantial changes in the levels of labour force participation of married women have had a negligible effect on the process of class mobility. This should not be taken as providing justification for the exclusion of women from mobility analysis. It does suggest, however, that as Erikson and Goldthorpe (1992a, p. 253) have argued, any adequate explanation of the disadvantages suffered by women as a consequence of gendered labour-market segmentation and the lack of continuity in their work histories is likely to be developed, for the most part, independently of class analysis.

We should stress that our analysis clearly recognises the disadvantages suffered by women as a consequence of gendered labour-market segmentation and the lack of continuity in their work histories. Indeed, it is precisely because of such features — and the consequent economic dependence of the majority of women within the family — that the family unit continues to be the appropriate one for class analysis. Our findings consistently support the argument of Erikson and Goldthorpe (1992b, p. 235) that 'the lines of class division run between but not through, families'.

6 Education, Class Origins and Entry to the Labour Force

INTRODUCTION

One of the most striking and significant state policies during this century has been the introduction of free education in all industrialised nations. Ireland was a late starter in the process of educational reform, but in the 1960s a series of changes was set in train that greatly increased state involvement in education. Although post-primary education in vocational schools had always been free of charge, it was not until 1967 that secondary schools agreed to forgo fees in exchange for a capitation grant from the state. In addition, physical access to post-primary schools was eased by the simultaneous introduction of free school transport. Such reforms gave an impetus to the pre-existing growth in educational participation rates, so that at present more than three-quarters of each age cohort complete full-time post-primary education (Breen *et al*, 1990, pp.123–30).

As a late industrialising, semi-peripheral nation, Ireland provides a useful test case for theories that seek to relate social change to economic development. The recency of Irish industrialization means that data are available relating to the periods both before and after this change. In this chapter we will be particularly concerned with the degree to which the Irish experience provides support for the so-called 'liberal theory of industrialism' (Kerr *et al* 1960; Kerr 1969; Parsons 1960, 1964, 1970; Treiman 1970). We test this by examining the extent to which two implications of the thesis can be seen to have occurred in Ireland. First is the belief that class origins will become less closely linked to class destinations as ascription gives way to achievement. Second is the belief that primarily educational (but also other impartially certified) credentials will increasingly be used to allocate individuals to positions in the class structure. These changes come about for two main reasons. First, there will be a composition effect as classes that own the means of production and in which the direct inheritance of class position is of paramount importance (notably farmers, the *petit bourgeoisie* and the self-employed) decline in number and the number of employees increases. Second, among employees jobs will increasingly be acquired on the basis of achievement. This, it is argued, is a functional necessity of capitalism. In order to compete with other nations an economy must ensure that optimum use is made of its population's abilities: hence the acquisition of position on the grounds of anything other than merit will be sub-optimal. In allocating positions on the basis of achievement, educational credentials will come to play a central role. This process is sometimes called 'expanding universalism' (Blau and Duncan 1967, p.430).

An alternative approach, while it accepts the increasing role of education in allocating people to positions, argues that education is not the only factor that plays this role. It further holds that there may be, at most, only a very modest change in the class of origin/class of entry relationship, and that the direction of such change will be indeterminate. In contrast to the liberal theory, then, this approach draws attention to the ability of those in positions of privilege and power to maintain their position against encroachment by outsiders, even in the face of the functional requirements of industrial society and specific State policies that might threaten them.

In this chapter we investigate whether these developments are evident in the transition from education to the class of entry to the labour force. We first focus on the relationship between class origins and educational attainment to see if there has been any change over time in the relationship between these two. Has the expansion of the educational system led to a weakening in the link between class origins and educational attainment? Then we turn to the relationship between class of entry to the labour force, on the one hand, and education and class origins on the other. Has there been any evident strengthening of the relationship between education and class of entry and has this been at the expense of the link between class origins and class of entry as the liberal theory implies?

VARIABLES USED IN THE ANALYSES

In order to examine change over time in these processes we define what are sometimes called 'synthetic cohorts'. In other words, using the data collected in 1987, we divide our sample into three age groups and treat these as separate cohorts. These cohorts are defined as follows:

Cohort 1:   those respondents born between 1922 and 1936, the bulk of whom would have entered the labour force between 1936 and 1957;

Cohort 2:   those respondents born between 1937 and 1949, and who would have entered the labour force between 1951 and 1970;

Cohort 3:   those respondents born between 1950 and 1962 and who would, therefore, have entered the labour force no earlier than about 1965.

Of these three cohorts, the third is distinguished in virtue of the fact that it is only the members of this cohort who would have had the opportunity of free post-primary education and who would have entered the labour force after the process of industrialization that commenced in the late 1950s.

We measure educational credentials in a relatively straightforward way, using the highest level of formal educational qualification possessed by the individual. We define four such levels:

1   Primary Certificate (the examination formerly taken at the end of primary education) or no qualifications;
2   Group or Intermediate Certificate (Junior Cycle);
3   Leaving Certificate or Matriculation (Senior Cycle);
4   Any post-second level qualification at sub-degree, primary or higher degree level.

Finally, we take as our measure of origin class the seven class categories that we have employed in previous chapters.

TRENDS IN EDUCATIONAL ATTAINMENT

As we would expect we see a good deal of change between our three cohorts in the distribution of men and women over the four educational categories. Table 6.1 shows the percentages of each sex at each of these levels. For both men and women we see a steady decline in the percentages of persons leaving school without any post-primary qualifications from around 70 to 30 per cent. However, most of this decline occurs between the second and third cohorts. This is coupled with a steady growth in the percentages of persons leaving with some form of qualification. The only significant difference between women and men is in the percentages of those leaving school after the junior cycle examinations.

However, the question of interest to us concerns the relationship between class origins and educational levels. Although the overall level of educational attainment has obviously increased greatly over the period, it does not necessarily follow that the relationship between class origins and educational attainment will also have changed. The distinction is the same as that between absolute mobility and social fluidity. Here we are interested in 'social fluidity in education': that is, in the question of whether inequalities in educational attainment as between people of different class origins have increased, widened or remained the same over time.

Table 6.1:   *Percentages of Men and Women at Each Educational Level by Cohort*

	No qualifications	Junior Cycle	Senior Cycle	Third Level
Men				
Cohort 1	72	11	7	9
Cohort 2	60	18	10	12
Cohort 3	32	33	22	13
Women				
Cohort 1	67	12	14	7
Cohort 2	51	22	17	10
Cohort 3	29	26	31	15

CHANGES IN THE CLASS ORIGINS, EDUCATIONAL ATTAINMENT LNK

One of the earliest attempts to tackle this question by Tussing (1978) suggested, that rather than providing improved access to education for working-class children, free secondary education involved a 'windfall' for middle-class families. More recently, Raftery and Hout (1993) have argued that what emerged in the Irish case was a pattern of maximally maintained inequality. By this they mean that inequalities between classes remain the same from cohort to cohort unless they are forced to change by increasing enrolments. What was involved was an across-the-board increase in access to secondary education without any change in the selection criteria. 'The equality of outcomes increased not because merit replaced class in the selection of who got ahead but because selection itself diminished' (1993, p. 60).

   In Table 6.2 we set out the relationship between class origins and educational achievement for men and women for our sample as a whole. Looking first at figures for men, we find that the percentage having a

Primary Certificate as their highest level of education rises from 6 per cent for those of professional and managerial class origins to 61 per cent for the non-skilled manual class; and finally to 77 per cent for agricultural workers. The reverse trend for third-level education sees the figure falling from 41 per cent for the professional and managerial class to 3.3 per cent for the non-skilled manual class; and to a mere 1 per cent for agricultural workers. Summarising in odds-ratio terms, the inequality of opportunity between the professional and managerial and non-skilled manual groups in terms of primary education and third-level destinations, we find that the former have an advantage of 120:1. After the service class, it is the *petit bourgeoisie* who display the highest level of educational achievement with 31 per cent having a third-level education. They are followed by those from the routine non-manual class. There is a significant gap between them and the skilled manual class. Finally, the remaining classes have, in each case, at least 60 per cent of their members who have not moved beyond the primary level. However, those from farming origins are much more likely than their counterparts in the remaining two classes to proceed to the Leaving Certificate or third level.

For women we again find very substantial inequalities of opportunity between those at the top and bottom of the class structure. Those from service class backgrounds are over six times less likely than their non-skilled manual counterparts to have terminated their education at the primary level and are nine times more likely to have achieved a third-level qualification; giving us an odds ratio of 55. Once again, it is those from *petit bourgeoisie* origins who are next in the pecking order. However, such women are only half as likely as male 'siblings' to have a third-level qualification. They are also less likely to be found at primary level and are heavily concentrated in the Intermediate or Group Certificate and Leaving Certificate categories. The educational distribution of women from farm backgrounds is also strikingly different from that of their male counterparts. They are only half as likely to have a Primary Certificate or less, and are twice as likely to have, at least, a Leaving Certificate. The remaining significant difference between the sexes concerns women from skilled manual backgrounds who are less likely to have exited at Group or Intermediate Certificate; a finding which is consistent with barriers to entry to traditional skilled manual work for women.

What is of central interest to us is the extent to which such patterns of educational fluidity have changed over time. We can test for change in the relationship between class origins and educational qualifications by forming, for men and for women, the three-dimensional table of class origins by educational attainment by cohort. In order to test for change

Table 6.2: *Educational Qualifications by Class of Origin by Gender Percentage by Column*

	Professional and Managerial (I + II)		Routine Non-Manual (III)		Petit Bourgeoisie (IVa+b)		Farmers (IVc)		Skilled Manual (V/VI)		Non-silled Manual (VIIa)		Agricultural Workers (VIIb)		Total	
	Men	Women	Men	Women	Men	Women	Men	Women	Men	Women	Men	Women	Men	Women	Men	Women
Primary Certificate	6.1	9.7	39.0	44.0	32.8	24.1	60.1	31.2	45.2	53.1	61.3	62.5	77.0	67.8	51.6	44.7
Group or Intermediate Certificate	14.0	7.5	17.3	22.3	16.5	29.6	19.0	24.8	32.3	23.8	26.6	20.4	17.8	14.7	22.7	21.4
Leaving Certificate or Matriculation	38.5	36.9	24.0	23.2	20.4	30.7	12.2	30.5	13.3	16.2	8.7	12.5	3.8	16.8	14.3	22.1
Third Level	41.5	45.9	19.7	10.5	30.3	15.6	8.8	13.6	9.2	6.8	3.3	4.6	1.4	0.8	11.4	11.8

over time we need to specify some underlying model which generates the observed frequencies in this three-way table. A simple model is one that allows for 'all two-way interactions'. This model has the same form as the constant social fluidity model which we have encountered earlier. So class origins and cohort are related, allowing for change in the origin distribution across cohorts. Equally, educational attainment and cohort are also allowed to be related, permitting change in the distribution of respondents across educational levels over cohorts in the way that was shown in Table 6.1. Class origins and education are also related, reflecting the association between the class in which a person is born and the level of education they attain. What this model does not include, however, is any form of change over time in this latter relationship. In other words, it posits that the link between class origins and educational attainment has remained the same over the three cohorts.

This model fits the data very well for women, returning a G^2 of 40.33 on 36 df, but not for men ($G^2 = 66.78$ on 36 df). Thus we conclude that, contrary to expectations, among women the relationship between class origins and educational attainment has not changed over the three cohorts, despite the major policy shifts in education and in industrial policy that would have influenced the youngest cohort.

Before discussing the situation among men, it is important to say something about the nature of this apparently unchanging class origins/ education association among women. Fortunately, it is relatively straightforward. If we rank our four levels of education from 1, for no qualifications, to 4, for a post-second level qualification, we find that the so-called 'row effects' model fits the data almost as well ($G^2 = 62.54$ with 48 df). In this case, rather than scoring the origins in terms of observed differences in resources, we estimate such differences through our statistical modelling procedures in order to find the set of scores which comes closest to fitting the observed pattern of frequencies. The resource measure used in the AHP model is replaced by a set of dummy variables which are entered in interaction with the education variable which is scored from one to four. This allows us to measure generalised effects relating to each specific origin class and the desirability of educational destinations. The row effects model specifies that the log odds on a higher status destination, relative to the next lower status destination, changes by a fixed amount for each shift of origins, regardless of the pair of destinations being compared (more detailed treatment of the row effects model can be found in Breen, 1984; Goodman, 1979 and Hout, 1983).

The model is useful for our purposes in that it allows us to rank origin classes relative to each other in terms of the odds of attaining a higher rather than a lower educational level. The reference category against which all others are compared is the professional and managerial class and is scored zero. The scores reported in Table 6.3 are those which generate the expected log frequencies and the model is in log-linear form. If we wish to predict actual frequencies, it is necessary to use the multiplicative form of the model. In that case, the differences in origin scores can be calculated by taking the anti-log of the additive differences. Thus, in the case of the comparison between the professional and managerial class versus the non-skilled manual class, the relative advantage in competition for desirable educational destinations will be reflected in the multiplicative model in a difference in scores of 5.9 ($e^{0-(-1.78)} = e^{1.78} = 5.9$). The relativities between each pair of classes can be expressed in either linear or multiplicative terms and it is, precisely, such *relativities* which convey the crucial information generated by the model. The pattern of scores tells a very straightforward story. The professional and managerial group have the highest odds of attaining higher rather than lower educational levels and the gap between them and all other classes is greater than that between any other pair of classes. They are followed by the *petit bourgeoisie* and farmers whose scores are virtually identical. These classes are separated from the routine non-manual class by a more modest, but substantial, difference and the latter, in turn, enjoy a slightly larger advantage over the skilled manual class. Finally, the gap between the skilled manual classes and the two non-skilled manual classes is equally significant.

Table 6.3: *Scoring of Origin Classes According to their Relative Advantage in Access to Higher Levels of Education among women*

Origin Class		Score	Scores in Multiplicative	Standard error
Professional and Managerial	(I+II)	0	1.00	-
Petit Bourgeoisie	(IVa+b)	-0.78	(2.18)	0.13
Farmers	(IVc)	-0.84	(2.32)	0.11
Routine Non-Manual	(IIIa)	-1.15	(3.15)	0.14
Skilled Manual	(V/VI)	-1.42	(4.14)	0.12
Non-Skilled Manual	(VIIa)	-1.70	(5.48)	0.12
Agricultural Workers	(VIIb)	-1.78	(5.93)	0.16

More simply, those women who come from the upper white-collar classes have the highest level of educational attainment, followed by those from classes that own the means of production. Beneath them come the remaining white-collar classes, followed by the manual classes, where daughters of skilled manual workers do better than daughters of the non-skilled. What is most striking about this result, however, is not this ordering of relative advantage, but the fact that it has remained completely unchanged across cohorts, despite the dramatic changes in overall levels of women's educational attainment, as shown in Table 6.1.

Among men, on the other hand, there has been some change. The relationship between class origins and educational attainment is also more complex than it is among women. A simple linear ranking of origin classes according to their relative advantage is not adequate to capture its nature which is best represented by the type of non-measured variable model we have referred to earlier. The type of model we employ is most frequently referred to as a levels model. This model allocates all cells in a table into mutually exhaustive and disjoint sets (each cell is allocated to one and only one level) by means of a set of dummy variables. Such a model provides explicitly for a number of different levels of interaction or differing tendencies towards particular types of flows. What the model requires is that each cell of the mobility table be allocated to a particular interaction level, so that all cells placed at the same level share a common interaction parameter which determines the expected frequency in the cell. The result is that odds-ratios formed from cells drawn from the same level will be equal to one, while odds-ratios formed from cells drawn from different levels will not. The model thus posits equality of opportunity for pairs of origins and destinations at the same level and inequality of opportunity for pairs of origins and destinations drawn from different levels.

The particular model we employ is set out in Table 6.4. This shows a crosstabulation of class origins by educational level, but the figures in the body of the table are not frequency counts: rather they represent six groupings or 'levels' of the cells of the table, according to the degree to which the frequencies in these cells are higher or lower than would be expected if class origins and educational level were unrelated. Those cells which have been allocated to level 0 are those which come nearest to representing this situation of independence of origin and destination. Those cells with frequencies higher than expected on the basis of the independence or equality of opportunity hypothesis are allocated to levels higher than 0, while those with lower than expected frequencies are placed at levels lower than 0. The extent of departure from zero is hypothesised to increase the further one moves in either direction from level zero.

Table 6.4:   Levels Model Specification of Class Origins/Educational
Attainment Relationship Among Men

		Educational Level			
		No Qualifications	Junior Cycle	Senior Cycle	Third Level
Origin Class					
Professional and Managerial	(I+II)	-2	0	2	2
Routine Non-Manual	(III)	1	0	1	1
Petit Bourgeoisie	(IVa+b)	0	0	0	1
Farmers	(IVc)	2	1	1	0
Skilled Manual	(V/VI)	2	2	1	1
Non-Skilled Manual	(VIIa)	3	2	1	-1
Agricultural Workers	(VIII)	3	2	0	-1

Cells allocated to level 3 are those with the highest levels of over-representation under the counterfactual of equality of opportunity. It applies to only two cells which involve termination of education without qualifications among the two non-skilled manual groups. On the other hand, the under-representation of these groups at third level is reflected in the allocation of these cells to level -1. The most extreme example of under-representation involves the flow from the professional and managerial class to the group lacking any qualification and this is represented by allocating the cell to level -2. A value of 2 also indicates over-representation, but not so extreme as the value of 3. This applies to men of professional and managerial origins having a higher post-primary or third-level qualification and it also captures the propensity for men of manual worker origins to leave school at the lower post-primary level. In many cases this arises because this was the traditional route into an apprenticeship. It also captures the tendency of farmers' sons — particularly those who inherit the farm — to leave school without any qualifications. Finally, level 1 also indicates over-representation, but at a yet less extreme level than level 2.

The magnitude of these levels is not determined in advance: rather, they are entered into the model as four dummy variables (see Chapter 4 for a discussion of these).   Returning to our initial model of all two-way interactions, i.e. hypothesising a constant relationship between class origin and educational level across cohort, we found that this yielded G^2 of 66.78 with 36 df for men. However, if in this model, we replace the class origins by educational level association with the levels model that specifies these four dummy variables, we find that the G^2 increases to 85.28 but so do the degrees of freedom — from 36 to 49. Because this model, like the 'all two-way interactions' model, does not allow for change over cohorts in the link between class origins and education it does not fit the data. However, it is as good a fit as the 'all two-way interactions' model (the difference in G^2 is 18.5 with 13 df which is not statistically significant) showing that the levels model which is a great deal more parsimonious does a good job of capturing the class origins/educational level relationship.

Given this, we can then go on to see how this relationship changes over time. It turns out that, in fact, the extent of change over cohorts has been very modest indeed. First, there is no change between cohorts one and two: all the change that there is in the link between class origins and educational attainment occurs as between the two oldest and the youngest cohort. The change which is apparent relates entirely to access to third-level qualifications. Consistent with our findings in Chapters 3 and 4, the relative chances of access to this level improve significantly for both the farming and *petit bourgeoisie* classes in the final cohorts. These gains are at the expense of routine non-manual class and, more particularly, the skilled manual group. These changes can be captured by moving the relevant farming cell from level 0 to level 1 and the *petit bourgeoisie* from 1 to 2. Correspondingly, the routine non-manual level is changed from level 1 to 0 and the skilled manual from 1 to -1. These changes give us a model that returns G^2 of 52.26 with 49 df, which provides an excellent fit for the data.

Table 6.5 displays both the additive and multiplicative parameter values for the final model. The table can be read as showing that, in terms of frequencies expected under the model, the density level of relative flows is 1.97 times greater at level 1 than 0, 3.46 times greater at level 2 and 6.69 times greater at level 3. Correspondingly, the density at level -1 is 0.71 times that at level 0, and at level -2 it is 0.25 times that of the reference category.

So, among men, the link between class origins and education is a little more complex than it is among women. The overall relationship has to be modelled using a set of levels that reflect several different factors. One of these is the distribution of relative advantages across origin classes. This encompasses both the differential ability to avoid less desirable educational outcomes (for example, men from the professional and managerial class are very markedly under-represented in the no-qualifications category, whereas non-skilled manual men are equally strongly under-represented in the highest qualification level) and the resources to secure a position in those which are most desirable (for example, men with service class origins are over-represented in the higher post-primary and third-level outcomes, compared with non-skilled manual men who are very strongly under-represented here). Another factor is the specific strategies that different classes pursue. The tendency for inheriting sons of farmers to leave school without qualifications and for male children of manual workers to pursue apprenticeships is also evident in the pattern of levels shown in Table 6.4. But this complex relationship has been remarkably enduring in so far as it relates to social fluidity in education. Despite the changes in the overall levels of educational attainment, there is only one significant shift in these fluidity patterns. This is the disappearance of the modest advantage enjoyed by men from lower white-collar and skilled manual classes in attaining third-level qualifications. In the two oldest cohorts they were disadvantaged relative to men from the professional and managerial class in attaining this level of qualifications, but were on an equal footing with men of *petit bourgeoisie* backgrounds, and were advantaged relative to farmers and, even more so, relative to non-skilled workers. But by the time of the third cohort, both classes had slipped down this ranking. The routine manual group remained ahead of the non-skilled manual groups but fell substantially behind the *petit bourgeoisie* and saw their position in relation to farmers reversed. The skilled manual class also lost out in competition with these groups and indeed in the final cohort were found at the same level as the two non-skilled manual classes. While those at the top and the bottom of the class hierarchy maintained their relative positions over time, among the intermediate classes the battle to take maximum advantage of the new opportunities provided by educational expansion at third-level was decisively won by the property-owning group.

Table 6.5: Values of the Parameters of Density Levels for the Six-Level Model of Class-Origin-Educational Qualifications for Men

Level	Additive Parameter Values	Values in Multiplicative Form
-2	-1.38	(0.25)
-1	-0.34	(0.71)
0	0.00	(1.00)
1	0.68	(1.97)
2	1.24	(3.46)
3	1.90	(6.69)

EDUCATION, ORIGIN CLASS AND ENTRY TO THE LABOUR FORCE

Given these findings, concerning the very limited extent of change in the relationship between class origins and educational attainment, we turn now to the link between educational qualifications and the class of entry to the labour force (or 'entry class' for short). The latter is the social class position that a person occupies in the first regular job obtained after completing full-time education.

Table 6.6: Percentages of Men and Women in Each Entry Class by Cohort

	Professional and Managerial (I+II)	Routine Non-manual (III)*	Entry Petit Bourgeoisie (IVa+b)	Class 3 Farming (IVc)	Skilled Manual (V/VI)	Non-skilled Manual (VIIa)**	Agricultural Workers (VIIb)
Men							
Cohort 1	6	16	1	5	18	29	25
Cohort 2	10	20	1	4	24	27	14
Cohort 3	11	18	1	1	30	31	9
Women							
Cohort 1	13	13	0	0	11	61	2
Cohort 2	14	17	0	0	11	57	1
Cohort 3	14	26	0	0	9	50	1

*   Includes IIIa and IIIb for men but only IIIa for women.
** Includes VIIa and IIIb for women but only VIIa for men.

For men we use the same class categories for entry class as for class origins — in other words the same seven-category schema. However, for women we make two changes. First, following Erikson and Goldthorpe (1992, p.241) we distinguish, within the class of routine non-manual employees, between IIIa and IIIb. Here IIIb comprises occupations which are largely filled by women, and involve straightforward wage labour, rather than the more service-orientated relationship characteristic of occupations in IIIa. Accordingly, for women, IIIb is placed in the same class category as non-skilled, non-agricultural manual employees, class VIIa. Second, when we examine the distribution of women and men across entry classes, we see one very striking difference. This is that, although the number of men entering classes based on ownership of the means of production (IVa+b and IVc) is small as is to be expected, almost

Table 6.7: Class of Entry by Class of Origin for Women Percentage by Column

| | Class of Origin | | | | | | | |
Class of Entry	Professional and Managerial (I + II)	Routine Non-Manual (III)	Petit Bourgeoisie (IVa+b)	Farmers (IVc)	Skilled Manual (V/VI)	Non-silled Manual	Agricultural Workers	Total
Professional and Managerial (I + II)	40.0	5.5	23.9	20.7	6.3	5.2	5.9	13.8
Routine Non-Manual (III)	30.4	30.3	23.9	26.4	19.6	11.5	8.8	20.4
Skilled Manual (V/VI)	0.9	10.6	4.5	4.7	17.4	15.1	11.2	11.2
Non-Skilled Manual (IIIb, VIIa)	28.6	53.7	47.7	48.2	56.8	68.3	74.1	55.5

no women enter these classes or the class of non-skilled agricultural workers (VIIb). The relevant figures are shown in Table 6.6. In practice women enter one of only four classes: service class (I+II); higher routine non-manual (IIIa); skilled work (V/VI) and the lower routine non-manual and non-skilled manual class (IIIb+VIIa). The concentration of women in this latter class is particularly marked. Thus for the analyses of women's entry into the labour force we confine ourselves to considering these four classes.

The relationship between class of origin and class of entry for women is shown in Table 6.7. Four out of ten of those from professional and managerial backgrounds enter this class on taking up their first job. This compares with one in twenty of those from non-skilled manual backgrounds. There is a sharp contrast between the service class and the property-owning class and all other classes in the extent of access to other professional and managerial positions. Women from routine non-manual backgrounds do rather better than their male counterparts while those originating in the non-skilled manual classes do a good deal better. Women are 50 per cent more likely than men to start their careers in the service class. However, their exclusion from the propertied classes and skilled manual work classes means that they are, nevertheless, twice as likely to be found in the non-skilled manual class. Almost seven out of ten of those from non-skilled manual backgrounds are located there, but so too are one in two women from the propertied classes, and three out of ten of those originating in the professional and managerial class. Entry to skilled manual work, where it does occur, is largely confined to those from routine non-manual and manual backgrounds.

Men, as we can see from Table 6.8, are dispersed across a wider range of class categories. Just less than one in three men from professional and managerial backgrounds are found in the service class. This figure declines to less than 3 per cent for men from non-skilled manual backgrounds. Men from farming backgrounds are significantly less likely than women to be found in this class. In contrast, as we have already indicated, men from the routine non-manual class do significantly better than women from such origins. At the bottom of the class hierarchy the percentage found in non-skilled manual work ranges from over 40 per cent for those from that class to 10 per cent for those from professional and managerial origins. Men from the white-collar classes display an equal tendency to women to be found in the routine non-manual classes; with one in three being located there. The main factor distinguishing the male mobility table from the female one is the evidence of male 'inheritance' patterns. In the first place, one in ten sons of farmers is found in farming. Even more striking is the

Table 6.8:   *Class of Entry by Class Origin for Men*
              Percentage by Column

| | Class of Origin | | | | | | | |
Class of Entry	Professional and Managerial (I + II)	Routine Non-Manual (III)	Petit Bourgeoisie (IVa+b)	Farmers (IVc)	Skilled Manual (V/VI)	Non-silled Manual (VIIa)	Agricultural Workers (VIII)	Total
Professional and Managerial	31.1	15.0	19.1	8.3	7.2	2.6	1.8	9.0
Routine Non-Manual	36.6	32.8	23.4	10.6	18.7	17.4	10.1	18.1
Petit Bourgeoisie	1.8	0.0	5.5	0.4	1.0	0.5	0.0	0.9
Farmers	0.0	0.0	0.0	9.8	1.0	0.2	0.0	3.1
Skilled Manual	19.1	21.4	35.1	15.4	42.3	27.1	18.7	25.2
Non-skilled Manual	10.0	28.6	13.9	25.2	26.5	43.8	24.6	29.0
Agricultural Workers	1.4	2.2	2.7	30.2	3.3	8.4	44.8	14.9

fact that 30 per cent of this group start out as agricultural workers. For many of this group this provides a starting point which will eventually lead them to farm ownership The importance of self-recruitment within agriculture is also shown by the fact that close to one in two of those originating in the agricultural workers' class are also found there on entry to the labour-market. Immobility in the skilled manual class is also extremely high, with over four out of ten inheriting such positions. Inheritance in the *petit bourgeoisie* class is more modest, with 5 per cent of men starting out in this fashion but, as we have already indicated, such inheritance is entirely restricted to men.

The next relationship on which we wish to focus attention is that between class of entry and educational qualifications. A substantial literature exists on the topic of the return to education. In economics this is often associated with human capital approaches while in sociology the status attainment approach has been particularly influential (Blau and Duncan, 1967). The latter approach focuses on how education helps to determine 'who gets ahead' in society's status hierarchy. Critics of the status attainment approach argue that such work illustrates a persistent ideological bias in functionalist themes of stratification. The bias involves a refusal to depict the occupational system as anything other than a hierarchical structure of positions with the assignment of rewards being determined by society's needs. It is this assumption which leads to a neglect of the social structural constraints which operate on the stratification process independently of individual characteristics. Critics have pointed to the failure to deal with the constraints imposed by the extent of the 'fit' between the patterns of occupational 'demand' and 'educational' supply (Crowder, 1974; Sorenson, 1977; Pawson, 1978). More particularly, it has been argued that the model contains no theory of the labour-market or presupposes a fully competitive labour-market (Horan, 1978; Bielby, 1981).

Another major criticism, as Breen *et al.* (1995) note, relates to the assumption that labour-markets and educational institutions operate as separate institutional spheres with the former 'purchasing' the latter's output. In fact, as they emphasise, recent research has shown substantial differences among countries in the nature and degree of institutional linkages between the labour-market and educational institutions. The nature of these linkages varies from the German situation, where a range of clearly-defined occupations is associated with relatively fixed educational and vocational preparation courses and qualifications, to the very loose connections in the United States where job definition and training are primarily defined by firms and training is largely carried out within them.

A number of conceptual schemes has been proposed to handle such cross-national variation. However, the Irish pattern of education/labour-market linkages does not fit neatly into either the 'qualification mobility space' or 'organisational mobility space' ideal types which have been proposed in the literature (Maurice, *et al*, 1986). The link between types of educational pathways and job entry is much looser in Ireland than in countries like Germany. The Irish apprenticeship system is very limited, accounting for no more than 5 per cent of the labour-market entrants. However unlike the United States, where a similarly weak relationship between educational courses and job entry exists, Ireland possesses a national curriculum and a set of standardized examinations which are widely used by employers for recruitment purposes. The system is thus characterised as involving a high degree of standardization but a low degree of stratification (Allemendinger, 1989). The examination system provides a mechanism whereby, despite the absence of any clear institutionalised connection, education/training institutions and job entry paths, there is nevertheless a very close link between educational success and labour-market prospects. Soskice (1993) argues that, in the absence of powerful employer organisations and co-operative industrial relations, mass post-18 and higher education provides the alternative to company-based initial training by providing the skills that companies want in an increasingly service- and client-dominated economy. This view is entirely consistent with the manner in which educational outcomes in Ireland appear to act '. . . as a signal of the potential productivity of job seekers which employers can use so minimizing their recruitment costs and allowing them to make as fine distinctions as are required in order to select among a possibly large field of job applicants in a very slack labour market' (Breen, *et al*, 1995, p.71).

In the Irish situation we would expect, on rational choice grounds, that the relationship between class of origin and educational achievement is likely to be strong because such achievement is critical in a number of respects. In the first place, the cost of educational failure is particularly high because it involves not only location at the bottom of the class hierarchy but also a high probability of being unemployed. In addition, in the absence of horizontal differentiation, vertical differentiation is extremely important, with employers using quite fine distinctions in examination results in deciding who to hire and how much to pay. Finally, the volume of applicants for access to third-level education substantially exceeds the number of available places and although access is based solely on the performance of the applicant in the Leaving Certificate since that is, in turn, strongly related to class origins, the overall class origin/educational achievement relationship is likely to be stronger than in a system where all who are qualified gain access to third-level education.

Given a strong link between class origins and education, and the available evidence relating to the comparatively limited degree of career mobility, we might also expect that the relationship between educational achievement and first class-position will prove to be particularly strong. One qualification which must be entered relates to the manner in which the relationship may be expected to vary across labour-market segments and, in particular, the likelihood of a looser connection between credentials and access to positions in farming or among the *petit bourgeoisie*. In addition, we might expect to observe significant interactions between class origins and gender.

The perspective we have adopted accords with Erikson and Goldthorpe's (1992a, p. 307) argument for taking into account the fact that the school-to-work transition is part of the process of intergenerational mobility where variations in component transitions are best viewed as capturing 'the effects of differing strategies pursued by individuals and families within cross-nationally varying institutional contexts, which lead them to apply such resources as they are able to devote to enhancing their mobility chances in differing ways and at different stages of the life-course.'

It also takes account of their further argument that while it is necessary to make a clear conceptual distinction between absolute and relative mobility, this does not require that relative mobility patterns are independent of the absolute mobility flows. Thus, in Ireland, the possibility exists that the long-term situation of an excess of labour influences class strategies and the outcome of these strategies and the series of competitions arising from them are then reflected in the pattern of relative mobility rates.

Table 6.9 shows the relationship between educational qualifications and class of entry for women. Almost two-thirds of those with third-level qualifications entered the service class at first-job stage. This figure falls to one in six for those with a Leaving Certificate and to fairly negligible levels for other qualifications. By far the highest probability of entering routine non-manual work, i.e. almost one in two, occurs for those terminating their education at Leaving Certificate level, with the Group or Intermediate Certificate holders significantly having the next highest level. For women, skilled manual work is mainly associated with primary education. The relationship between non-skilled manual work and education is a straightforward one, with the percentage in such work declining from 76 per cent for those with primary education to 16 per cent for third-level respondents.

Table 6.9:   *Class of Entry by Educational Qualifications for Women Percentage by Column*

	Primary Certificate	Group or Intermediate Certificate	Leaving Certificate or Matriculation	Third Level	Total
Professional and Managerial (I + II)	2.6	6.3	16.9	63.0	13.8
Routine Non-Manual (IIIa)	3.7	28.0	45.9	21.0	20.4
Skilled Manual (V/VI)	18.1	8.8	2.0	0.0	10.4
Non-Skilled Manual (IIIb, VIIa)	75.7	56.9	35.7	16.0	55.5

For men, as set out in Table 6.10, the probability of starting in the service class declines from almost six out of ten for those with third-level qualifications to zero for those with primary education. Men with such qualifications differ from their female counterparts primarily in the significantly higher probability of being found in skilled manual work and the lesser likelihood of starting out in non-skilled manual work. This pattern is observed for each level of qualification. In addition, particularly below Leaving Certificate level, men are much more likely to be found in agricultural work. Finally, for men, there is a very strong link between Intermediate or Group Certificate qualifications and entry to skilled manual work.

What is crucial for our present purposes is the trends in the relationships we have examined in this section. If the liberal theory of industrialism is correct, we ought to detect an increase over time in the importance of educational credentials in securing an entry class position at the expense of ascriptive features. Our final analyses look at how the impact of class of origin, and of educational qualifications, on entry class position has changed over time. To do this we analyse the four-way table of class origins by educational qualifications by entry class by cohort among both men and women. For men we have a seven (class origins) by four (educational qualifications) by seven (entry classes) by three (cohorts) table, while for women we have a seven by four by four by three table.

*Table 6.10: Class of Entry by Educational Qualifications for Men
           Percentage by Column*

	Primary Certificate	Group or Intermediate Certificate	Leaving Certificate or Matriculation	Third Level	Total
Professional and Managerial (I + II)	0.0	0.1	16.6	56.0	9.0
Routine Non-Manual (III)	12.1	16.7	42.1	18.1	18.1
Petit Bourgeoisie (IVa+b)	0.6	1.0	1.6	1.1	0.9
Farmers (IVc)	4.7	1.6	1.8	0.3	3.1
Skilled Manual (V/VI)	19.3	49.1	16.7	14.8	25.2
Non-Skilled Manual (VIIa)	39.6	22.4	18.1	7.6	29.0
Agricultural Workers (VIIb)	23.6	8.2	3.1	2.1	14.7

We carry out these analyses separately for the two sexes. Turning first to men, we begin by fitting the model of 'all two-way interactions' within each cohort. This model hypothesises that, given the relationship between class origins and educational attainment (discussed earlier), the impact of class of origin on entry class does not vary according to educational level, and equally, the impact of educational level on entry class does not vary according to class of origin. In other words, the effects of origin class and education on entry class are additive. This means, for example, that the difference in the chances of entering, say, the Professional and Managerial class as between someone with the Leaving Certificate and someone without any qualifications, is the same regardless of their class background. This is not to say that the absolute chances of someone entering the service are unaffected by class origins: clearly they are, but the *differences* in such chances as between people of different educational levels are not sensitive to class of origin.

Such a model fits the data for all three cohorts. It has 108 degrees of freedom and returns G^2s of 104.03, 92.23 and 102.21 respectively. Such a model, however, is not a very parsimonious one in that it does not specify precisely the nature of the relationship between origin class and entry class or between educational qualifications and entry class. All we know is that a model which constrains such relationships to be constant across cohort fits the data. So we have a model of no change but have no precise knowledge of the pattern of relationship which has remained invariant. Our first step in seeking a more parsimonious model involves specifying the origin class–entry class relationship. The next step is to seek to model the origin class–entry class relationship in some more parsimonious fashion. We do this by using the AHP model. We include, as before, measures of an overall class inheritance effect (INH1), a specific inheritance effect for farmers (INH2), a barrier to entry into the agricultural sector (AGB) and an effect that captures specific advantages associated with origins in the propertied classes in relation to access to the service class (SLP). In place of the other two effects, that we had previously included in the AHP model (namely XY and P), we now include the set of interactions between the dummy variables representing origin classes and the scoring of the entry classes using the measure Y. Recall that Y is meant to capture the overall desirability of classes and some of the barriers to entry to them. By including this in the model, in interaction with each class origin, we are saying that the chances of entering a more rather than a less desirable entry class varies according to class origin; but we are not specifying, in advance, the nature of this variation. This is a less restrictive specification than we used earlier, where we also scaled the origin classes using the measure X. In effect we are letting the data tell us the magnitude of the origin class differences in resources for mobility. We refer to these terms as the origin specific desirability effect. This version of the AHP model is considerably more parsimonious than the full set of interaction terms between class origins and entry class. The latter fits 36 parameters compared with 10 for the AHP model.

Our second step is to seek to model the education–entry class relationship more parsimoniously. Among men we find that using the interactions between the dummy variables for the different educational levels and the Y scoring for entry classes is adequate. This is directly analogous to the origin specific desirability effect, except that we now have an education specific desirability effect. So we are now saying that the chances of entering a more desirable entry class vary according to educational level. This model uses 3 parameters as compared with 18 for the full set of education–entry class interactions.

These two specifications, of the origin–entry and education–entry relationships, are very parsimonious, but together with the full set of origin class–educational level interactions they fit the data for each cohort just as adequately as the model of all two-way interactions (see Breen and Whelan 1993, p. 12 for details).

So far, we have been looking at each cohort separately. Now we turn to change over time. It is clear from Table 6.6 that there has been some change over cohorts in the distribution of men over the entry classes. For example, there has been a pronounced decline in the percentages of men entering farming, while there has been a less marked decrease in the percentages entering non-skilled manual work and some growth in skilled manual work. Our concern is not with these shifts but with the question of the degree to which there is change over cohorts in the impact of education on class of entry and of class origins on entry class. Given the specifications of these effects, this amounts to asking whether the component effects of the AHP model change over time, and whether the education specific desirability effect changes over time. The answer is that of the origin class effects only the SLP term, which measures the additional advantages enjoyed by the *petit bourgeoisie* and farming classes in gaining access to the professional and managerial class, shows any change over cohorts: the inheritance effects, the agricultural barrier and the origin specific desirability effects are all constant over cohorts. The education effects do change over cohorts, however (see Breen and Whelan 1993, pp.11–13 for details of this analysis).

Table 6.11: Parameter Estimates of Final Model for Men
(Asymptotic Standard Errors in Parentheses)

A: **Parameters constant over cohorts**			
INH1	0.562	(0.08)	
INH2	3.677	(0.39)	
AGB	-1.446	(0.38)	
Origin Class:			
Professional and Managerial	1.00	–	
Routine Non-Manual	-0.407	(0.16)	
Petit Bourgeoisie	-0.072	(0.18)	
Farmers	-0.679	(0.15)	
Skilled Manual	-0.278	(0.13)	
Non-Skilled Manual	-0.271	(0.15)	
Agricultural Workers	-0.625	(0.19)	

B. **Parameters varying over cohorts**		*Cohorts*	
	1	2	3
SLP	1.269	0.668	0.508*
	(0.36)	(0.30)	(0.26)
Education effects:			
No qualifications	0.000	0.000	0.000
Junior cycle	0.925	0.686	0.446*
	(0.18)	(0.15)	(0.12)
Senior Cycle	1.888	1.784	1.066*
	(0.25)	(0.21)	(0.13)
Third-Level	2.409	2.337	1.668*
	(0.28)	(0.23)	(0.16)

* Indicates significantly different from coefficient in cohort 1 ($p < 0.05$).

Table 6.11 shows the parameter estimates for this model. Panel A reports those coefficients that do not change as between cohorts: panel B shows those that change. We see a strong overall inheritance effect (INH1) and a very large inheritance effect for farmers (INH2). This latter arises because, although relatively few men enter farming as their first job, those who do are all the sons of the farmers. Once again the origin class effects run from zero (for the professional and managerial class) downwards, providing a simple ranking of relative advantage. Broadly speaking, these scores are all reasonably close together. On the other hand, if we leave the education effects out of the model, they become much more widely spaced. This indicates that much of the class difference in access to more desirable entry classes is in fact mediated through educational qualifications. There are large class differences in educational attainment, as we have seen, and these feed through to cause large class differences in access to entry classes. Once we partial out this channel of class origin effects (as has happened in the results reported in panel A) the remaining class origin effect (i.e. that which does not operate via the educational system) is relatively weak.

In panel B we see that the pattern of change in both the SLP term and the effects of education is a contrast between, on the one hand, cohorts 1 and 2, and cohort 3 on the other. The SLP effect diminishes over cohorts. Recall that this captures specific advantages linked to being born in the classes that own the means of production. That this has weakened suggests that such advantages have declined. However, we know from other analyses (Breen and Whelan 1993, p.10) that the simple relationship between class origins and entry has shown no change over cohorts, suggesting that the weakening in SLP must have been compensated for by the acquiring of advantage, for the members of these origin classes, elsewhere. One way in which this may have come about concerns our earlier result showing that, in relative terms, the chances of access to third-level qualifications for the routine non-manual and skilled manual classes worsened in the youngest cohort, while those of the property-owning groups improved. More generally, the shift, on the part of members of the *petit bourgeoisie* and farming classes from direct advantage to advantage mediated *via* education provides a good example of how class advantage can persist in the face of change through the use of other channels of mobility. Lastly, we see that the coefficients for the different educational levels (all of which are measured relative to the coefficient for 'No qualifications' which is set to zero) come closer together as we move from cohort 1 to cohort 3.

The contraction of social classes whose members own the means of production and, in particular, the dramatic decline in agriculture have substantially reduced the absolute impact of direct inheritance in shaping mobility flows. Within the employee sector educational qualifications are increasingly important as a prerequisite for specific occupational positions. Notwithstanding such structural effects, the question still remains whether education has become more or less salient as a reproduction mechanism. Over our cohorts the distribution of individuals over the education categories comes to display diminishing variation; and at the same time the variance of the returns to different levels of education has also declined. As Boudon (1974) has discussed, the rational decisions of individuals to acquire more education have had an unforeseen (and negative) aggregate effect: higher levels of educational qualifications have become less valuable over the three cohorts as greater proportions of each cohort have come to acquire them. Educational credentials have undoubtedly come to be increasingly necessary for recruitment to occupations. At the same time, educational level, as measured here, has come to exercise less influence in shaping inequalities in social fluidity. The relative advantage associated with a higher level of education has declined over time as the number possessing such qualifications increases. However, the advantages enjoyed by property-owning groups are increasingly transmitted through educational qualifications. In the final cohort, even though the property effect is now, more than ever, mediated by education, the partial effect of education declines. But the overall inheritance effect, the inheritance effect for farming, the barrier to entry to agriculture and the partial origin effects remain constant across cohorts.

Turning to women the position is somewhat different. We find that,as with men, the model of all two-way interactions within each cohort provides a good fit to the data (G^2s of 56.56, 49.79 and 60.23 respectively, on 54 df). However, to model the class origins–entry class relationship we can only use some elements of the AHP model — notably INH1, SLP and the origin specific desirability effects. We cannot include the term for class inheritance among farmers or the agricultural barrier since we have no one in the propertied or agricultural worker classes. Similarly, the scoring of Y now applies to only four classes, professional and managerial, routine non-manual, skilled manual and non-skilled manual. It has the values 1.22, 0.50, -0.32 and -0.67.

When we come to model the education–entry class relationship we find that the simple pattern of education specific desirability effects does not hold for women. Rather we have to model this relationship using the matrix of levels shown in Table 6.12. The interpretation of this is the same as that for the matrix given in Table 6.4. The figures in the body of the table represent five groupings or 'levels' of the cells of the table, according to the degree to which the frequencies in these cells are higher or lower than would be expected if entry class and educational level were unrelated. The figure 3 indicates cells whose frequency is much higher than would be expected under this counterfactual. It applies to only one cell in the table — educational level 4 (third-level) and the professional and managerial class. At the other extreme, the cells which have the value -1 are those where the frequency is very much lower than would be the case if independence held. These apply to the cells relating to entry to the service class and the routine non-manual class among women who have no qualifications and to the cells relating to entry into the skilled manual class among women who have an upper post-primary or third-level qualification.

Table 6.12: Levels Model Specification of Educational Attainment/Entry Class Relationship Among Women

	Entry Class			
	Professional and Managerial	*Routine Non-Manual*	*Skilled Manual*	*Non-Skilled Manual*
Education:				
No qualifications	-1	-1	2	1
Junior Cycle	0	0	0	1
Senior Cycle	2	1	-1	0
Third-Level	3	2	-1	0

In general terms what this matrix is modelling is the very marked tendency for women without qualifications to enter manual work or low-level routine non-manual work. A similar picture holds for women who have a junior cycle qualification, although they are rather less likely to be found in the skilled manual class, and marginally more likely to be found in other white-collar work. Women with a senior cycle qualification are concentrated in routine non-manual and, to a lesser extent, the service class, while those with a third-level qualification are overwhelmingly found in the professional and managerial class.

If we make these two substitutions — of the partial AHP model for the origin–entry association and of the levels matrix given in Table 6.12 for the education–entry association — we find that the model still provides a good fit to the data within each cohort of women (G^2s of 91.53, 70.01 and 80.54, respectively on 69 df). The final step is to test whether there has been any change over cohorts. Referring once again to Table 6.6, we can certainly discern some change in the marginal distribution of women over entry classes, with a marked increase in the percentage in the routine non-manual class and a decline in the percentage in the non-skilled manual class. However, as before, our interest is in the effects of class origins and education on entry class chances. And here we find no evidence of any such change. If we simply allow for changes between cohorts in the marginal distributions of all the variables (origin class, education and entry class) and in the origin class – education relationship (which, as we saw earlier, does not in fact change over cohorts) we arrive at a model that fits the data (G^2 of 272.25 with 231 df). The parameter estimates for this model — all of which are constant over cohorts — are given in Table 6.13.

Table 6.13: Parameter Estimates of Final Model for Women
(Asymptotic Standard Errors in Parentheses)

Class origin effects		
INH1	0.306	(0.11)
SLP	0.675	(0.26)
Origin Scores		
Profession and Managerial	0.000	–
Routine Non-Manual	-0.306	(0.24)
Petit Bourgeoisie	-0.176	(0.24)
Farmers	-0.134	(0.20)
Skilled Manual	-0.207	(0.19)
Non-skilled Manual	-0.217	(0.23)
Agricultural Workers	-0.465	(0.27)
Education effects:		
Level:		
-1	-2.092	(0.19)
0	0.000	–
1	0.389	(0.09)
2	0.538	(0.16)
3	2.989	(0.28)

    Turning to the origin class effects we see a very considerable tendency for class inheritance (INH1) and substantial advantages to those born in the propertied classes. However, the origin specific desirability effects are all non-significant. In other words, with the exception of the foregoing advantages, class origins have no impact on a woman's relative chances of access to a more rather than a less desirable entry class, once we take into account the impact of educational qualifications. In a sense this is what the liberal theory would predict — except that it posits a movement towards something like this state of affairs over time whereas our data suggest that this has been the situation for most of this century. The education effects are largely as we would have expected, with increasing parameter values the higher the level, reflecting the pattern of association between specific educational levels and specific entry classes shown in Table 6.12. Noteworthy is the very large value for level 3 showing the very strong link between having a third-level qualification and the chances of access to the service class.

By and large, among women, and with the exception of the overall inheritance effect and the specific additional advantages enjoyed by the propertied classes in gaining access to the professional and managerial class, origins have no impact on entry class once education is taken into consideration. But, if we omit education, then origin and entry class are strongly associated. The reason why the inclusion of education makes this relationship almost vanish is the strong association that exists between origin class and education. Recall that earlier we saw that this relationship had not changed over our three cohorts among women and that it could be captured in the form of a ranking of origin classes in terms of their relative advantage in placing their children in higher rather than lower educational levels. So, among women, class origins strongly influence educational attainment, and in turn, the latter strongly influences entry class. This is a relationship that has remained unchanged despite all the changes in educational, economic and industrial policy that have occurred over the recent past.

CONCLUSION

We began by asking to what extent the data from the Republic of Ireland in respect of the class people first enter on coming into the labour force could be used to support the predictions of the liberal theory of industrialism. We focused on two sets of issues. First, has the relationship between class origins and educational attainment shown any change over the period covered by our three cohorts? A weakening of this relationship would seem to be predicted by the theory in so far as, it is suggested, nations will have to make the optimum use of the talents of their populations. Second, has there been the predicted weakening in class origin effects on class of entry and the predicted strengthening in the impact of educational credentials?

In relation to the first issue it is evident that, among women, there has been no change whatsoever. Despite increasing overall levels of educational attainment the pattern of educational social fluidity has remained unaltered. There is a continuing strong link between class origins and educational attainment very simply captured in the hierarchical ranking of class advantage shown in Table 6.3. Among men there has been some change, but this has been modest, nor can it necessarily be counted as a weakening of the influence of class origins. Rather we see a shift in the pattern of relative advantage in third-level attainment away from the lower non-manual and skilled manual classes towards the propertied classes.

In relation to the second issue once again among women there is no change. The effects of class origin and educational qualifications on entry to the labour-market remain unchanged over time. For women, however, property effects are much less important than for men. A relatively straightforward pattern is observed whereby class origins are largely translated into educational qualifications which then determine the distribution of relative chances of access to more desirable classes. Not least of the remarkable features of this relationship is that it pre-dates the period of massive change in the Irish economy and society. Among men there has been some change but it is both limited and not all of it has been in the direction that would have been predicted. Several class origin effects persist unaltered over time (notably class inheritance effects, the strength of the agricultural barrier and the origin specific resource effects). There is evidence that the one class effect which does decline over time — namely the SLP term which captures additional advantages enjoyed by the propertied groups in access to the professional and managerial class — is partly compensated for by improvement in the relative chances of access of children in the *petit bourgeoisie* and farming classes to third-level education, at the expense of those from routine non-manual and skilled manual backgrounds. In any event, the overall origin class–entry class relationship has shown no change over time, indicating that any decline in the impact of specific property effects has been compensated for by the acquisition of advantage, for the members of such origin classes, elsewhere.

Paradoxically, as at least one type of class background effect is increasingly mediated through educational qualifications, and educational qualifications are increasingly a prerequisite of access to occupations, education has come to be a less powerful influence in shaping inequalities in social fluidity. As the number of men possessing particular qualifications increases, the relative advantage enjoyed by those who possess them has declined. This is a finding that has also been established in Britain and Sweden (Heath, *et al*, 1992; Jonsson, 1993). Comparison of the Irish and British cases indicates that such a diminution can occur in very different economic circumstances. Thus Heath *et al*. (1992) point to the possibility that in a period of rapid growth the strict application of meritocratic principles may not be entirely rational. The results we have presented documenting strong associations between class origins and educational qualifications, and the latter and class of entry, is entirely consistent with the available evidence that employers use fine distinctions in educational performance in making recruitment decisions. It remains possible that the decline in the impact of education, which is observed employing this particular set of class and educational categories, may obscure the fact that the kind of labour-market discriminations that were previously made on the basis of gross educational level, are now based on rather finer distinctions — such as those of type rather than (or in addition to) level of qualifications. Similarly, education now increasingly influences not only class destination but the risk of unemployment among members of the same class (Breen, 1991) and the class destinations of emigrants (Sexton, *et al*, 1991). Nevertheless, the Irish evidence also suggests that, in circumstances of a substantial excess supply of labour, many employers may find it unnecessary, or indeed too costly, to recruit through formal competition; or it may be that, where such competition occurs, other qualities (for which employers may previously have believed education to act as a proxy) come into play.

The results of our analysis, however, unlike those reported by Heath *et al*. (1992) for Britain, do not point to the increasing importance of luck relative to merit. Rather, attention is directed to the importance, for men, of class background influences other than those mediated by property and educational effects; these influences are reflected in the partial inheritance and origin effects, which show no sign of declining over time. These results suggest that, as the game changes, not only are the players most motivated to succeed able to adapt their strategies but the advantages associated with traditional strategies, relating to the use of social networks and specialized knowledge of the labour-market, may indeed become relatively more important (Halsey, 1977).

7 Work-Life Mobility

INTRODUCTION

In this chapter we will focus on intragenerational mobility. In particular we examine mobility from class origin to class at first job and then to current class. During the 1980s the argument was increasingly made that the standard 'parent-to-child' tables, which we have employed in the previous chapters, are seriously flawed as sources of information on mobility (Sorenson, 1986). The basic argument is that such a snapshot picture is incapable of capturing the complex temporal sequences which are actually involved in work-life mobility. In this chapter we go some way towards addressing this criticism by looking at two component parts of origin to current class mobility. We focus first on movement between class origins and the class in which a man's first job places him. Thus we are here looking at the start of the individual's career: how strongly is his first foothold in the labour-market influenced by his class origins? We then go on to examine mobility from this point to his current (or destination) class. So here interest centres on the issue of how strongly a man's subsequent class position is shaped by the class in which he enters the workforce, and also of course, whether, over and above this, the class in which he was brought-up continues to exercise an influence.

We undertake these analyses without accepting the validity of the critiques made by Sorenson and others. It is, of course, clear that the conventional origin to current class mobility table records less movement than would a study that counted each and every change of class position during persons' careers. But this does not invalidate the conventional approach. As Erikson and Goldthorpe (1992, pp. 278–83) have argued, the purpose of standard mobility tables is not to provide evidence about the details of individual careers but, rather, about the mobility rates and patterns displayed by societies at particular points in time.

Cross-national variation in fluidity patterns is significantly greater in the component transitions from origin to entry, and entry to destination, than in the overall movement from origin to destination. The fact that the variation observed in the component transitions is not cumulative, however, leads Erikson and Goldthorpe (1992a) to question whether macro patterns of intragenerational mobility can fruitfully be understood as no more than the unconstrained aggregation of individual trajectories. An alternative interpretation is that variation in the component transitions, over and above that reflected in the standard mobility table, derives from macro constraints on life-course mobility processes. In other words the likelihood that particular 'career' strategies will be successful is crucially dependent on cross-nationally varying institutional contexts. Thus an emphasis on societal constraints that are relatively similar across industrial societies leads them to conclude that while viewing

'. . . intragenerational mobility as a life-course process' may in regard to certain problems be especially revealing . . . in treating others . . . greater insight may be gained from taking just the reverse perspective: life-course mobility as an intergenerational process' (Erikson and Goldthorpe, 1992, p. 306).

DATA PROBLEMS AND CHOICE OF COMPARISON

A number of problems arise in measuring 'first' employment. The first relates to whether this should relate literally to the first paid work that an individual ever undertook or whether there should be exceptions. The Irish data relate to first employment after the completion of full-time education as does the English data. Other surveys, however, follow rather different procedures. The second problem arises in the case of those men whose first employment took the form of working in a family business or on a family farm. Where the distinction between self-employed and relatives assisting can be made the usual practice of treating the former as employees can be followed. However, the accuracy with which this distinction can be made varies from one data set to another. While such a lack of comparability is of no great consequence in the case of the *petit bourgeoisie* since the number involved is small, the effects in the case of agricultural work may not be negligible. We have therefore excluded from our analysis those whose first occupation was in agriculture.

A further restriction of the sample arises from the fact that, among younger respondents, there is a much higher number for whom their current job is also their first job and their inclusion in the analysis will tend to give an exaggerated idea of the degree of immobility that prevails. We have therefore excluded respondents aged twenty to thirty-four. Our detailed analysis is also restricted to men because, when our other restrictions are implemented, taken together with the pattern of women's labour force participation, we are left with less than 300 women who are currently in the labour force. We will, however, provide some descriptive information on the situation of women.

Data considerations have also been influential in our decisions to concentrate, in our analysis of intragenerational mobility, on comparisons between Ireland and England with agricultural occupations excluded at the entry stage. There is, however, a further reason for choosing England as a comparison point. This is that both countries have linkages between the educational system and employment that are of a notably unspecific kind. This is largely because, in both England and Ireland, educational institutions and the scale of provision have evolved with considerable autonomy relative to the economy, in marked contrast to countries (such as Germany) where education and training systems were developed as instruments of manpower policy, and where the education–labour-market linkages are much more specific and formalised. From our point of view, however, it is more interesting to ask whether, despite such institutional similarity, the Irish pattern of career mobility might still differ significantly from that observed in England; and, if so, whether such differences can contribute to an understanding of the overall differences in mobility regimes which have been discussed earlier.

CROSS-NATIONAL COMPARISONS OF THE THREE TWO-WAY TRANSITIONS

Our analysis distinguishes between four classes.

(i)   Professional, Managerial and Administrative or the Service Class (I and II);

(ii)   Intermediate Class: Routine non-manual and *petit bourgeoisie*: (IIIa, IVa+b);

(iii) Working-Class: Lower routine non-manual, lower grade technicians and supervisors of manual workers, skilled and non-skilled manual workers, agricultural workers, (IIIb, V/VI, VIIa+b).

(iv)   Farmers (IVc).

Table 7.1: *Class Mobility Chances by Class of Origin: Outflow*
Percentages for Men aged thirty-five to sixty-four
(Excluding Respondents Entering Agricultural Classes at
First Job)
(Percentages in Parentheses Relate to England 1972)

Current Class	Class of Origin				Current Class Percentage
	Professional, Managerial, Administrative	*Intermediate Non-Manual*	*Farmers*	*Working-Class*	
	Per Cent by Column				
Professional, Managerial and Administrative	68.1 (62.3)	45.4 (32.4)	19.8 (32.8)	11.5 (19.0)	22.0 (26.5)
Intermediate Non-Manual	12.6 (15.1)	23.9 (26.6)	15.1 (14.3)	11.8 (12.7)	13.7 (15.1)
Farmers	0.0 (0.3)	0.7 (0.5)	22.0 (5.0)	0.6 (0.2)	5.1 (0.4)
Working-Class	19.2 (22.3)	30.1 (40.6)	43.1 (47.9)	76.8 (68.1)	59.2 (58.0)
Origin Percentage	9.7 (12.1)	9.5 (15.2)	21.3 (2.2)	59.5 (70.6)	

Respondents in agricultural occupations at point of entry are excluded from the analysis giving a three-class schema at that point. Tables 7.1 to 7.3 display the pattern of class mobility chances for each of the transitions. Table 7.1 relating to the overall origin-destination transition shows a pattern which is familiar from analyses employing more detailed schemas. Thus the outflow patterns from the service class are quite similar in the two countries, although in the Irish case immobility is somewhat higher. On the other hand, the upward mobility rates for the intermediate class are significantly superior in Ireland and the risk of downward mobility into the working-class is correspondingly lower. In contrast the upward mobility prospects of the working-class in Ireland are significantly worse than those in England and levels of immobility are higher. Not surprisingly the outflow patterns for farmers are quite dissimilar with levels of immobility significantly higher in Ireland and mobility into the service class significantly less likely.

Table 7.2: *Class Mobility Chances at First Job by Class of Origin:*
Outflow Percentages for Men aged thirty-five to sixty-four
(Excluding Respondents Entering Agricultural Classes at
First Job)
(Percentages in Parentheses Relate to England 1972)

Class at First Job	Class of Origin				First Job Percentage
	Professional, Managerial, Administrative	Intermediate Non-Manual	Farmers	Working-Class	
	Per Cent by Column				
Professional, Managerial and Administrative	30.1 (29.3)	25.3 (12.2)	11.5 (20.0)	3.6 (4.9)	9.9 (9.3)
Intermediate Non-Manual	31.3 (22.9)	14.6 (18.0)	7.2 (15.8)	7.8 (8.2)	10.6 (11.7)
Working-Class	38.6 (47.8)	60.1 (69.8)	81.3 (6.2)	88.6 (86.8)	79.4 (79.0)

In Table 7.2 we direct our attention to the transition from origin to point of entry. There is little difference between Ireland and England in immobility rates in the service class with 30 per cent immobile in both cases but downward mobility into the working-class is significantly less likely in Ireland; 39 per cent versus 48 per cent. Once again members of the intermediate class in Ireland are seen to enjoy striking advantages over their English counterparts in that they are twice as likely to be mobile into the service class; 25 per cent versus 12 per cent. The working-class in Ireland are again less likely to experience long-range upward mobility but the differences appear modest in comparison with those evident in the overall mobility tables: 4 per cent versus 5 per cent. For those from farming backgrounds the Irish group are substantially less likely to enter the service class; 12 per cent versus 21 per cent.

Finally in Table 7.3 we look directly at career mobility. It is clear that career immobility in the service class in Ireland is substantially higher than in England, 91 per cent versus 81 per cent. It is this factor which almost entirely accounts for higher levels of immobility in the final mobility table. On the other hand the ultimate advantage enjoyed by the intermediate class in Ireland is almost entirely due to differences in the outflow from origin to entry since the patterns for career mobility are almost identical. For the working-class on the other hand, comparatively restricted access to the service class is evident in both component transitions and the final disparity involves an accumulation of these advantages. Finally it is worth noting that it is the pattern of career mobility that differs between the two countries rather than the absolute level of mobility where very little difference exists with 69 per cent of the Irish respondents having been mobile compared to 66 per cent of their English counterparts.

Table 7.3:   *Class Mobility Chances by Class at First Job: Outflow Percentages for Men aged thirty-five to sixty-four (Excluding Respondents Entering Agricultural Classes at First Job) (Percentages in Parentheses Relate to England 1972)*

Current Class	Class at First Job		
	Professional, Managerial, Administrative	*Intermediate Non-Manual*	*Working-Class*
	Per Cent by Column		
Professional, Managerial and Administrative	90.5 (81.3)	53.5 (53.4)	9.3 (15.7)
Intermediate Non-Manual	2.6 (7.5)	28.7 (26.3)	13.1 (14.2)
Farmers	0.9 (0.9)	1.0 (0.4)	6.1 (0.3)
Working-Class	6.1 (10.3)	16.9 (19.8)	69.8 (71.4)
Class at First Job Percentage	22.1 (26.0)	10.6 (11.7)	79.2 (79.5)

The situation for women over thirty-five in the labour force is that their current class distribution is more skewed towards the upper end of the class hierarchy than is that for comparable males. The difference by sex is, however, substantially greater at first job: 30 per cent of these women had entered the service class at the time of their first job compared to 10 per cent of men. Correspondingly only half of the women had started out in the working-class compared to the corresponding male group.

This group of women thus start out as substantially advantaged in comparison with men in their age group but this advantage is almost entirely eroded as they experience significantly less upward mobility over time. From Table 7.4 we can see that the women who had started out in the professional and managerial class were almost as likely as their male counterparts to remain there. However, while 54 per cent of men who started out in the intermediate class were upwardly mobile into the professional and managerial class this was true of only 28 per cent of women. Similarly, women who started out in the working-class were much more likely to remain there; the respective percentages being 83 per cent and 70 per cent. Women over thirty-five in the labour force are, like men, able to hold on to their positions at the 'top' once they have been achieved but are less likely than men of comparable class origins to break into this class in the course of their careers.

Table 7.4:   Employment Mobility Chances by Class at First Job: Outflow Percentages for Women Aged aged thirty-five to sixty-four in the Labour Force
(Excluding Respondents Entering Agricultural Classes at First Job)

Current Class	Class at First Job			Current Class Position Percentage
	Professional, Managerial, Administrative	*Intermediate Non-Manual*	*Working-Class*	
	Per Cent by Column			
Professional, Managerial and Administrative	84.5	28.4	6.2	29.9
Intermediate Non-Manual	8.6	50.6	10.0	18.8
Farmers	0.3	0.4	0.8	0.6
Working-Class	6.6	20.6	83.0	50.8
'Class' at First Job Percentage	23.8	22.4	53.7	

PATTERNS OF SOCIAL FLUIDITY

The outflow patterns reported in Tables 7.1 to 7.3 are a consequence of differences in overall (or absolute rates) of mobility and are influenced by structural differences in the class distribution of the two societies as well as differences in relative rates (or social fluidity). As we have explained earlier the appropriate measure of relative mobility chances are the odds-ratios which are captured in the parameters of log-linear models.

We use these models to assess the importance of relative and absolute cross-national differences at each transition, and to assess the extent to which relative differences remain significant when we control for absolute differences. We apply them to tables of origin by current (or destination) class; origin by entry class; and entry class by current class. In each case we fit the models of conditional independence (IND) and constant social fluidity (CnSF). The former allows for variation in origins and destinations between countries but no association between origin and destination i.e. complete equality of opportunity. The constant social fluidity model, on the other hand, assumes that there is an association between origins and destinations but this is the same in both countries, although the marginal distributions are allowed to differ between countries. We thus have variation in absolute mobility but cross-nationally constant relative mobility. Not surprisingly, as the results in Table 7.5 show the bulk of the cross-national variation for each transition is accounted for by structural differences — that is to say, it is mainly due to differences in the marginal distributions. However, in no case does the constant social fluidity model provide a satisfactory fit to the data. Thus at each stage cross-national differences in relative rates of mobility are statistically significant. The indicator shown in the final column, G^2/df, suggests that the constant social fluidity model fits least well for the entry to destination table.

Table 7.5: *Results of Fitting the Constant Social Fluidity Model to Tables Representing Different Transitions for Ireland 1987 and England 1972*

Model*	G^2	df	G^2/df
Origin-Destination			
ON DN (IND)	1,084.2	18	3.3
ON DN OD (CnSF)	29.3	9	
Origin-Entry			
OE EN (IND)	714.3	12	4.8
ON EN OE (CnSF)	28.8	6	
Entry-Destination			
EN DN (IND)	1,939.3	12	5.3
EN DN ED (CnSF)	31.5	6	

* O = Origin Class; D = Destination Class; E = Entry Class; N = Nation.

These results show that cross-national variation in relative rates is less in the overall origin-destination transition than in either of the two component transitions. 'Thus, underlying the mobility that is observed between origin class and entry-class there are clear cross-national differences in fluidity patterns, and if such differences are yet greater in the case of work-life mobility itself, why are these differences reduced, rather than heightened when an intergenerational view is taken?' (Erikson and Goldthorpe, 1992a, pp. 295–6).

While in the comparison that Erikson and Goldthorpe make (between England and France on the one hand, and Hungary and Poland on the other) the differences can be explained by the fundamentally different institutional contexts, the pattern of differences between Ireland and England will clearly require a somewhat different explanation. In order to explore this we now compare the results arising from analyses of three-way mobility tables.

In order to take up the analysis of cross-national variation in relative rates of mobility we first combine the Irish and English three-way tables into a single four-way table in which nation is also a variable. The outcomes derived from applying a variety of models to this table are set out in Table 7.6. Model A is that proposing (conditional) independence of origin, entry and destination class. Model B contains two 3-way interaction terms. This model implies that there is cross-national variation in relative rates in the origin-entry transitions and again in the entry-destination transition; but that the association between origin class and destination class and the cross-national variation in this association derive entirely from variation in the component transitions. Crucially, this model assumes that one's mobility chances in moving from first to current class is unaffected by one's class of origin. As we shall see this is an unrealistic assumption. Nevertheless that model accounts for about 80 per cent of the deviance associated with the conditional independence model.

Table 7.6:   *Results of Fitting Models to Three-Way Mobility Tables for Ireland and England*

	Model*	G^2	df	G^2/df
A	OE* EN* DN			
	(Independence)	3,201.0	78	41.0
B	OEN* EDN	634.2	54	11.7
C	OEN* EDN* OED	28.4	27	1.1
D	O*N + O*E + E*D*N + O*E*D	80.4	33	2.4
E	O*E*N + D*N + E*D + O*E*D	55.1	33	1.7

*   O = Origin Class; E = Entry Class; D = Destination Class; N = Nation.

Model C removes one of the major restrictions imposed by Model B in that it allows for association between origin class and destination class over and above that created by the component effects and for this association to vary by entry class. However, since the OED term is one that applies across nations, it remains the case that Model C allows for no cross-national variation in relative rates in the overall origin-destination tables other than that deriving from variation in their constituent origin-entry and entry-destination tables. This model provides a satisfactory fit to the data for Ireland and England with a G^2 of 28.4 with 27 degrees of freedom. The implication of the fit to the data provided by Model C is that all cross-national variation in mobility is accounted for by variations in the component traditions. In Models D and E the origin-entry term and the entry-destination term respectively are constrained to be cross-nationally invariant. Neither model fits but it is the entry-destination term which proves to be slightly more important.

Table 7.7: *Level of Educational Qualification by Class Origin for Those Entering Work in the Manual Class*

Level of of Education	Class of Origin			
	Professional, Managerial, Administrative	*Intermediate*	*Working- Class*	*Farming*
Primary or Less	10.6	35.7	62.5	65.8
Intermediate or Group Certificate	41.6	44.0	31.4	26.1
Leaving Certificate	27.2	8.7	2.3	5.6
Third Level	20.6	11.6	3.8	2.5

The Irish pattern of career mobility is clearly such as to undermine any notion of a series of open-ended life-course movements. Rather it is consistent with the Erikson and Goldthorpe argument, for the operation of constraints across nations, which shape the way in which the transition from origin class to entry class and entry class to destination class are related to each other. Thus the Irish pattern of mobility involves the operation of comparatively strong class advantages, which are clearly related to the mobilisation of class resources, for each of the transition components. It also involves the interaction of class origin with the entry-origin association as reflected in the levels of career counter-mobility to class of origin — in other words the tendency for those men who are initially mobile out of their class of origin to return to it at some later point.

This is very common among, for example, the inheriting children of farmers and the *petit bourgeoisie*. Such counter-mobility is hardly surprising when we take into account the relationship between class origin and education level even when we hold class of entry constant. In Table 7.7 we illustrate this fact for those entering work in the manual class. Thus only one in ten of those from service class backgrounds who enter work in the manual class have primary education, or less, while almost one in two have a Leaving Certificate or third-level education; in contrast for those from working class or farming class backgrounds two-thirds had primary education, or less, and somewhat less than one in twelve had proceeded to Leaving Certificate or beyond.

However, while counter-mobility is a very significant factor in shaping the Irish pattern of career mobility, in this respect Ireland does not appear to differ greatly from England. The ultimate difference in the pattern of mobility observed in the Irish and English origin to destination tables is a consequence, predominantly, of a straightforward accumulation of the greater inequalities displayed in Ireland for each of the component transitions. In Table 7.8 this point is illustrated for the service class/working-class 'competition' for each of the transitions. For the origin-entry transition the Irish odds-ratio comes close to 20 and is almost twice as great as the corresponding figure for England; for the entry to destination transition the Irish figure rises to close to 70 and is once again almost double the odds-ratios found in England. These inequalities, together with the processes of counter-mobility, combine to produce a situation where the Irish odds-ratios for the final origin to destination transition is 23.4 while the corresponding figure for England is 8.5.

Table 7.8: A Comparison of Odds-Ratios for the Service Class and Working-Class for Each of the Two-Way Transitions

	Ireland 1987	England 1972
Origin-Entry	19.2	10.9
Entry-Destination	68.4	35.8
Origin-Destination	23.4	8.5

EXPLAINING WORK-LIFE PATTERNS OF MOBILITY IN IRELAND

We have provided a more detailed treatment of the Irish pattern of social fluidity and comparisons with the experience of other European countries in Chapter 4. Here we concentrate our attention on attempting to provide an explanation of variations in relative mobility in the entry-destination transition between Ireland and England in the absence of significant differences in counter-mobility patterns in the two countries. A number of possibilities suggest themselves.

The first points to the possibility of structural differences which are concealed by the class schema we have employed. That differences in career mobility patterns may be related to basic differences in the occupational structure has been raised in previous work (Whelan and Whelan, 1984, p. 51). In addition, the evidence for England and Wales pointed to the continuing importance of skilled manual occupations as an initial training ground both for higher-grade technicians and for professionals in engineering and related areas (Goldthorpe, 1980, pp. 132–4). The evidence for England shows that the distinction between skilled and non-skilled employment appears as an important one as far as work-life mobility is concerned. For men aged thirty-five to sixty-four, in England skilled manual positions clearly exceed non-skilled as entry points whereas in Ireland non-skilled positions are almost twice as frequent.

In Table 7.9 we break down the working-class into its constituent elements and show the levels of long-range upward mobility for both countries. Both the size of the lower non-manual group and the technicians' group, and the outflows from them are very similar. The remaining groups vary in size and in outflows. Thus the percentage of skilled manual workers is twice as great in England and career mobility to the service class is over twice as likely. The non-skilled manual groups are

Table 7.9: *Work-Life Mobility from the Working Class to the Professional and Managerial Class–Men Aged aged thirty-five to sixty-four*
(Figures in Parentheses Related to the Size of the Occupational Group at First Job)

	Ireland 1987		England 1972	
	%	%	%	%
Routine Non-Manual Lower-Grade	21.6	(8.7)	21.6	(6.5)
Technicians and Supervisors of Manual Workers	20.0	(5.2)	23.8	(5.3)
Skilled Manual	7.8	(16.8)	16.6	(34.6)
Non-Skilled manual	4.4	(29.2)	11.2	(25.2)
Agricultural Workers	2.2	(17.5)	7.3	(9.5)

of similar size but upward mobility is two-and-a-half times more probable in England. Finally, the agricultural worker group which, in relative size is almost twice as great in Ireland, has a mobility probability which is three-and-a-half times greater in England. Thus, while variations in occupational structure are undoubtedly of great importance, differential outflows from corresponding groups also play a major role.

One further possibility which must be considered relates to structural differences within the groups we have identified. Although we could find no appreciable differences between England in 1972 and Ireland in 1987 in the percentages of skilled workers located in manufacturing there is a striking difference in the composition of the non-skilled manual groups. While unskilled manual and agricultural workers make up one-fifth of the English non-skilled manual class, the corresponding figure for Ireland is one-half. However, the possibility of long-range upward career mobility is identical for both categories. Thus we can find no evidence for further structural effects which are hidden by our categorisation. Other possible explanations of the distinctiveness of the Irish situation include:

(i) the fact that the small size of Irish private-sector organisations sets strict limits to the potential role of internal-labour markets in facilitating career mobility; while the continued significance of family ownership is likely to inhibit the application of universalistic criteria in determining career advancement.

(ii) The Irish educational system is particularly rigid with little or nothing in the way of second chance opportunities being offered.

A final possibility is that the long-term situation of an excess supply of labour in Ireland influences the outcome of the competitions whose results are reflected in the observed pattern of odds-ratios.

Unemployment in Ireland has been characterised by a high overall rate and a high level of long-term unemployment. The degree to which unemployment has been concentrated in the working classes is striking. Unemployment among non-agricultural unskilled workers has hardly fallen below 30 per cent since 1961, while that for the upper middle-class has only once exceeded 3 per cent. Thus among those classified as entering work in the manual classes are significant proportions who will have had their opportunities for career mobility impeded by the experience of long-term or recurring levels of unemployment.

The excess of labour supply is also related to the extent of qualification inflation and the use of qualifications as a screening mechanism. Thus Murray and Wickham (1983, p. 100), in their study of Irish electronics firms, found that in Ireland entry to technicians' jobs required the completion of two or three years of full-time technical education. In Britain, on the other hand, technicians have frequently been recruited via apprenticeship and subsequent promotion, providing an important channel of upward mobility. Similar findings have been reported for Italy. There is evidence that such screening can influence career mobility not only directly but also through its impact on the probability of being unemployed. Thus while we do not have detailed life-history data on unemployment experience we have shown elsewhere that in Ireland, unlike England, class of origin does have an independent effect on the risk of unemployment even when current class is taken into account (Whelan *et al.* 1992).

The results presented here confirm that work-life mobility, rather than being viewed as an open-ended process, needs to be located in the context of societal constraints. In Ireland the pattern of career mobility and how it differs from the English one, must be understood in terms of the manner in which it contributes to the overall level of social closure in the conventional origin-destination table rather than as a process which is obscured by it. Understanding this pattern requires that it be viewed in the light of the limited levels of intergenerational mobility and indeed limited opportunities to participate in the labour-market that prevail in Ireland.

8 The Continuing Relevance of Class Analysis

INTRODUCTION

In the previous chapters we have documented the extent of social mobility in Ireland, the degree of social closure and the determinants of existing patterns of social fluidity. Class was defined solely in terms of employment relationship and the extent of class-related socio-cultural variation was considered to be an empirical issue. A great deal of our interest in mobility issues is motivated by our belief that life-chances, defined following Giddens (1973, pp. 130–31) as the 'chances an individual has for sharing in the socially created economic or cultural "goods" that typically exist in any given society', are significantly related to class position. In the absence of evidence for such relationships class mobility analysis would undoubtedly attract a good deal less attention. In recent years critics have, indeed, argued that such analysis is becoming unproductive and increasingly less relevant. For example Clark and Lipset (1991, p. 397) argue that 'Social class was the key theme of past stratification work. Yet class is an increasingly outmoded concept.' Similarly, in Britain, Pahl (1989, p. 710) argues that in modern societies 'class as a concept is ceasing to do any useful work for sociology'.

Goldthorpe and Marshall (1992) provide a defence of class analysis against the critiques of Pahl (1989), Holton and Turner (1989), Offe (1985), Hindess (1987) and others (see also Hout et al., 1993). Their defence involves distinguishing class analysis, as conducted by those such as Goldthorpe, from the class analysis of Marxist sociology. The former involves neither a theory of history, in which class conflict serves as the engine of change, nor a theory of class exploitation. Furthermore, the relationships between class structure, consciousness and action is seen to be contingent. From this perspective class analysis can be understood as involving exploration of

. . . the interconnections between positions defined by employment relations in labour markets and production units in different sectors of national economies; the processes through which individuals and families are distributed among these positions over time; and the consequences thereof for their life chances and for the social identities they adopt and the social values and interests that they pursue. (Goldthorpe and Marshall, 1992b, p. 382)

Issues relating to values and social interests go beyond our brief and thus our concern will be with the remaining part of the programme (see Whelan, 1994). Our attention is therefore focused on claims that the explanatory power of class is waning and has been overtaken by that of factors, such as consumption patterns or life-styles, and that inequalities in life-chances are no longer significantly structured by class position: there is a 'classlessness' of social inequality (Beck,1992; Pahl,1989).

Before proceeding to empirically examine such issues we will first deal with the theoretical justification for class analysis. Goldthorpe and Marshall's (1995, p. 382) assertion, that class analysis as they understand it does not entail a commitment to any particular theory of class, has been taken by some as abandoning any pretensions to theory in favour of placing complete faith in empirical analysis. In fact, as our discussion in Chapter 2 has shown, the CASMIN class schema, developed by Goldthorpe and his associates, is based on a particular understanding of the manner in which employment-related inequalities emerge as a consequence of the way in which work is organised within capitalist organisations and the nature of control in such organisations. Class position, and consequently, differential rewards follow a line of cleavage between employers, the self-employed and employees,and within the latter group, according to the nature of the employment relationship. Here a distinction is made between the service class relationship and a labour contract. The greater rewards accruing to the former are associated with the need for employers to engender long-term relationships of trust and commitment with employees who, by virtue of their specialised knowledge or exercise of delegated authority, cannot be directly supervised (Erikson and Goldthorpe, 1992a, p. 42; Goldthorpe, 1982). Breen and Rottman (1995b) point to the similarity between this formulation and that of 'efficiency wage' in economics. Here the argument is that in certain jobs the direct monitoring by employers of employees is difficult. This leads to employers rewarding employees in such jobs at a rate above what they could get elsewhere. Through such processes relations based in production become central to understanding how life-chances are distributed.

CLASS AND LIFE-CHANCES

In our analysis of variation in life-chances by class position it would be possible to provide evidence of such variation across the highly detailed class schema that we have used earlier. This is to some extent demonstrated by our ability to successfully utilise a measure of hierarchy in modelling the pattern of social fluidity using the fourteen-class schema. However, most of the variation that is central to our argument can be captured using a four-class schema which distinguishes:

1. The professional and managerial or service class (I + II)

2. The intermediate non-manual group, the *petit bourgeoisie* and farmers with more than 50 acres. (IIIa, IV a+b, IVc > 50 acres)

3. Skilled and semi-skilled manual workers and small farmers (IIIb, IVc, V, VI, VIIa(i) < 50 acres)

4. Unskilled manual workers. (VIIa (ii), VIIb)

We proceed to apply this class schema to households where the Head of Household (HOH) is aged less than 65 years and the relevant class position is in both cases that of the HOH.

Economic Resources

The obvious starting point in an analysis of life-chances involves an examination of variations in the level of resources. In Table 8.1 we show the breakdown of household income, savings and net house value. By employing this range of measures we hope to capture variations, not just in current income, but in longer term command over resources which is crucial for life-chances. The income measure employed is net equivalent household income where each additional adult has been given a weight of 0.66 and each child a weight of 0.33. Income varies systematically across social class and overall it accounts for 21 per cent of the variance. The incomes of the professional and managerial group are twice that of the unskilled manual class. A fairly sharp division exists between the manual and non-manual classes; the intermediate non-manual and property-owning classes have an advantage of almost 1.5:1 over the skilled manual class. The scale of the difference within the manual group is of a similar magnitude. For savings and deposits a rather similar pattern emerges. In relation to the former those at the peak of the hierarchy enjoy an advantage of over 4:1 over those at the bottom; with regard to the latter the differential is somewhat weaker at just over 2:1. The unskilled manual group is distinguished by a particularly low level of savings.

Table 8.1:   Household Economic Resources by Social Class

	Net Equivalent Household Income	Savings	Net House Value
	£	£	£
Professional and Managerial [I+II]	131.2	3,023	27,964
Intermediate Non-Manual, *Petit Bourgeoisie* and Farmers [IIIa, IVa+b, IVc, > 50 acres]	117.3	2,875	21,577
Skilled and Semi-Skilled Manual Workers and Small Farmers [IIIb, IVc, V, VI, VIIa(i), < 50 acres]	79.1	1,380	15,579
Unskilled Working Class [VIIa(ii), VIIb]	55.3	743	12,628
Proportion of Variance Explained	0.211	0.025	0.094

Life-Style

At this point we shift our focus from resource measures to outcome measures. Initially, we look at a set of measures whose enforced absence has elsewhere been described as involving secondary deprivation. (Callan, Nolan and Whelan 1993; Nolan and Whelan, 1986). The items involved are a telephone, a car, a colour television, a week's annual holiday away from home, central heating, being able to save some of one's income regularly, and a daily newspaper. For each of these items it was established whether the item was possessed by the household; where this was not the case it was further established whether its absence was because it could not be afforded. An additional question dealt with being able to afford an afternoon or evening out in the previous two weeks. Table 8.2 describes the distribution across the social classes of the enforced absence of such items. Inability to afford a telephone rises gradually from a level of 7 per cent among the professional and managerial class to 53 per cent in the unskilled manual class. Similarly, the latter are six times more likely than the former to be unable to afford a car; the respective percentages being 41 and 7. The number being unable to afford a colour television is much lower than in the case of any of the other items. It remains as low as 3 per cent in both of the non-manual classes but rises to 8 per cent for the skilled manual class and to 14 per cent for the unskilled manual class. The opportunity of enjoying a holiday is strongly class related. Just over one in five of those at the top of the class hierarchy are denied this opportunity; the figure remains at a

Table 8.2: *Life-Style Deprivation by Social Class: Percentage of Households Lacking Steins Because They could not Afford Them.*

	Telephone	Car	Colour TV	Holiday	Central Heating	Savings	Daily Newspaper	Night or Afternoon Out in Previous Two Weeks	Secondary Deprivation Score
	%	%	%	%	%	%	%	%	%
Professional and Managerial [1+II]	7	7	3	22	9	30	4	7	0.9
Intermediate Non-Manual Workers, *Petit Bourgeoisie* and Farmers [IIIa, IVa+b, IVc, >50 acres]	20	23	3	29	17	44	11	10	1.7
Skilled and Semi-Skilled Manual Workers and Small Farmers [IIIb, IVc, < 50 acres, V, VI, VIIa(i)]	43	31	8	62	32	61	18	23	3.0
Unskilled Working Class [VIIa(ii), VII(b)]	53	41	14	77	54	82	28	40	4.3
Proportion of Variance Explained									0.220

relatively low level of three out of ten for other non-manual workers and property-owning groups. Among manual workers, on the other hand, being deprived of a holiday is the norm. It is true of over 60 per cent of the skilled manual class and over three-quarters of the unskilled class. Being in a position to avail of central heating is also directly related to class position. While only 9 per cent of the professional and managerial class indicate that they cannot afford this facility the figure rises steadily so that it is eventually six times higher at the bottom of the class hierarchy. Similarly while over four out of five of unskilled manual class households are unable to save this drops to three out of ten of service class households. Being able to afford a newspaper displays a familiar pattern, with those at the bottom of the hierarchy being seven times more likely than those at the top to report this deprivation; the respective figures being 28 per cent and 4 per cent. Class differences in ability to afford an afternoon or evening out in the previous fortnight are even more extreme. Among the white-collar and property-owning classes the number of household heads who must forego this pleasure does not rise above one in ten; for the skilled manual class, however, it reaches one in four, and finally peaks at the level of four out of ten for the unskilled working class. Class differences in access to these consumer items and activities are summarised in the scores on the nine-item secondary deprivation index. The service class group, on average, suffers an enforced lack of one item; the figure then rises gradually to in excess of four for the unskilled working class.

Poverty, Economic Strain and Fatalism

The findings set out in the previous section provide evidence of substantial life-style variation by social class. However, in general, the items involved are not ones which would be considered by most people to be essentials. Elsewhere we have identified such a set which is comprised of the following items:

- whether there was a day during the previous two weeks when the household manager did not have a substantial meal at all from getting up to going to bed;

- whether the household manager had to go without heating during the past year through lack of money, that is, having to go without a fire on a cold day, or go to bed early to keep warm or light the fire late because of lack of coal/fuel;

- whether the household had experienced any of the following

- current arrears on rent, mortgage, electricity or gas;

- had to incur debt in the past 12 months to meet ordinary living expenses (such as rent, food,Christmas or back-to-school expenses);

- had to sell or pawn anything worth £50 or more to meet ordinary living expenses; or

- had received assistance from a private charity in the past year.

- Enforced absence of:

- new not second-hand clothes;

- a meal with meat chicken or fish;

- a warm waterproof overcoat;

- two pairs of strong shoes;

- a roast or its equivalent once a week.

In all cases where information was available the vast majority of respondents considered such items to be social necessities. This dimension of life-style deprivation we label 'basic deprivation'.

Information on this measure has been combined with information on equivalent disposable household income to provide a measure of household poverty. Poverty is here defined as involving *exclusion* arising from *lack of resources*, from *socially defined necessities*. The poor must therefore be defined using both a deprivation and an income criterion. Poverty is consequently, defined as a situation where a household falls below a specified income line (in this case the 60 per cent relative income line) and experiences an enforced absence of at least one of the basic life-style items. (Callan, Nolan and Whelan,1993; and Nolan and Whelan, 1996).

From Table 8.3 it is clear that poverty varies dramatically by social class. Among the professional and managerial class the rate is less than 2 per cent. It then rises to 10 per cent among the intermediate non-manual and property-owning group. The rate the skilled manual class reaches is double this figure. Finally, for the unskilled manual class the level of risk is almost one in two and is close to thirty times higher than that observed for the service class. The objective experience of extreme deprivation and the need to constantly engage in economic brinkmanship is reflected, although not exactly paralleled, in the subjective experience of economic strain. Six out of ten households located in the unskilled manual class report that they experience extreme difficulty in making ends meet. The figure drops to just below four out of ten for the skilled manual class, and to one in four and one in ten for the lower and higher non-manual classes respectively. That these class differences reflect more than short-term economic difficulties is demonstrated by comparable variations in the probability of the head of household reporting that the family in which she/he had grown up had experienced extreme financial difficulties.

Table 8.3:   Poverty and Economic Stress By Social Class

	Poor	Experiencing Extreme Difficulty in Making Ends Meet	Severe Financial Problems in Family When Growing Up
	%	%	%
Professional and Managerial [I+II]	1.6	10.7	13.5
Intermediate Non-Manual, *Petit Bourgeoisie* and Farmers [IIIa, IVa+b, IVc, > 50 acres]	10.2	26.1	10.3
Skilled and Semi-Skilled Manual and Small Farmers [IIIb, IVc, < 50 acres, V, VI, VIIa(i)]	20.6	38.7	25.9
Unskilled Working Class [VIIa(ii), VIIb]	46.0	59.6	42.2

The influence of current and long-term financial difficulties and strain are in turn reflected in the relationship between social class and feelings of powerlessness or fatalism which has been documented by social scientists of varying disciplinary backgrounds (Mirowsky and Ross, 1990; Whelan, 1992 a & b). The set of items we employed to measure fatalism is set out in Table 8.4, as is variation by social class in the percentage of heads of households agreeing with each item. The level of fatalism varies systematically by social class. Further analysis suggests that, unlike psychological distress which we will look at later, it is the cumulative realities of working-class life and the difficulties involved in imposing one's will on an intractable environment that are crucial rather than the current experience of deprivation *per se*.

The first and most important conclusion which emerges from an examination of Table 8.4 is that what one is confronted with is not complete helplessness and passivity. Bearing in mind that each of the individual items is a rather imperfect measure of the underlying concept of fatalism, we direct our attention, initially, to some of the positively-worded

Table 8.4: Responses to Fatalism Items by Social Class for Heads of Household

	Percentage Agreeing			
	Professional and Managerial (I & II)	Intermediate Non-manual Petit Bourgeoisie and Farmers (III, IVb, IVc < 50 acres)	Skilled & Semi-skilled Manual and Small Farmers (IIIb, IVc, < 50 acres, V, VI, VIIa(i))	Unskilled Working-Class (VIIa(ii), VIIb)
	%	%	%	%
1. I can do just about anything I set my mind to	72	72	66	58
2. I have little control over the things that happen to me	19	34	43	50
3. What happens to me in the future depends on me	82	77	73	62
4. I often feel helpless in dealing with the problems of life	16	38	41	54
5. Sometimes I feel I am being pushed around	21	28	32	37
6. There is a lot I can do to change my life if I want to	69	64	45	23
7. There is really no way I can solve some of the problems I have	23	33	45	62

items. The percentage agreeing that *'I can do just about anything I set my mind to'* declines from 72 per cent for the professional and managerial class to 58 per cent for the working-class. Similarly, while 82 per cent of the former express agreement with the statement that *'What happens in the future depends on me'* the figure drops to 62 per cent for the latter. However, despite such class differences, the results are not consistent with a picture of the working class as a demoralised apathetic mass.

There is another side to the picture. Focusing on the remaining positively-worded items, one finds that while seven out of ten of the professional and managerial group feel that *'there is a lot I can do to change my life if I want to,'* the figure drops to less than one in four for the lower working-class. For all of the negatively-worded items the differences are just as dramatic. One in two of the lower working-class accept the views that *'I have little control over the things that happen to me'* and *'I often feel helpless in dealing with the problems of life'*; the corresponding figures at the peak of the class hierarchy range between one-fifth and one-sixth. Similarly, the lower working-class are almost twice as likely as their professional and managerial counterparts to indicate that *'sometimes I feel I am being pushed around'*; the respective figures being 21 per cent and 37 per cent. Finally, almost two-thirds of the lower working-class accept that *'there is really no way I can solve some of the problems I have'*; a level almost three times higher than that displayed by the professional and managerial class.

The pattern of results points to the fine line we must walk in avoiding portraying the working-class as passive victims of external circumstances rather than, as they frequently are, active, interpreting, striving agents, without at the same time, ignoring the extent to which the erosion of economic resources undermines the capacity to cope (Fryer, 1986, 1992; Whelan, 1992c). Neither does fatalism appear to be significantly related to location in urban rented public sector housing but rather appears to be a consequence of broader working-class experience (Whelan, 1996).

Physical and Mental Health

One of the most basic life-chances relates to being able to enjoy good physical and mental health. A comprehensive discussion of the determinants of physical and mental health and of issues relating to the role of selection and structural and cultural differences, would take us well beyond the scope of the current volume (Blane *et al*, 1993; Davey-Smith *et al*, 1990; Whelan, 1994b). Although we will refer briefly to such issues in our discussion of class and causality later in this chapter, for the moment, we will concentrate on simply documenting class inequalities.

Our measure of physical status was derived from responses to the following question: '*Do you have any major illness, physical disability or infirmity that has troubled you for at least a year or that is likely to go on troubling you in the future?*' This type of question on chronic illness has been widely used in surveys elsewhere, for example, in the UK General Household Survey and in regular health surveys carried out in France and the Scandinavian countries. Blaxter (1989) categorises this type of question as fitting into what she terms the 'medical model' since — although self-reported rather than medically assessed — ill health is being defined in terms of deviation from physiological norms rather than limitations to functioning, or subjectively in terms of the individual's perception and experiences. While self-reporting might be thought likely to be problematic, where comparisons have been made, the agreement with doctors' assessments or medical records has been high. (Blaxter, 1989, pp. 209–210).

Substantially higher rates of self-reported chronic illness in the lower rather than the higher social classes have been found in various countries, the gap being particularly pronounced in the middle age ranges. The Irish results for men in the age range forty to fifty-four as set out in Table 8.5 are entirely in line with such findings. The number reporting such illness rises gradually from 9 per cent among the professional and managerial group to 22 per cent among the unskilled working-class.

Table 8.5: Physical Health by Social Class for Heads of Households Aged 40–54 Years

	Percentage Ill
Professional and Managerial [I+II]	9.1
Intermediate Non-Manual, *Petit Bourgeoisie* and Farmers [IIIa, IVa+b, IVc, > 50 acres]	15.0
Skilled and Semi-Skilled Manual Workers and Small Farmers [IIIb, IVc, < 50 acres, V, VI, VIIa(i)]	18.8
Unskilled Working-Class [VIIa(ii), VIIb]	21.7

To provide information about psychological health we rely upon a version of the widely-used General Health Questionnaire (GHQ), (Whelan *et al*, 1991; Whelan, 1992c, 1994). This comprises a twelve-item set of questions, which are designed to give information about the respondent's current mental state. It is neither a measure of long-standing personality attributes nor an assessment of the likelihood of falling ill in the near future. On the other hand it is most definitely not merely a complaints inventory. It consists solely of items that have been chosen from a substantial battery on the basis of their ability to discriminate between groups of respondents in terms of their likelihood of being assessed as non-psychotic psychiatric cases. The items which provided such discrimination did not deal with traditional psychosomatic phenomena but rather were inextricably linked with the respondent's sense of being unable to cope with problems and to deal with social difficulties (Goldberg,1972, p. 91). There are six negative and six positive items, and each consists of a question asking whether the respondent has experienced a particular symptom or behaviour pattern more often or less often than usual. The GHQ was designed by Goldberg (1972) as a screening test for detecting minor psychiatric disorders in the community. The results of our analysis are presented in the terms of the distinction between those scoring above two and all others. This provides the most appropriate threshold score for those who are likely to be classified as non-psychotic psychiatric cases and all others. The results which are set out in Table 8.6 show the substantial impact of social class. The service class is distinguished from all others by a particularly low level of psychological distress; less than one in thirteen are located above the threshold. For other non-manual groups and the property-owning groups the figure rises to one in six, and for the skilled manual class it is almost one in five. Finally for the unskilled manual class it comes close to one in four.

Table 8.6: *Mental Health of Heads of Households by Social Class*

	Percentage Above Psychological Distress Threshold
Professional and Managerial [I+II]	7.8
Intermediate Non-Manual, *Petit Bourgeoisie* and Farmers [IIIa, IVa+b, IVc, > 50 acres]	16.7
Skilled and Semi-Skilled Manual Workers and Small Farmers [IIIb, IVc, < 50 acres, V, VI, VIIa(i)]	19.5
Unskilled Working-Class [VIIa(ii), VIIb]	22.5

The evidence available to us provides decisive confirmation of the continuing importance of social class for life-chances. Economic resources, life-style deprivation, poverty, economic stress and physical and mental health are all strongly related to social class. Whether these differences are increasing or declining is a question which could be answered decisively only if we were in a position to make such comparisons across time. In the absence of the kind of data that we would ideally like to have it is important to remember that there is no inevitable logic of industrial development leading inexorably towards reduced class differences (Goldthorpe,1992). One factor which it is increasingly necessary to take into account is the growth of large-scale and long-term unemployment.

SOCIAL CLASS AND UNEMPLOYMENT

A persistent theme in class analysis is the existence of an excluded sector or an 'underclass'. Such a class has often been conceived of as consisting of positions sufficiently detached from the labour-market as to make it difficult to incorporate them into conventional class categories. The very high rate of male unemployment, and more particularly, its increased duration have been matters of sociological concern for over a decade. By the end of the 1980s the spectre of long-term unemployment provided a substantial challenge for class analysis. A large number of positions exist that offer very poor prospects of re-entry into the labour-market. As Morris and Irwin (1992, p. 401) note, the questions raised by non-employment and non-standard forms of employment have been central to the debate on gender and class analysis, but with the increasing incidence of male unemployment they have now led to a questioning of the extent to which class models are capable of 'adequately portraying and theorising structured inequality'.

In Ireland between 1980 and 1987 the numbers unemployed soared to 230,000 or almost 18 per cent of the work force. The dramatic increase in the level of unemployment was accompanied by a steady increase in the proportion who were long-term unemployed. Statistics on the registered unemployed show that in April 1980, 35 per cent of those on the Live Register had been registered continuously for over a year. By April 1987 the figure had reached 44 per cent. While the overall unemployment rate was well above average for those aged under 25, most of the long-term unemployed were aged 25 or over and 80 per cent were men. The increasing importance of long-term unemployment was accompanied by a shift in the pattern of social welfare support. Whereas in 1980 47 per cent of those on the Live Register were in receipt of insurance based Unemployment Benefit (UB) and 48 per cent received the means-tested Unemployment Assistance (UA), by 1987 only 37 per cent were on UB and the percentage on UA had risen to 58 per cent (O'Connell and Sexton, 1994).

The Irish Survey data for 1987 therefore provide a particularly interesting testing-ground for competing responses to the problems posed to class analysis by the changing nature of unemployment. Positions in the class structure traditionally refer to persons who are in gainful employment. The unemployed are usually allocated to a class on the basis of their last job. The assumptions involved are, that when the persons involved re-enter the work force, they will occupy a position similar to that which they last held, and perhaps, more importantly, that 'the class effects associated with prior positions are extraordinarily durable' (Marshall, *et al.* 1994). This is the approach we have adopted throughout this volume and it can be distinguished from that of Runciman(1990, p. 88), where the long-term unemployed, being among 'those whose roles place them more or less permanently at the level where economic benefits are paid by the state to those who are unable to participate in the labour-market', are placed in a residual category. With this definition, as with Smith's (1992, p. 1), the long-term unemployed fall *outside* the class structure. These definitions as Morris and Irwin (1989, p. 402) note 'fail to engage with conventional class analysis' and with the fact that vulnerability to unemployment and, in particular, long-term unemployment is a feature of location in the working-class. Approaches which obscure this connection undermine our ability to understand the dynamics of labour-market experience (Morris,1993, p. 408; 1994).

Evidence for this argument is provided by the results set out in Table 8.7 showing the relationship between social class and the labour-market experience of heads of households, (excluding those currently in farming or the *petit bourgeoisie*). The risk of unemployment is close to zero for those located in the service class and remains at a relatively modest level of 6 per cent for the intermediate non-manual group. For the skilled manual group it rises dramatically to over 20 per cent but this still remains at a level of only half that of the unskilled manual group where over four out of ten household heads are unemployed. Viewed in terms of the composition of the unemployed, rather than the risk of unemployment, analysis shows that almost one-third of unemployed heads of household are drawn from the unskilled working-class and just less than two-thirds from the skilled and semi-skilled class; with a mere 3 per cent being located in the non-manual classes. It is not just current unemployment status which is stronglyassociated with class. The number of weeks unemployed rises, in the previous year, from less than 1 for those at the peak of the hierarchy to 19.3 for those at the bottom. Similarly, the total number of 'career' years unemployed rises from 0.21 to 4.0 and the proportion of potential of labour-market time unemployed rises from 1 per cent to 16 per cent. In

Table 8.7: Labour-Market Experience of Heads of Households by Social Class (Excluding Farming and Petit Bourgeoisie Households)

	Percentage Unemployed	Number of Weeks Unemployed in Previous Twelve Months	Career Unemployment: Number of Years Unemployed	Career Unemployment: Proportion of Part-Time Labour-Market Time Unemployed
Professional and Managerial [I+II]	0.8	0.8	0.21	0.01
Higher Routine Non-Manual [IIIa]	5.9	3.0	0.43	0.02
Skilled and Semi-Skilled Manual [IIIb, V, VI, VIIa(i), < 50 acres]	20.7	8.9	1.47	0.07
Unskilled Working Class [VIIa(ii), VIIb]	41.6	19.3	4.00	0.16
Proportion of Variance Explained		.099	.137	.129

each case the working class are quite sharply distinguished from the non-working-class and, within the working-class the unskilled manual group suffer particularly extreme disadvantages. In fact our subsequent analysis shows that the relevant class experiences go beyond current class situation. Elsewhere, in order to explore the implications of unemployment for class mobility analysis, we have introduced unemployment as a destination and compared Irish and English class mobility chances (Whelan, Breen and Whelan, 1992). The three-class schema which includes all routine white-collar workers and the technicians' group in the intermediate category has been chosen to facilitate comparison with the English data; for this reason also the analysis is restricted to men aged between twenty and sixty-four. The results of this exercise are set out in Table 8.8. The probability of unemployment varies by class origin for both countries but there is a particularly high probability, of one in four, for those of manual work origins in Ireland. On the basis of the English data Goldthorpe and Payne (1986, pp. 17–18) concluded that mobility chances for manual workers had polarised between 1972 and 1983 with more experiencing upward mobility, but more too being downwardly mobile into unemployment. The

Table 8.8: Percentage of Class Mobility Chances: Outflow Rates, Including to Unemployment

Class of Origin	Percentage by Row Social Class			
	Professional, Administrative and Managerial [I + II]	*Other Non-Manual workers and Farmers [III + IVa, b, c + V]*	*Manual and Agricultural Workers [VI + VIIa+b]*	*Unemployed*
Professional: Administrative and Managerial [I + II]				
Ireland 1987	56.3	28.5	11.8	3.4
England 1983	63.1	23.2	9.3	4.4
Other Non-Manual Workers and Farmers [III + IVa, b, c +V]				
Ireland 1987	16.5	44.2	27.8	11.4
England 1983	32.7	36.2	22.8	8.2
Manual and Agricultural Workers [VI + VIIa, b]				
Ireland 1987	10.3	23.1	41.4	25.1
England 1983	20.5	29.5	39.5	10.5

Sources: For English figures, Goldthorpe and Payne (1986), for Irish figures, Whelan, Breen and Whelan (1992, p. 119).

return of mass unemployment 'has had the general effect of "raising the stakes"'. In Ireland no such improvement in the prospects of upward mobility has occurred for those from manual work backgrounds. In England men from manual work origins were twice as likely to appear in the service class as to be unemployed but in Ireland this probability was reversed. It is for the intermediate non-manual class that such polarisation has occurred while at the top relatively little change is observed. Such results confirm that a perspective on unemployment which fails to relate the risk of exposure to unemployment to class position and, indeed, class origins can be seriously misleading. As Marshall *et al* (1994) argue, critiques of the treatment of the unemployed in class analysis frequently tend to suffer from a tendency to think of class in static rather than dynamics, or as structure rather than process. The fact that people are not in employment at a particular point in time does not mean that they have dropped out of the class structure or that their previous class experience is irrelevant.

A reasonable expectation would be that the effect of class origin on the risk of unemployment would operate through its relationship to current class position. Thus we could hypothesise that any relationship, which is found between unemployment and class of origin, can be accounted for entirely by the association between class of origin and present class, and between the latter and unemployment, leaving no independent or 'carry-over' effect for class origins. In this situation a log-linear model, which embodies the hypothesis that the odds on a man being unemployed are dependent upon his current class but not his class of origin (although allowing for the association between origin and destination), should provide an adequate fit to the data. Such a model does reproduce the English data but does not come close to fitting the Irish data. Earlier we suggested that the most plausible hypothesis regarding the manner in which class origin has an independent effect on unemployment was that 'in a country where a situation of a long-term excess of labour supply exists, class origin may serve not only as a good predictor of current class position but also distinguish within classes between those with stable and unstable work histories'. (Whelan, Breen and Whelan 1992, p. 121).

In fact, it is within the working-class that we would expect such differentiation to be of importance. In Table 8.9 we show the effect of class origins on labour-market experience for working-class heads of households. The underlying relationship can be most easily presented employing a three-class schema for class origins in which all property-owning groups including small farmers are assigned to the intermediate class, and a single class incorporates all of the elements of the working-

Table 8.9: Labour-Market Experience of Heads of Households by Social Class and Class Origins

Class Origins	Social Class							
	Percentage Unemployed		Number of Weeks Unemployed in Previous Twelve Months		Number of Years Unemployed		Proportion of Potential Labour-Market Time Unemployed	
	Skilled and Semi-Skilled	Unskilled Manual	Skilled and Semi-Skilled	Unskilled Manual	Skilled and Semi-Skilled	Unskilled Manual	Skilled and Semi-Skilled	Unskilled Manual
Professional and Managerial [I+II]	10.2	-	4.68	-	0.86	-	0.05	-
Higher Routine Non-Manual Workers, Petit Bourgeoisie and Farmers [IIIa, IVa,b,c]	15.8	27.1	6.03	13.9	1.39	2.00	0.06	0.09
Working-Class and Small Farmers [IIIb, V, VI, VII]	22.5	45.8	9.67	20.8	1.53	4.58	0.07	0.18

class. The former decision is consistent with the evidence, discussed earlier, regarding the more successful adaptive strategies of small-scale landholders in Ireland in comparison with the working-class. For unemployment the risk rises gradually among those currently in the skilled manual class from 10 per cent for those from professional and managerial origins to 23 per cent for those who come from the working class. For those from the unskilled working-class the relevant contrast is between those originating in the higher routine non-manual and property-owning groups and those with working-class backgrounds; with the respective percentages unemployed being 27 per cent and 46 per cent. The independent effect of class of origin can therefore be seen to be quite substantial. A similar pattern is observed for the number of weeks unemployed in the previous twelve months. Within the skilled manual class the figure rises from 5 weeks to 10 weeks depending upon class of origin; while within the unskilled manual class the figure rises from 14 to 21 weeks as one moves from origins in the intermediate class to working-class origins. The number of years unemployed also varies in relation to both current class and class of origin. The level almost doubles within the skilled manual class as one moves down the class-origin hierarchy; rising from 0.9 to 1.5. Furthermore, it more than doubles for unskilled manual HOHs with working-class backgrounds in comparison with those from higher routine-non-manual or property-owning class origins. Finally, the percentage of time unemployed rises from 5 per cent for skilled manual workers with professional and managerial origins backgrounds to 18 per cent for unskilled manual workers with their roots in the working-class: a figure which is twice that of the next highest group. Such results confirm that a perspective on unemployment which fails to relate the risk of exposure to unemployment and the severity of the experience to class location and indeed class origins is likely to be seriously misleading. It is equally true, however, that the increasing marginalisation of a significant sector of the working-class is likely to be associated with an increasing degree of heterogeneity within the working-class. Aggregated class schema which conceal such differences are also less than satisfactory.

WORKING-CLASS MARGINALISATION

This issue of working-class marginalisation has been pursued elsewhere. (Whelan, 1996). Restricting attention to working-class non-farm households with a HOH aged less than 65, the focus is as Buck (1992, p. 11) puts it, on 'stable absence of relationship to employment, on the one hand, and unstable relationship with employment on the other'. Arriving at a definition of the marginalised working-class involves taking a number of criteria into account. The first criterion relates to stability of membership of the unemployed; here two years of unemployment is chosen as the cut-off point. With regard to stable relationship to employment, use is made of the measure of proportion of potential labour-market spent unemployed. The cut-off point chosen is 20 per cent of potential labour-market with the additional condition that the HOH must have been at least five years in the labour market. The choices have been made because the notion of labour-market marginalisation implies severe problems in connecting with the labour-market. Varying the cut-off points does not have a dramatic effect on the results and such differences as do exist are further moderated by the requirement that a household satisfy other criteria in order to be so categorised. Thus where the head of household is currently in employment and has not experienced a spell of unemployment in the previous twelve months the household is excluded from the marginalised working-class. Furthermore, since we are seeking to identify households having no stable relationship with legitimate gainful employment, those households where the spouse of the HOH is in employment have been excluded.

The definition of working-class marginalisation is then as follows:

1. The head of household is in the working-class.

   and

2. The head of household has been unemployed for two years or more or has spent 20 per cent or more of his/her potential labour-market time, since leaving full-time education, unemployed and has been in the labour-market for at least five years.

   and

3. The spouse of the head of household is not in full time employment.

   In addition

4. Where the head of household is currently employed and has not experienced a spell of unemployment in the previous twelve months the household is excluded.

Such households constitute 11 per cent of non-farm households where the HOH is aged under 65. Previous analysis also showed that the consequences of relatively persistent labour-market difficulties throughout one's time in the labour-force may be rather different from those arising from a limited number of spells of long-term unemployment. Consequently a further distinction is introduced between what we term *pervasive* and *restricted* working-class marginalisation. The former refers to a situation where the HOH has been unemployed for at least 20 per cent of his/her potential labour-market time, while the latter refers to the situation where this does *not* hold, but the conditions for marginalisation are still fulfilled. The pervasively marginalised working-class contains 7.9 per cent of non-agricultural households where the HOH is aged less than 65 and the restricted marginalisation group contains 3.2 per cent.

The threefold distinction between the middle-class, the working-class and the marginalised working-class, and the more detailed schemes involving further distinction within these groups, will be referred to as class situation. In order to establish precisely to what extent the marginalised working-class are distinctive we provide a further breakdown within the non-marginalised working-class by labour-market status: differentiating between those in employment, the unemployed and those aged between fifty and sixty-four who are retired or ill or disabled. Previous analysis shows that the marginalised working-class is distinctive in terms of a low level of economic resources and the extent of life-style deprivation even in comparison with the unemployed and those in early retirement or ill/disabled. Within the marginalised working-class, the pervasively marginalised are further distinguished by the extent to which they are characterised, not only by a shortfall in current income, but also by a particularly low level of longer-term resources and by distinctive high levels of basic deprivation, i.e. enforced absence of socially defined necessities.

The cumulative effect of class situation on life-chances is best captured by the extent of variation in the risk of poverty, as set out in Table 8.10. Less than 4 per cent of middle-class households are below the 60 per cent relative income line and are also experiencing basic deprivation. The figure rises to just over one in six of the non-marginalised working-class as a whole; although among those not employed it is as high as three in ten. For the marginalised working-class as a whole, the level of risk reaches two out of three; with the respective figures for restricted and pervasive marginalisation reaching one in two and almost three out of four.

On the basis of such results it is not difficult to see why even some Marxists have come to argue that in late welfare-state capitalism job assets have become central to mapping the class structure and understanding the implicit dynamics of change. (Breen and Rottman, 1995b, p. 93). It is equally true that our evaluation of the relevance of working-class marginalisation for class analysis will be crucially dependent on our understanding of the underlying dynamics. Right wing proponents of the 'underclass thesis' have sought to explain such developments as a consequence of the perverse interventions of the welfare state, that seduce in the short-term, but have the long-term consequence of creating a dependency culture (Murray, 1984, 1990). More radical exponents of the thesis have pointed to the importance of geographical concentration and, in particular, to the manner in which certain groups occupying marginal positions in the labour-market have 'their economic position uniquely reinforced by their milieu' (Wilson, 1987, 1991).

Table 8.10: Risk of Poverty by Class Situation

	Percentage Poor
Middle-Class	3.7
Non-Marginalised Working-Class	17.5
(i) In Employment, etc.	12.3
(ii) Unemployed	30.7
(iii) HOH aged 50-64 and Retired or Ill and Disabled	30.9
Marginalised Working-Class	66.7
(i) Restricted Marginalisation	50.1
(ii) Pervasive Marginalisation	73.8

Elsewhere an analysis of the Irish situation has been offered which rejects such explanations and argues that it provides a good example of a case where the search for an underclass proves less fruitful than a concentration on the larger scale processes affecting all class groups. (Whelan, 1996). Furthermore, fatalism does not appear to be significantly related to location in urban rented public sector housing *per se* but rather appears to be a consequence of a much broader set of working-class experiences. In particular, members of the pervasively marginalised are not concentrated in urban centres. Pervasive marginalisation is concentrated among those households where the HOH is aged under forty while restricted marginalisation, on the other hand, is predominantly found among households where the HOH is aged over forty. The pattern reflects the uneven nature of the pattern of class transformation in Ireland whereby the labour-market experiences of the younger cohorts have come to have a qualitatively different character to those of their predecessors. What we are confronted with in Ireland is the outcome, in a situation involving a substantial surplus of labour, of the competition between classes for secure positions. This competition now takes place in circumstances where the traditional option of exporting marginalised labour is no longer a feasible option.

CLASS RELATIONSHIPS AND CAUSAL MECHANISMS

Despite the weight of evidence we have presented up to this point it can be argued, as Pahl (1989, p. 710) does, that demonstrating associations between poverty and class position and class origins simply 'conflates a number of distinct processes which should be kept analytically distinct'. However, as Goldthorpe and Marshall (1992, p. 386) stress, it does not necessarily follow that the completely successful 'unpacking' of the effects of class, through a specification of the manner in which class relationships are mediated, would not necessarily reduce its sociological importance. In order to illustrate this point we draw on some earlier work to elaborate on the findings we have reported regarding the relationship between class and physical and mental health. In trying to 'unpack' these relationships use was made of the measures of class situation and basic life-style deprivation referred to earlier. (Whelan and Whelan, 1995).

As soon as the question of causality is faced it is clear that the direction of the relationship may run from health to class rather than *vice versa*. The available evidence suggests that this is more likely to be the case in relation to physical health. Our interest at this point is not affected by the possibility of reciprocal relationships since what is at issue is simply the extent to which rather different types of causal processes may underlie the relationships between class and specific dimensions of health.

In attempting to assess the extent to which this may be true, we start by examining the relationship between our indicators of mental and physical health and class situation and basic deprivation. From Table 8.11 we can see that the percentage of household heads coming above the psychological distress threshold climbs gradually from a low of 11 per cent among middle-class households to an intermediate level of 18 per cent among the non-marginalised working-class, eventually peaking at 30 per cent among the marginalised working-class. Similarly, the level of psychological distress rises steadily as the degree of basic deprivation, i.e. enforced absence of socially defined necessities such as food, clothing and heat, experienced by the household increases. Only 9 per cent of individuals in households suffering an enforced lack of none of these items are found above the GHQ threshold, but this figure rises to 20 per cent for those lacking one such item, 30 per cent for those lacking two items before finally reaching a level of 43 per cent for those deprived of three or more basic items. The risk of experiencing psychological distress moves steadily upward as basic deprivation increases and as we move across the categories of class situation. Further analysis shows that the impact of class situation is modest among those households experiencing no deprivation but for all others continues to play a crucial role.Thus the influence of class situation, and in particular, working-class marginalisation is mediated by, but by no means entirely accounted for, by basic life-style deprivation. The influence of social class,on the other hand,is almost entirely accounted for by its association with such deprivation. Psychological distress appears to be particularly responsive to the extremes of life-style deprivation or labour-market situation (Whelan, 1992b, 1994).

Table 8.11: Psychological Distress and Physical Illness by Basic Life-Style Deprivation and Class Situation of Household

	Basic Deprivation Scale				*Class Situation*		
	0	*1*	*2*	*3+*	*Middle-Class*	*Non-Marginalised Working-Class*	*Marginalised Working-Class*
% Above GHQ Threshold	9	20	30	43	11	18	30
% Reporting Major Illness	11	17	20	21	9	16	18

Source: Whelan and Whelan (1995).

The situation in relation to physical health is rather different. From Table 8.11 we can see that the major contrast is between those in middle-class and working-class households; and between those not experiencing basic deprivation and all others. The percentage reporting physical ill-health problems rises from 11 to 17 per cent as the basic deprivation score moves from zero to one but then changes rather slowly before reaching a peak of 21 per cent for those reporting deprivation scores of three or above. Similarly, the percentage reporting ill-health increases from 9 per cent for the middle-class to 16 per cent for the non-marginalised working-class but then rises a mere 2 per cent before reaching its highest value among the marginalised working-class. These findings suggest that, in relation to this indicator, shared aspects of the experience and culture of the working-class are more important than the extent of extreme deprivation or labour-market marginality.

Before concluding our attempt to 'unpack' the influence of relationship of social class to our indicators of health it is necessary to take into account that influence on physical health may develop over a much longer period than is the case in relation to psychological distress. In particular, it is necessary to consider that childhood economic circumstances, which was shown to be strongly related to social class, may be a factor (Lundberg, 1991, 1993). In Table 8.12 we show the effect of this variable on physical health status while controlling for class situation. Within each category of the latter variable, representing current labour-market situation, those reared in situations of extreme financial strain are more likely to report ill-health. This relationship cannot be explained away by the fact that older groups are more likely to have reported such experiences. The influence of economic hardship in childhood is not simply a consequence of its relationship to current labour-market marginality nor, as further analysis shows, its association with class of origin. The results suggest that our measure of childhood economic circumstances is tapping processes of accumulating disadvantage over and above those represented by such factors. The significance of this finding is enhanced by the fact that marginalised households containing children aged under fifteen suffer extreme rates of poverty with almost 4 out of 5 of such households falling below the poverty line we have employed. While labour-market marginality is not a decisive factor in relation to our measure of current physical health, it seems highly probable that it is contributing significantly to class inequalities in health among the future generations of adults.

Table 8.12: Physical Illness by Family's Economic Circumstances When Person was Growing Up and Class Situation

	Percentage Reporting Major Physical Illness		
	Class Situation		
Family's Economic Circumstances	*Middle-Class*	*Non-Marginalised Working-Class*	*Marginalised Working-Class*
Great Difficulty in Making Ends Meet	14	23	23
Other	8	14	16

Source: Whelan and Whelan (1995).

The analysis reported in this section provides a relatively simple example of an attempt to do as Breen and Rottman (1995b) suggest and develop our understanding of class analysis by moving beyond documenting associations and attempting to understand the processes which generate such associations. The health indicators chosen have allowed us to demonstrate quite clearly that the immediate causes of the observed relationships with social class are far from being the same; in one case extreme life-style deprivation and labour-market marginality seem central while in the other more general class influences and childhood economic circumstances are more important. While teasing out the nature of such processes is crucial to the development of class analysis, unless the original relationships to social class are shown to be spurious, such analysis in no way undermines the significance of social class. As Goldthorpe and Marshall (1992, p. 386) argue, to the extent that the *immediate* and necessarily diverse causes of a range of class associations can be traced to the location of individuals and families in particular class positions 'then the importance of class is enhanced rather than diminished. The pervasiveness of class is underlined'.

CONCLUSIONS

In this chapter we have shown the continuing importance of social class for a range of life-chances including economic resource, poverty, life-style and health. Furthermore, while entirely accepting the need to go beyond documenting such associations in order to focus on causal processes, the evidence we have presented in relation to physical and mental health supports the view that an understanding of the variety of ways in which class relationships are mediated is likely to convince one not of the redundancy of class but of the 'promising future of class analysis'.

In particular we have argued that the emergence of large-scale and long-term unemployment appears to undermine the relevance of class analysis only if the nature of the structural processes, which lead to its concentration in particular class positions and among those from working-class backgrounds, are ignored. It is, however, necessary to take into account differences within the working-class which may, to some extent, be concealed by conventional class classifications. In the Irish case we have argued that this has more to do with the manner in which the costs of economic change have been disproportionately borne by members of the younger working-class cohorts rather than with any sort of underclass theory whether of a conservative or radical variety. Precisely because of these cohort effects we could find no evidence by 1987 of a substantial degree of intergenerational transmission of unemployment. Such household concentration of unemployment is found in older working-class households rather than marginalised households. However, given the low rate of exit from unemployment for young household heads, located in the pervasively marginalised working-class, and the relationship between such marginalisation and deprivation and educational failure, a clear danger exists of the emergence of a significant group of unemployed people whose formative years will have been spent in conditions of extreme deprivation, and in households effectively detached from the labour-market. In such circumstances the notion of an 'underclass', displaying distinctive sub-cultural characteristics may become more relevant; but our understanding of the emergence of such a group is unlikely to be enhanced by theories which fail to locate it in the wider problematic of the transformation of the Irish class structure. The agenda for the future seems entirely consistent with Goldthorpe and Marshall's (1992b, p. 382) definition of class analysis as a *research programme* which represents a specific way of investigating interconnections 'between historically formed macrosocial structures, on the one hand, and,on the other, the everyday experience of individuals within their particular social milieux, together with the patterns of action which follow from that experience'.

9 CONCLUSIONS

THE SIGNIFICANCE OF CLASS MOBILITY

Social class, as we have defined it, involves a position of social power based on relationships within labour-markets and production units and the resources and constraints associated with that position. The significance of social class for the distribution of life chances is intimately connected to the extent of class mobility. Restrictions on mobility opportunities are a crucial mechanism by which resource and constraint differences between families become perpetuated across generations. Inequalities of mobility are not just one additional inequality but are a central mechanism through which classes become identifiable through shared and distinctive life-styles. Since a knowledge of these processes is central to the understanding of any society the study of social mobility could be justified on these grounds alone.

Apart from enhancing our knowledge of society, however, there are several other more pragmatic reasons for paying attention to social mobility. A number of authors have been concerned about the inefficiency involved in highly stratified societies. They emphasise that talent and ability should be rewarded by higher status and that it is important that elite positions be occupied by those with the highest levels of ability irrespective of their social origins. Others, including many with a more directly political orientation, have underlined the injustice of high levels of immobility. A society with restricted opportunities for upward social mobility automatically denies many the opportunity of sharing in important socially created goods while guaranteeing the privileged positions of certain groups. More recently concern has grown that those who are denied the opportunity for upward mobility are not simply trapped at the bottom of the class hierarchy but are, in an important sense, forced outside the class system and come to constitute an 'underclass'.

INDUSTRIALISATION AND MOBILITY

Given the extent of social change in Ireland in the past thirty years it is hardly surprising that many people would have expected such change to be associated with an historic enlargement of opportunity — the 'rising tide that would raise all boats' — and a process of 'creative destruction' in which the old order is crushed and a new one, based on principles relating to achievement rather than inherited status, is brought into being. That these expectations are not entirely unreasonable is shown by the fact that they were shared by many sociologists who posited a direct relationship between economic growth and mobility and an inevitable trend towards more meritocratic principles in industrial societies.

The reality is more complex. Mobility is related not to economic growth *per se* but to restructuring of the occupational structure, in particular the decline of agricultural employment, and the expansion of the professional and managerial class. Levels of mobility are substantially affected by variations in the speed, rhythm and phasing of such change. However, perceptions of a substantial degree of mobility in recent years are, indeed, accurate. Employing a three-class schema which divides men into professional and managerial, intermediate and working-classes, we find that over two-fifths of them had experienced mobility across generations. Mobility is not an unusual phenomenon. Given this finding, it is hardly surprising that we found little evidence to support the thesis of extreme social closure of elite groups. This finding was sustained whether we looked at the professional and managerial group as a whole or its upper stratum: over two-thirds of the latter group being recruited from outside the class. While a more finely-graded class schema might reveal higher levels of *elite* self-recruitment it seems likely that at that point we would be dealing with occupational rather than class closure. The extent of structural change in recent decades has created sufficient room at the top to ensure that the professional and managerial class is a heterogeneous group. Almost one in three of this class originate in the working-class and a further one in five have agricultural origins. This is not a closed *elite* group. Similarly, the *petit bourgeoisie* (not including farmers) have become a relatively heterogeneous group. Its members are increasingly likely to have farming and working-class backgrounds.

It is in fact among the working-class rather than at the peak of the class structure that we observe self-recruiting blocks. Almost two-thirds of the working-class are second generation, even though almost one in four are recruited from the agricultural classes. Over recent decades a significant increase in self recruitment has occurred matched by a corresponding drop in recruitment from the agricultural classes. A mere 7 per cent of the industrial working-class are drawn from outside that class or from the class of small farmers.

While structural change has been associated with large-scale mobility, it remains true that the creation of increased room at the top and a contraction of places at the bottom can lead to a general shift upwards without, necessarily, reducing the relative advantages enjoyed by those families which experienced privileges in the old class system. Economic change, no matter how deep, may not be associated with an alteration in relative advantages. It is relative rather than absolute mobility rates — the outflow from class origins rather than the inflow into current classes — which allows us to assess whether social change has enhanced the ability to compete of those for whom the dice were unfavourably loaded. In fact, when we focus on such rates, the evidence from the 1973 and 1987 surveys points to a remarkable degree of similarity in mobility chances at both points in time. Just over one-half of those from professional and managerial origins were found in that class and just over one-fifth in the industrial working-class. These figures are very close to those for other western European countries in the early 1970s. Focusing on men from the industrial working-class we find that one in nine is located in the professional and managerial class; while seven out of ten have remained in their class of origin. The Irish figure for immobility is comparatively high. However, what marks Ireland out as distinctive is the extremely low level of upward mobility from the working-class to the professional and managerial class.

The picture of stability in mobility patterns at the top and the bottom of the class hierarchy contrasts with the substantial improvement in the mobility chances of those from *petit bourgeoisie* and farming origins. Over the 1970s and 1980s a substantial improvement took place in the chances of entry to the professional and managerial class for the sons of small employers and, more particularly, the self-employed. This was associated with a sharp drop in the numbers remaining in this class. Those from farming backgrounds displayed lower levels of mobility over time and an increased tendency to move into both the professional and managerial classes and the skilled manual class.

EXPLAINING PATTERNS OF SOCIAL FLUIDITY

The approach we have adopted to explaining patterns of social fluidity or relative mobility chances is a rational choice one. This approach views actors as utilizing the resources available to them in order to make choices between differentially preferred destinations each of which has costs associated with it in terms of barriers to entry. The important aspects of desirability, resources and barriers in shaping fluidity include the hierarchical ordering of classes in terms of the resources they confer as origins, their desirability as destinations and the barriers that exist to entry in terms of capital required, access to social networks and educational qualifications. Such hierarchical factors are only one element. Other significant factors include inheritance and sector. Inheritance factors include not just direct inheritance of property but all those factors which favour 'insiders' against 'outsiders'. Finally, movement into the farming sector is likely to be particularly weak even when we allow for the influence of hierarchy and inheritance.

From this perspective class mobility chances are seen as the outcome of a series of competitions between classes to achieve access to more desirable class locations and to avoid being consigned to less favourable locations. The outcome of such competitions is summarized in the odds-ratio statistic which measures how strongly class origins influence destinations independently of any change in the size of such classes. Hence, they provide a measure of how open the class structure is. The closer is the value of the odds-ratio to one the more equal or 'perfect' is the competition to which it refers. Our analysis shows that the higher professional and managerial group enjoys advantages in the order of 2000:1 over the unskilled manual class in the competition to gain access to the former class and avoid being located in the latter. The corresponding figure for the lower professional and managerial group is 1500:1; for the *petit bourgeoisie* 200:1 and for the higher routine non-manual class 100:1. For the remaining classes the advantages enjoyed are a good deal more modest but the unskilled manual class still emerges as a particularly disadvantaged group. Openness in terms of a substantial level of absolute mobility and heterogeneity of the professional and managerial class turns out to be consistent with very substantial inequalities of opportunity associated with a persistence of the underlying pattern of relative advantages.

In attempting to develop a model of the underlying pattern of social fluidity or relative mobility chances we start by taking the distribution of class origins and destinations as fixed. The factors that shape the context of relative mobility patterns are taken as exogenous. The task we are then faced with is accounting for the pattern of frequencies that appear in the body of the table taking the marginal distributions as given.

The model which we use to explain the Irish pattern of social fluidity identifies hierarchy, property and barriers to entry to agriculture as the crucial dimensions. We refer to this as the AHP model. The cumulative effect of these dimensions is to give those from the upper professional and managerial group backgrounds a distinctive profile in terms of their ability to achieve positions in their class of origin (with over four out of ten so doing), to be mobile into *the petit bourgeoisie* and to avoid long-range downward mobility. The lower professional and managerial group are only slightly less likely to be found in the professional managerial class as a whole (55 per cent versus 60 per cent), but not surprisingly are concentrated in the lower stratum. They are,however, much less likely to be found in the *petit bourgeoisie* and are substantially more likely to be found in manual work. The higher routine non-manual class display the lowest tendency of all to inherit their class. Furthermore, although the actual flows are much weaker, like the higher professional and managerial group they display a tendency to move into classes associated, at least to some degree, with ownership of property. In both sections of the *petit bourgeoisie*, about one-third of their members enter the professional and managerial class. The lower stratum are much less likely to remain in their class of origin and a good deal more likely to be mobile into technician and skilled manual work positions. Farmers display a distinctive profile, with just over one-third remaining in farming. These are rather similar to the lower *petit bourgeoisie* in their tendency to enter the professional and managerial classes and the skilled working-class. The probability of being found at the bottom or the top of the class hierarchy is significantly related to farm size. Finally, a striking contrast exists between the manual classes and all others in mobility chances, with a further sharp division observable between the unskilled manual class and all other manual positions.

The results we have presented are consistent with a range of evidence that points to particulary low levels of social fluidity in Ireland where, once again, we are referring to the extent of inequality in the outcomes of competitions between classes rather than to aggregate levels of mobility. It has been suggested that Irish deviations from the core international tendencies might be accounted for by the existence of wide variation in farm size and a distinctive rural working-class and the particular salience of status differences between white-collar and blue-collar classes. The explanation of the distinctiveness of the Irish pattern of social fluidity is, therefore, seen to be a consequence of historical peculiarities. Our own analysis, though, convinces us that this distinctiveness is open to explanation in terms of the general theoretical dimensions captured in the AHP model. The strength of the hierarchy effect is consistent with the available evidence on inequalities of condition, both historical and current, which our measures of resources and attractiveness/barriers seek to capture. Similarly the strength of the property effects we have observed, as captured both by the measure of self-employment and the term capturing the additional advantages such groups enjoy in gaining access to the professional and managerial class, are entirely consistent with our understanding of the particular advantages enjoyed by property-owning groups in Ireland. Taken together with the barriers to entry to agriculture and tendencies towards class inheritance we have specified these factors are sufficient to account for the Irish pattern of fluidity without any reference to historical peculiarities.

The Irish case, as we have noted, provides a particularly useful test of theories that seek to relate social change to economic development because of the recency of Irish industrialisation. The data available allow us to adjudicate between the liberal theory of industrialism, which implies greater openness associated with the functional requirements of industrial society, and the class analysis perspective, which directs attention to the manner in which those who occupy positions of relative privilege can use their power and advantage to maintain their positions with the consequence that systems of social stratification display powerful self-maintaining properties (Erikson and Goldthorpe, 1992a, p. 393). Our analysis of changes in mobility patterns, based on a comparison of the data from 1973 and 1987 and analysis by cohort for the latter date, provides substantial support for the latter perspective. The advantages associated with class resources, whether of a strictly hierarchical or property-owning nature, show virtually no change over time. One possible reason for the absence of such change is that even by 1987 it may still have been too early to see the effect of the introduction of free secondary education in 1967. Set against this possibility is the alternative interpretation that middle-class and, in particular, property-owning families may have benefited disproportionately from such reforms as they responded to the changing stratification system by seeking to preserve their traditional advantages by new means.

In any event some policies did have a impact. The evidence of the particular success of the offspring of property-owning groups in taking advantage of the industrial and educational opportunities created in recent decades is entirely consistent with the taxation advantages enjoyed by such groups. The balance of cash transfers and tax paid favoured propertied classes over employees . Given the impact of such policies on inequality of condition, it is hardly entirely surprising that inequality of opportunity should have proved so particularly resilient.

WOMEN AND MOBILITY

Gender, as we have noted, has frequently been identified as the most controversial issue confronting class analysis. In presenting our understanding of the issues involved and the outcomes of our analyses, we have stressed that it is necessary to achieve clarity on certain fundamental issues before engaging in debate. The fundamental issue relates to the unit of class composition. Should we focus on the individual or the family? The position we have taken is that if our concern is with class rather than occupational mobility, then the latter option should be chosen. An entirely work-centred view fails to capture the extent to which members of a conjugal family share both current life-chances and prospects of affluence or deprivation. The choice of individual, whose occupation and employment status determines the class position of other family members, is made in the light of the key role of the family as a unit of strategic action in terms of consumption and production. The decision to operate with the family as the unit of analysis does not involve a denial of differences in power and resources within families. Rather, it is precisely the extent to which other family members remain economically dependent on the male 'head' which provides justification for this approach.

When, however, we do focus on women's own occupations, we find that the most striking change in recent decades relates not to their distribution across 'class' categories but to the marked increase in the number of married women participating in the labour-market. Nevertheless, women continue to be concentrated in a restricted set of occupational categories. On the basis of their own occupations, women are, predominantly, found in the professional and managerial, white-collar and semi-skilled manual classes and are largely excluded from farming, the *petit bourgeoisie* and technician and skilled manual classes. As a consequence of their exclusion from those classes in which inheritance has its greatest influence women experience more mobility than men and, in particular, are a good deal more likely to experience downward mobility. Labour-market segmentation is associated with a significantly greater tendency for women in the professional and managerial classes to come from farm backgrounds. Correspondingly, women from non-skilled manual backgrounds make up a significantly lower percentage of the service class than do their male counterparts. Women in the professional and managerial class are, therefore, a much more homogeneous group than is the case for men.

The major question which must be addressed in any comparison of male and female mobility rates is whether the variation we observe can be accounted for solely by differences in the objective opportunity structure arising from gender segregation in the labour-market or whether, in addition to such differences, it is necessary to posit gender differences in the underlying mobility regimes. In fact, it is possible to account for gender differences in relative mobility rates simply by allowing for variation in the origins and destination distributions while assuming that the underlying pattern of relative mobility is the same for both men and women. Class inequalities in relative mobility opportunities operate in a 'gender blind' fashion (Erikson and Goldthorpe, 1992a, p. 253).

The pervasiveness of class effects is also evident when we consider marital mobility. The suggestion has been made that women's 'class fate is more loosely linked to their social origins than is the case for men' (Heath, 1981, p.114). The reasoning underlying this argument is basically that marriage 'markets' may operate, particularly for women, according to rather different principles than labour-markets because physical or personality attributes, which can make women more or less attractive as marriage partners, are less closely associated with social origins than are those that mainly influence mens' achievements in the labour-market. However, applying the AHP model to women's marital mobility experiences we find that it does a remarkably good job. The results show that women are more likely to change class through marriage than are men to change class through employment; and that it is easier (*ceteris paribus*) for women to marry farmers and farm workers than it is for men not born in agriculture to become farmers and farm workers. These rather modest differences, however, do not detract from the importance of the finding that the processes which distribute married women across class destinations, defined in terms of their husbands' situations, are only marginally different from those by which men's class fate is determined through employment. The consequences of 'marriage markets' for women are strikingly similar to those of labour-markets for their 'brothers'.

We have also applied the AHP model to a 'complete' mobility table constructed on the basis of the dominance procedure where information on the class position, employment status and number of hours worked by both husband and wife were used to select the 'dominant' individual. Such tables do give somewhat higher rates of mobility with both upward and downward mobility being more frequent. In addition, mobility to the professional and managerial classes and the higher routine white-collar class is somewhat higher. Overall though, what is striking are the similarities rather than the differences. Furthermore, the differences we observe arise almost entirely as a consequence of gender segregation in the labour-market rather than in underlying patterns of social fluidity. In order to achieve an adequate fit to the 'complete' mobility it is necessary merely to allow for weaker inheritance effects and allow for a stronger relative flow from the propertied classes to the higher routine white-collar work class.

Our findings point clearly to the disadvantages suffered by women as a consequence of gendered labour-market segmentation and lack of continuity in their work histories. It is precisely because of the economic dependence which women suffer as a result of these disadvantages that the family continues to be the appropriate unit for class analysis. Changing patterns of female participation in the labour-market and a transformation of the current practices in relation to child care and domestic labour may at some point make this assumption untenable. For the moment though the evidence in relation to women's mobility, marital mobility and 'complete' mobility tables provide substantial support for Erikson and Goldthorpe's argument that 'the lines of class division run between but not through families'.

CLASS MOBILITY AND EDUCATION

Ireland, as we have noted, is a particularly useful test case for the predictions of the liberal theory of industrialism. The educational reforms of the 1960s led to a situation where, at present, more than three-quarters of each age cohort complete post-primary education. This expansion might have been expected to be associated with a movement from ascription to achievement — from the importance of who you know to what you know. In particular it might seem reasonable to hypothesise that class origins would become less closely linked to class destinations and that educational credentials would become increasingly important in allocating individuals to occupations. These changes could be expected to follow both from the decline in the size of the property-owning classes and the increasing need for nations to make optimum use of their populations' abilities. The data on which we base our analysis covers the periods both before and after the relevant educational and class structural changes.

Despite the apparent plausibility of such reasoning, the expectations are not borne out. For women, the relationship between class origins and educational qualifications has remained unchanged over time. Among men, the only discernible change over time involves an improvement in the relative advantages in access to third-level education of those from farming and *petit bourgeoisie* backgrounds and a corresponding decline in the chances of those from the routine non-manual class and, more particularly, the skilled manual class. The absence of change relates to relative chances. It is, of course, true that the numbers achieving higher levels of qualification has grown rapidly. The number reporting a complete absence of educational qualifications declines across the three cohorts from 63 per cent to 30 per cent. The educational system has become less selective but, to the extent to which selection operates, there is no evidence that it is increasingly based on meritocratic principles rather than factors associated with class background. The chances of working-class men having completed the Leaving Certificate improved across the cohorts in our study from 14 per cent to 20 per cent. On the other hand, the percentage of those without qualifications who were from working-class backgrounds rose from 60 to 72. To take another example, in our oldest cohort those from professional and managerial backgrounds were 9.2 times more likely to at least complete the Leaving Certificate than were those from non-skilled manual backgrounds. This figure had declined to 4.6 for our youngest cohort, suggesting a substantial reduction in the impact of social class. However, it is also true that while in the oldest cohort the non-skilled manual group were 3.6 times more likely to lack any qualification, this figure rose to 12.7 for the youngest cohort. Our modelling procedures which are based on odds-ratios take into account both types of inequalities. As in other countries, across the board expansion in educational participation has proved ineffective in reducing class inequalities.

Our analysis was extended to take into account the direct and indirect relationships between class origins, educational qualifications and class of entry and the manner in which such relationships vary across cohort. For women a clear, simple and unchanging pattern is observed whereby the resources associated with specific class origins are translated into educational qualifications which then determine the distribution of relative chances of access to more desirable classes. The impact of class background influences other than those mediated by educational qualifications is a good deal less potent than in the case of men. Allowing for the fact that educational qualifications are significantly associated with class background, this is the closest we came to observing the dominance of achievement over ascription. It cannot, however, be taken as evidence of expanding universalism and a trend towards more efficient use of talent since the pattern predates the period of substantial social change.

For men, a range of class origin effects which are independent of educational qualifications persist unaltered over time. The one effect of this kind which does weaken over time is in some part compensated for by the relative improvement in the access to third-level education of those from propertied backgrounds. In any event, the overall relationship between class origins and class of entry remains unchanged over time. While class origin effects are increasingly mediated through education, and educational qualifications have increasingly become a prerequisite of access to occupations, the relative advantages associated with such qualifications appears to have declined. The rational decisions of individuals to acquire more education has the unforeseen aggregate effect that higher levels of educational qualifications become less valuable as greater proportions come to acquire them. The weakening of the education effect while many of the indirect effects of class maintain their strength suggest that, in a situation of a substantial surplus of qualified labour, the advantages associated with traditional strategies relating to the use of social networks and specialized knowledge of the labour-market may have become relatively more rather than less important. Our findings reinforce what is becoming an increasingly widely-reported result: that is, that the introduction of across-the-board free education will not reduce educational inequalities. If all families are given the same opportunities regardless of differences between them in their own resources such inequalities will at best persist and may even widen (Shavit and Blossfeld, 1993).

Overall then, the evidence available to us provides no support for the existence of a trend towards increasing meritocracy. Instead it is entirely consistent with a class perspective which draws attention to the ability of those in positions of privilege and power to maintain their position against encroachment by outsiders. In this regard, it is important to keep in mind the rational choice perspective we have adopted in attempting to explain patterns of social fluidity. There is no need to hold that the action taken by dominant groups is necessarily concerted or foresightful in the sense of leading to collective action aimed at obstructing movement towards equality of opportunity. All that is required is that they succeed in sufficient numbers, in maintaining 'their own and their family's position by setting their superior resources strategically against whatever changes — in institutional arrangements, public policy, etc. — may appear threatening to them.' (Erikson and Goldthorpe, 1992a, p. 394).

WORK–LIFE MOBILITY

In recent years the question has been increasingly posed as to whether the standard 'parent-to-child' table and the snapshot picture it provides is capable of capturing the complex pattern of work–life mobility. However, such critiques have, in turn, tended to ignore how strongly a person's subsequent class position is shaped by their class origins over and above its impact on class entry. The available evidence suggests that the fact that we observe substantially greater cross-national variation in origin-entry and entry-destination transitions than in the overall origin-destination relationships is a consequence of the fact that cross-nationally varying institutional contexts lead to considerable variation in career strategies, but substantially less variation in the outcomes to which these strategies lead.

A comparison of career mobility in Ireland and England, focusing mainly on men aged thirty-five or over, shows immobility in the professional and managerial class is much higher in Ireland than in England and it is this which almost entirely accounts for higher levels of mobility in the final table. In contrast the ultimate advantage enjoyed by those in the intermediate classes over their English counterparts is a consequence of differences in the outcome of the origin to entry transition since the entry to destination patterns are almost identical in both countries. The working-class, on the other hand, are disadvantaged in comparison with their English counterparts in relation to both transitions, experiencing less mobility on entry to the labour-market and less subsequent work–life mobility.

The situation for women aged thirty-five or over who are currently in the labour-market is somewhat different. They are much more likely than men to have started their careers in the professional and managerial classes and they are as successful as men in remaining in this class. However, women who start out outside the professional managerial class are much less likely than men to experience upward mobility during their work-life. Thus women who are currently active in the labour-market initially display a profile which shows them to be substantially advantaged in comparison with men but this advantage is almost entirely eroded over time.

Analysis of the Irish pattern of social fluidity for men undermines any notion of career mobility as a series of open-ended life-course movements. There is clear evidence of comparatively strong class advantages for each transition consistent with the mobilisation of class resources in pursuit of career strategies. It addition, we observe strong tendencies towards career counter mobility with downward mobility being followed by a subsequent return to class of origin. The extent of counter mobility is, at least in part, due to the superior educational qualifications held by those from more favoured class origins in comparison with others with whom they share their current class situation. However, direct inheritance and other transfers of property are also likely to play a significant role. While counter mobility is a significant factor in shaping the Irish pattern of career mobility in this respect Ireland does not differ significantly from England. The ultimate difference in the pattern of mobility observed in both countries is, predominantly, a consequence of an accumulation of the inequalities observed for each of the component transitions.

In attempting to provide an explanation of variations in mobility at the entry to destination transition between Ireland and England we have drawn attention to basic differences in the occupational structures of the two countries. In particular we have focused on the greater proportion of skilled manual workers in England especially in light of the evidence for the importance, in that country, of such occupations as a training ground for higher-grade technicians and for professionals in engineering and related areas. Other possible explanations of the lower levels of career mobility in Ireland include the small size of Irish private sector organisations, the continuing significance of family ownership, and the rigid nature of the Irish educational system which provides little in the way of second chance opportunities. Finally, it seems entirely possible that high levels of unemployment in Ireland and associated qualification inflation may well have contributed to a restriction in career mobility opportunities, particularly for those from working-class backgrounds.

THE CONTINUING RELEVANCE OF CLASS ANALYSIS

We have deliberately not built differences in income or life-style into our definition of class. From the outset though we have made it clear that our interest in class mobility is motivated by our conviction that the location of individuals and families in the class structure is the most significant determinant of their life-chances. It is, precisely, this assumption which has been challenged by those who see class as an 'outmoded' concept in an era where there is a 'classlessness of social inequality' (Pahl, 1989; Beck, 1992).

The class schema we have employed throughout this volume is based on a particular understanding of the manner in which employment-related inequalities emerge as a consequence of the way in which work is organised within capitalist organisations and the nature of control in such organisations. Class positions and, consequently, differential rewards follow a line of cleavage between employers, the self-employed and employees; within the final group further differentiation takes place on the basis of the nature of the employment relationship. Greater rewards accrue to those employees involved in a service class relationship based on long-term relationships of trust and commitment than to those whose relationship is defined in terms of a very specific exchange of wages for effort.

Analysis of the available Irish data, for households where the head of household is aged less than sixty-five, reveals striking evidence of class variation in economic resources whether defined in terms of income, savings or house property. Class differences extend to access to a range of life-style items ranging from items such as cars, telephones and holidays which are part of a reasonably affluent life-style, to necessities such as basic requirements in relation to food, heating and clothing which form part of a minimally acceptable standard of living. Thus unskilled manual working-class households were between six to seven times more likely than professional and managerial households to be unable to afford a telephone, a car, central heating and an afternoon or evening out in the past two weeks. Combining information in relation to household income and what we have termed basic life-style deprivation we constructed a poverty line below which fall 1.6 per cent of professional and managerial households and, on the other hand, 46 per cent of unskilled manual households. The differences in objective circumstances were reflected in substantial variation in the degree of economic stress reported, in the extent to which such strain had been a feature of childhood circumstances and in levels of fatalism.

Significant class differences were also found in relation to physical and mental health. Just less than one in ten professional and managerial households in the age range forty to fifty-four years reported current physical health problems in comparison with over one in five of those located in the skilled manual working-class. Similar differences are observed for all households in relation to the percentage found to be above a psychological distress threshold. The causal mechanisms involved in each case appear to be rather different but the identification of a diversity of causal processes underlying the range of class associations we observe, rather than diminishing the importance of class, underlines its pervasiveness (Goldthorpe and Marshall, 1992).

The results we have presented provide unambiguous evidence of the continuing significance of social class for life-chances. Economic resources, life-style deprivation, poverty, fatalism and physical and mental health are all strongly associated with social class. Whether these differences are increasing or decreasing is a question which could be answered decisively only if we were in a position to make the appropriate comparisons across time. In the absence of the kind of data that we would, ideally, like it is important to keep in mind that there is no inevitable logic of industrial development leading towards reduced class inequalities (Goldthorpe,1992).

One factor which it is increasingly necessary to take into account is the emergence of large-scale and long-term unemployment. In particular the increasing incidence of male unemployment has led to a questioning of the adequacy of class models which are based on employment relationships. A persistent theme in recent debates has been the existence of an 'underclass'. A number of authors have conceived the long-term unemployed as falling *outside* the class system (Runciman, 1990; Smith, 1992). However, this approach obscures the extent to which unemployment and, in particular, long-term unemployment is directly related to class position.

Our own analysis shows that a variety of indicators of labour-market experience are strongly related to social class. The percentage unemployed ranges across classes from 0.8 per cent in the professional and managerial class to 41.6 per cent among the unskilled working-class. The number of weeks unemployed in the previous year ranges from 0.8 to 19.3 and the number of years unemployed from 0.21 to 4.00. Finally, the proportion of labour-market time unemployed rises from 0.01 for the professional and managerial class to 0.16 for the unskilled manual class. Furthermore, unlike the English case, the risk of unemployment varies by class of origin and this effect is not adequately accounted for by the cumulative impact of the association between class origins and class on the one hand and class and unemployment on the other. The persisting impact of class origin arises from the fact that, in a situation where a long-term excess of labour supply exists, class origin is not only a good predictor of current class position but also allows one to distinguish within classes (particularly the working-class) between those with stable and unstable work histories.

Such results show the limitations of thinking of class in static rather than dynamic terms. The fact that people are not in employment at a particular time does not mean that they fall outside the class system (Marshall, forthcoming). It is equally true, however, that the increasing marginalisation of a significant section of the working-class will lead to a greater degree of differentiation within the working-class which is not capable of being captured within aggregated class schemata. We have identified what we have described as a set of marginalised working-class households where two out of three of such households fall below the poverty line. Within that class is a group of households, which we have termed the pervasively marginalised working-class, where the risk of poverty rises to three out of four.

The implications of such marginalisation for the relevance of class analysis depends on the nature of the underlying dynamics. Right-wing exponents of the 'underclass' thesis have directed attention to the perverse effects of the welfare state and the creation of a dependency culture. More radical exponents of the thesis have focused on geographical concentration, social isolation and increasing fatalism. In the Irish case, however, we have argued that working-class marginalisation has more to do with the manner in which the costs of uneven economic change have been borne by the younger working-class cohorts than with the emergence of an 'underclass'. A possibility exists that the emergence of a significant group of unemployed people, whose formative years will have been spent in conditions of extreme deprivation, and in households effectively detached from the labour-market will make the notion of an 'underclass' displaying distinctive sub-cultural characteristics more relevant to Ireland. However, what our analyses suggest is that our understanding of the emergence of such a group will require precisely the type of class analysis we described in Chapter 8 which allows one to relate, in Mills' (1959) terms, biography to history and 'personal troubles' to 'public issues'.

References

ABBOT, P. and PAYNE, G. (1990), 'Women's Social Mobility: The Conventional Wisdom Reconsidered', in G. Payne and P. Abbot (eds), *The Social Mobility of Women*, London: The Falmer Press.

ABBOT, P. and SAPSFORD, R. (1987), *Women and Social Class*. London: Tavistock.

ACKER, J. (1973), 'Women and Social Stratification: A Case of Intellectual Sexism', *American Journal of Sociology*, 78, 4:936–45.

ALLMENDINGER, J. (1989), 'Educational Systems and Labour Market Outcomes', *European Sociological Review*, 5, 3:231–50.

ARBER, S. (1989), 'Gender and Class Inequalities in Health: Understanding the Differentials', in J. Fox (ed.), *Health Inequalities in European Countries*, Aldershot: Gower.

ARBER, S. (1993), 'Inequalities Within the Household', in D. Morgan and L. Stanley (eds), *Debates in Sociology*, Manchester University Press.

BAXTER, J. (1994), 'Is Husband's Class Enough? Class Location and Class Identity in the United States, Sweden, Norway and Australia', *American Sociological Review*, 59, 2:220–35.

BECK, U. (1992), *The Detection of Psychiatric Illness by Questionnaire*, London: Oxford University Press.

BIELBY, W.T. (1981), 'Models of Status Attainment', in D.J. Treiman and R.V. Robinson (eds), *Research in Social Stratification and Mobility*, Volume 1, Greenwich, Connecticut: JUI Press.

BISHOP, Y.M.M., FINEBERG, S.E. and HOLLAND, P.W. (1975), *Discrete Multivariate Analysis: Theory and Practice*, Cambridge, MA: MIT Press.

BLANE, D., DAVEY SMITH, G. and BARTLEY, M. (1993), 'Social Selection: What Does it Contribute to Social Class Differences in Health', *Sociology of Health and Illness,* 15:2–5.

BLAU, P.M. and DUNCAN, O.D. (1967), *The American Occupational Structure,* New York: Wiley.

BLAXTER, M. (1989), 'A Comparison of Measures of Inequality in Mobility' in A.J. Fox (ed.), *Health Inequalities in European Countries,* Aldershot: Gower.

BLAXTER, M. (1990), *Health and Lifestyle,* London: Tavistock-Routledge.

BOUDON, R. (1974), *Education, Opportunity and Social Inequalities,* New York: John Wiley and Sons.

BREEN, R. (1984a), 'Fitting Non-Hierarchical and Association Log Linear Models Using GLIM', *Sociological Methods and Research,* 13:77–107.

BREEN, R. (1985), 'A Framework for the Comparative Analysis of Social Mobility', *Sociology* 19:93–107.

BREEN, R. (1991), *Education, Employment and Training in the Youth Labour Market,* Dublin: The Economic and Social Research Institute, General Research Series, Paper No. 152.

BREEN, R., HANNAN, D.F. and O'LEARY, R. (1995), 'Returns to Education: Taking Account of Employers' perceptions and use of Educational Credentials', *European Sociological Review,* 11, 1:59–74.

BREEN, R., HANNAN, D.F., ROTTMAN, D.B. and WHELAN, C.T. (1990), *Understanding Contemporary Ireland: State, Class and Development in the Republic of Ireland,* London: Macmillan.

BREEN, R. and ROTTMAN, D. (1995a), *Class Stratification: A Comparative Perspective,* London: Harvester Wheatsheaf.

BREEN, R. and ROTTMAN, D. (1995b), 'Class Analysis and Class Theory', *Sociology*, 29, 3:453–73.

BREEN, R. and WHELAN, C.T. (1985), 'Vertical Class Mobility and Class Inheritance in the British Isles', *British Journal of Sociology*, 36:175–92.

BREEN, R. and WHELAN, C.T. (1992), 'Explaining the Irish Pattern of Social Fluidity', in J.H. Goldthorpe and C.T. Whelan (eds), *The Development of Industrial Society in Ireland*, Oxford: Oxford University Press.

BREEN, R. and WHELAN, C.T. (1993), 'From Ascription to Achievement? Origins, Education and Entry to the Labour Force in the Republic of Ireland During the Twentieth Century', *Sociologica*, 36, 1:3–19.

BREEN, R. and WHELAN, C.T. (1994), 'Gender and Class Mobility: Evidence from the Republic of Ireland', *Sociology*, 29, 1:1–22.

BREEN, R. and WHELAN, C.T. (1995), 'Measuring Trends in Social Fluidity: The Core Model and a Measured Variable Approach Compared', *European Sociological Review*, 10, 3:259–72.

BRITTEN, N. and HEATH, A. (1983), 'Women, Men and Social Class', in E. Gamarnikow, D. Morgan, J. Purvis and D. Taylorson (eds), *Gender, Class and Work*, London: Heinemann.

BUCK, N. (1992), 'Labour Market Inactivity and Polarization: A Household Perspective on the Idea of an Underclass' in D.J. Smith (ed.), *Understanding the Underclass*, London: Policy Studies Institute.

CALLAN, T. and FARRELL, B. (1992), *Women's Participation in the Irish Labour Market,* Dublin: National Economic and Social Council.

CALLAN, T., HANNAN, D., NOLAN, B., WHELAN, B. and CREIGHTON, S. (1989), *Poverty and the Social Welfare System in Ireland*, Dublin: The Economic and Social Research Institute.

CALLAN, T., NOLAN, B. and WHELAN, C.T. (1993), 'Resources, Deprivation and the Measurement of Poverty', *Journal of Social Policy,* 22:141–72.

CLARK, T.N. and LIPSET, S.M. (1991), 'Are Social Classes Dying?', *International Sociology,* 6, 4:397–410.

CROMPTON, R. (1980), 'Class Mobility in Britain', *Sociology,* 14:117–119.

CROMPTON, R. (1993), *Class and Stratification: An Introduction to Current Debates,* Cambridge: Policy Press.

CROMPTON, T. (1989), 'Class Mobility in Britain', *Sociology,* 14:117–19.

CROMPTON, T. (1989), 'Class Theory and Gender', *British Journal of Sociology,* 40:565–87.

CROWDER, N.D. (1974), 'A Critique of Duncan's Stratification Research', *Sociology,* 8:19–45.

DALE, A., GILBERT, G.N. and ARBER, S. (1985), 'Integrating Women into Class Theory', *Sociology,* 19:384–408.

DAVEY SMITH, G., BARTLEY, M. and BLANE, D. (1990), 'The Black Report on Socio-Economic Inequalities in Health 10 Years On', *British Medical Journal,* 301:373–77.

DAVIS, K. and MOORE, W.E. (1990), 'Some Principles of Stratification', *American Sociological Review,* 10.

DEX, S. (1990a), 'Goldthorpe on Class and Gender', in J. Clarke, C. Modgill and S. Modgill (eds), *John H. Goldthorpe: Consensus and Controversy,* London: Falmer Press.

ERIKSON, R. (1984), 'Social Class of Men, Women and Families', *Sociology,* 18:500–514.

ERIKSON, R. and GOLDTHORPE, J.H. (1987a), 'Commonality and Variation in Social Fluidity in Industrial Nations, Part I: A Model for Evaluating the "FJH Hypothesis"', *European Sociological Review*, 3:56–77.

ERIKSON, R. and GOLDTHORPE, J.H. (1987b), 'Commonality and Variation in Social Fluidity in Industrial Nations, Part II: The Model of Core Social Fluidity Applied', *European Sociological Review*, 3:145–66.

ERIKSON, R. and GOLDTHORPE, J.H. (1992a), *The Constant Flux: A Study of Class Mobility in Industrial Societies*, Oxford: Clarendon Press.

ERIKSON, R. and GOLDTHORPE, J.H. (1992b), 'Individual or Family? Results from two Approaches to Class Assignment', *Acta Sociologica,* 35:95–106.

EVANS, G. (1992), 'Testing the Validity of the Goldthorpe Class Schema', *European Sociological Review*, 8, 3:211–32.

FEATHERMAN, D.L., JONES, F.L. and HAUSER, R.M. (1975), 'Assumptions of Social Mobility Research in the US: The Case of Occupational Status', *Social Science Research*, 4:329–60.

FIENBERG, S.E. (1977), *The Analysis of Cross-Classified Categorical Data*, Cambridge, Mass.: MIT Press.

FRYER, D. (1986), 'Employment Deprivation and Personal Agency During Unemployment', *Social Behaviour,* 1: 3–23.

FRYER, D. (1992), 'Psychological or Material Deprivation: Why Does Unemployment have Mental Health Consequences?' in E. McLaughlin (ed.), *Understanding Unemployment: New Perspectives on Active Labour Market Policies*, London: Routledge.

GAGLIANI, G. (1990), 'Class and Economic Development: A Critique of Marxist Theories' in J. Clarke, C. Modgill and S. Modgill (eds), *John H. Goldthorpe: Consensus and Controversy*, London: The Falmer Press.

GIDDENS, A. (1973), *The Class Structure of the Advanced Societies,* London: Hutchinson.

GOLDBERG, D.P. (1972), *The Detection of Psychiatric Illness by Questionnaire,* London: Oxford University Press.

GOLDBERG, D. (1973), *The Detection of Psychiatric Illness by Questionnaire,* Oxford: Oxford University Press.

GOLDTHORPE, J.H. (1982), 'On the Service Class: Its Formation and Future' in A. Giddens and G. McKenzie (eds), *Classes and the Division of Labour,* Cambridge: Cambridge University Press.

GOLDTHORPE, J.H. (1985), 'On Economic Development and Social Mobility', *British Journal of Sociology,* 36:549–73.

GOLDTHORPE, J.H. (1980/1987), *Social Mobility and Class Structure in Britain,* Oxford: Clarendon Press.

GOLDTHORPE, J.H. (1990), 'A Response' in J. Clark, C. Modgill and S. Modgill (eds), *John H. Goldthorpe; Consensus and Controversy,* London: The Falmer Press.

GOLDTHORPE, J.H. (1992), 'The Theory of Industrialisation and the Irish Case', in J.H. Goldthorpe and C.T. Whelan (eds), *The Development of Industrial Society in Ireland,* Oxford: Oxford University Press.

GOLDTHORPE, J.H. and MARSHALL, G. (1992), 'The Promising Future of Class Analysis: A Response to Recent Critiques', *Sociology,* 26, 3:381–400.

GOLDTHORPE, J.H. and PAYNE, C. (1986), 'Trends in Intergenerational Class Mobility in England and Wales 1972–1983', *Sociology,* 20:1–24.

GOODMAN, L.A. (1979), 'Simple Models for the Analysis of Association in Cross-Classifications having Ordered Categories', *Journal of the American Statistical Association,* 74, 537–52.

GRANOVETTER, M. (1985), 'Economic Action and Social Structure: The Problem of Embeddedness', *American Journal of Sociology*, 91, 3:381–400.

HAKIM, C. (1992), 'Explaining Trends in Occupational Segregation: The Measurement, Causes and Circumstances of the Sexual Division of Labour', *European Sociological Review*, 8:127–52.

HALSEY, A.H. (1977), 'Towards Meritocracy? The Case of Britain', in A.H. Halsey and J. Karabel (eds), *Power and Ideology in Education*, New York: Oxford University Press.

HANNAN, D.F. and COMMINS, P. (1992), 'The Significance of Small Scale Land-holders in Ireland's Socio-Economic Transformation', in J.H. Goldthorpe and C.T. Whelan (eds), *The Development of Industrial Society in Ireland*, Oxford: Oxford University Press.

HAUSER, R.M. (1984a), 'Vertical Class Mobility in England, France and Sweden', *Acta Sociologica*, 27:87-110.

HAYES, B.C. and JONES, F.L. (1992), 'Marriage and Political Partisanship in Australia: Do Wives' Characteristics Make a Difference?', *Sociology*, 26:81-101.

HAYES, B. (1990), 'Intergenerational Mobility Among Employed and Non-Employed Women: The Australian Case', *Australian and New Zealand Journal of Sociology*, 26:368–88.

HAYES, B.C. and MILLER, R.L. (1993), 'The Silenced Voice: Female Social Mobility Patterns with Particular Reference to the British Isles', *British Journal of Sociology*, 44:653–72.

HEATH, A. (1981), *Social Mobility*, London: Fontana.

HEATH, A. and BRITTEN, R. (1984), 'Women's Jobs Do Make a Difference', *Sociology*, 18:475–90.

HEATH, A., MILLS, C. and ROBERTS, J. (1992), 'Towards Meritocracy? Recent Evidence on an Old Problem', in C. Crouch and A. Heath (eds), *Social Research and Social Reform*, Oxford: Clarendon Press.

HINDESS, B. (1987), *Politics and Class Analysis,*
    Oxford: Blackwell.

HOLTON, ROBERT J. and TURNER, BRYAN S. (1989), 'Has Class
    Analysis a Future? Max Weber and the Challenge of Liberalism to
    Gemeinschaftlich Accounts of Class', in Holton and Turner (eds),
    Weber on Economy and Society, London: Routledge and Kegan
    Paul.

HOPE, K. (1982), 'Vertical and Non-Vertical Class Mobility in Three
    Countries', *American Sociological Review,* 47:100–113.

HORAN, M. (1978), 'Is Status Attainment Research Atheoretical',
    American Sociological Review, 43, 1:95–110.

HOUT, M. (1983), *Mobility Tables,* London: Sage.

HOUT, M. (1989), *Following in Father's Footsteps: Social Mobility in
    Ireland,* London: Harvard University Press.

HOUT, M. (1984), 'Status Autonomy and Training in Occupational
    Mobility', *American Journal of Sociology,* 89/6: 1379–409.

HOUT, M., BROOKS, C. and MANZA, J. (1993), 'The Persistence of
    Classes in Post-Industrial Societies', *International Sociology,*
    8:259–68.

HOUT, M. and HAUSER, R.M. (1992), 'Symmetry and Hierarchy in
    Social Mobility: A Methodological Analysis of the Casmin
    Model of Class Mobility', *European Sociological Review,*
    83:239–66.

HOUT, M. and JACKSON, J. (1986), 'Dimensions of Occupational
    Mobility, in the Republic of Ireland', *European Sociological
    Review,* 2:114–37.

HUMPHREYS, P.C. (1983), *Public Service Employment: An
    Examination of Strategies in Ireland and Other European
    Countries,* Dublin: Institute of Public Administration.

JONSSON, J.O. (1993), 'Education, Social Mobility and Social Reproduction in Sweden: Patterns and Changes', in E.J. Hansen, S. Ringen, H. Uusitalo and R. Erikson (eds), *Welfare Trends in the Scandinavian Countries*, Armonk, New York: M. E. Sharpe.

KENNEDY, K. and McHUGH, D. (1984), 'Unemployment' in J. O'Hagan (ed.), *The Economy of Ireland: Policy and Performance*, Dublin: Irish Management Institute.

KERR, C. (1969), *Marshall, Marx and Modern Times*, Cambridge: Cambridge University Press.

KERR, C., DUNLOP, J.T., HARBISON, F. and MYERS, C.A. (1960/1973), *Industrialism and Industrial Man: The Problems of Labour and The Management of Economic Growth*, Cambridge, Mass.: Harvard University Press/London: Penguin.

KURZ, K. and Müller, W. (1987), 'Class Mobility in the Industrial World', *Annual Review of Sociology*, 13:417–42.

LIPSET, S.M. and BENDIX, R. (1959), *Social Mobility in Industrial Society*, Berkeley: University of California Press.

LUNDBERG, O. (1993), 'The Impact of Childhood Living Conditions on Illness and Mortality in Adulthood', *Social Science and Medicine*, 36:385-393.

LUNDBERG, O. (1991), 'Childhood Living Conditions, Health Status, and Social Mobility: A Contribution to the Health Selection Debate', *European Sociological Review*, 7, 2:149–62.

McRAE, S. (1990), 'Women and Class Analysis', in J. Clarke, C. Modgill and S. Modgill (eds), *John H. Goldthorpe: Consensus and Controversy*, London: The Falmer Press.

MACK, J. and LANSLEY, S. (1985), *Poor Britain*, London: George Allen and Unwin.

MARSHALL, G. (1990), 'John Goldthorpe and Class Analysis', in J. Clarke, C. Modgill and S. Modgill (eds), *John H. Goldthorpe: Consensus and Controversy*, London: The Falmer Press.

MARSHALL, G. (forthcoming), *British Journal of Sociology.*

MARSHALL, G., NEWBY, H., ROSE, D. and VOGLER, G. (1988), *Social Class in Modern Britain,* London: Unwin Hyman.

MARSHALL, G., ROBERTS, S., BURGOYNE, C. and ROUTH, D. (1994), *Social Class and Underclass in Britain and the United States,* Oxford: Nuffield College.

MAURICE, M., SELLIER, F. and SILVESTRE, J.J. (1986), *The Social Foundations of Industrial Power: A Comparison of France and Germany,* Cambridge: MIT Press.

MILLS, C.W. (1959), *The Sociological Imagination,* Oxford: Oxford University Press.

MIROWSKY, J. and ROSS, C. (1986), 'Social Patterns of Distress' in R. Turner, J.J. Short Jnr (eds), *Annual Review of Sociology,* 12:23–45.

MIROWSKY, J. and ROSS, C. (1989), *Social Causes of Psychological Distress,* New York: Aldine de Gruyter.

MIROWSKY, J.E. and ROSS, C.E. (1990), 'The Consolation Price Theory of Alienation', *American Journal of Sociology,* 95, 6:1,505–35.

MITCHELL, J.C. and CRITCHELEY, F. (1985), 'Configuration Similarity in Three Class Contexts in British Society', *Sociology,* 19, 1:72–92.

MORRIS, L. (1993), 'Is there a British Underclass?', *International Journal of Urban and Regional Research,* 17, 3:404–12.

MORRIS, L. (1994), *Dangerous Classes: The Underclass and Social Citizenship,* London: Routledge.

MORRIS, L. and IRWIN, S. (1989), 'Employment Historics and the Concept of the Underclass', *Sociology,* 28, 3:401–21.

MURGATROYD, L. (1984), 'Women, Men and the Social Grading of Occupations', *British Journal of Sociology*, 35:473–97.

MURRAY, C.A. (1984), *Losing Ground*, New York: Oxford University Press.

MURRAY, C.A. (1990), *The Emerging British Underclass*, London: I.E.A.

MURRAY, P. and WICKHAM, J. (1983), 'Technical Training and Technical Knowledge in an Irish Electronics Factory' in G. Winch (ed.), *Information Technology in Manufacturing Industry: Case Studies in Technological Change*, Aldershot: Gower Press.

NOLAN, B. (1990), 'Socio-Economic Mortality Differentials in Ireland', *The Economic and Social Review*, 21, 2:193–208.

NOLAN, B. (1991), *The Utilisation and Financing of Health Services in Ireland*, Dublin: The Economic and Social Research Institute.

NOLAN, B. and WHELAN, C.T. (1986), *Resources, Deprivation and the Measurement of Poverty*, Oxford: Clarendon Press.

O'CONNELL, P. (1995), The Transformation of Class Positions of Males and Females at Work in Ireland 1961–1990, unpublished paper.

O'CONNELL, P.J. and SEXTON, T.J. (1994), 'Labour Market Developments in Ireland 1973–1993' in S. Cantillon, J. Curtis, J. Fitzgerald (eds), *Economic Perspectives for the Medium Term*, Dublin: Economic and Social Research Institute.

O'CONNELL, P.J. and ROTTMAN, D.B. (1992), 'The Irish Welfare State in Comparative Perspective' in J.H. Goldthorpe and C.T. Whelan (eds), *The Development of Industrial Society in Ireland*, Oxford: Oxford University Press.

OFFE, C. (1985), 'Work: The Key Sociological Category' in C. Offe *Disorganised Capitalism*, Cambridge: Policy Press.

PAHL, J. (1989), *Money and Marriage*, Basingstoke: Macmillan.

PAHL, J. (1990), 'Household Spending, Personal Spending and the Control of Money in Marriage', *Sociology,* 24:119–38.

PAHL, R.E. (1989), 'Is the Emperor Naked? Some Comments on the Adequacy of Sociological Theory in Urban and Regional Research', *International Journal of Urban and Regional Research,* 13:709–20.

PAHL, R.E. (1991), 'R.E. Pahl Replies', *International Journal of Urban and Regional Research,* 15:127–29.

PARKIN, F. (1972), *Class Inequality and Political Order,* London: Paladin.

PARSONS, T. (1960), *Structure and Process in Modern Society,* Glencoe Ill.: Free Press.

PARSONS, T. (1964), 'Evolutionary Universals in Society', *American Sociological Review,* 29:339–57.

PARSONS, T. (1967), *Sociological Theory and Modern Society,* New York: Free Press.

PAYNE, G. (1990), 'Social Mobility in Britain: A Contrary View', in J. Clarke, C. Modgill and S. Modgill (eds), *John H. Goldthorpe: Consensus and Controversy,* London: Falmer.

PAWSON, R. (1993), 'Social Mobility', in D. Morgan and L. Stanley (eds), *Debates in Sociology,* Manchester: Manchester University Press.

RAFTERY, A.E. and HOUT, M. (1993), 'Maximally Maintained Inequality: Expansion, Reform and Opportunity in Irish Education, 1921–1975', *Sociology of Education,* 66, 1, 41–62.

RINGEN, S. (1987), *The Possibility of Politics,* Oxford: Clarendon Press.

RINGEN, S. (1988), 'Direct and Indirect Measures of Poverty', *Journal of Social Policy,* 17:351–66.

ROBERTS, H. (1993), 'The Women and Class Debate', in D. Morgan and L. Stanley (eds), *Debates in Sociology*, Manchester: Manchester University Press.

ROTTMAN, D.B. and O'CONNELL, P.J. (1982), *The Changing Social Structure in Unequal Achievement*, Dublin: Institute of Public Administration.

ROTTMAN, D. and REIDY, M. (1988), *Redistribution Through State Social Expenditure in the Republic of Ireland*, Dublin: National Economic and Social Council.

RUNCIMAN, W.G. (1990), 'How Many Classes are there in Contemporary British Society', *Sociology*, 24, 3:377–96.

SAUNDERS, P. (1990), *Social Class and Stratification*, London: Routledge.

SEXTON, J.J. (1982), 'Sectoral Changes in the Labour Force Over the Period 1961–1980', *Quarterly Economic Commentary*, August, Dublin: Economic and Social Research Institute.

SEXTON, J.J., WALSH, B.M., HANNAN, D.F. and McMAHON, D. (1991), *The Economic and Social Implications of Emigration*, Dublin: National Economic and Social Council.

SHAVIT, Y. and BLOSSFELD, H.P. (1993), *Persistent Inequality: Changing Educational Attainment in Thirteen Countries*, Boulder, Colorado: Westview Press.

SØRENSON, A.B. (1977), 'The Structure of Inequality and the Process of Attainment', *American Sociological Review*, 42:965–78.

SØRENSON, A.B. (1986), 'Theory and Methodology in Social Stratification' in U. Hemmelstrand (ed.), *Sociology from Crisis to Science?*, London: Sage.

SØRENSON, A.B. (1991), 'On the Usefulness of Class Analysis in Research on Social Mobility and Socioeconomic Inequality', *Acta Sociologica,* 34:71–87.

SØRENSON, J.P. (1992), 'More Matter with Less Art: A Rejoinder to Erikson and Goldthorpe', *European Sociological Review,* 8, 3:307–11.

SOSKICE, D. (1993), 'Social Skills from Mass Higher Education: Rethinking the Company Based Initial Training Paradigm', *Oxford Review of Economic Policy,* 9, 3:101–113.

SMITH, D.J. (1992), 'Defining the Underclass', in D.J. Smith (ed.), *Understanding the Underclass,* London: Policy Studies Institute.

STANWORTH, M. (1984), 'Women and Class Analysis: A Reply to John Goldthorpe', *Sociology,* 18, 2:159–70.

TOWNSEND, P. (1979), *Poverty in the United Kingdom,* Harmonsworth: Penguin.

TREIMAN, D.J. (1970), 'Industrialisation and Social Stratification', in E.O. Laumann (ed.), *Social Stratification: Research and Theory for the 1970s,* Indianapolis: Bobbs Merrill.

TUSSING, A.D. (1978), *Irish Educational Expenditure — Past, Present and Future,* Dublin: The Economic and Social Research Institute, Paper No. 92.

WHELAN, C.T. (1992a), 'The Role of Sense of Control and Social Support in Mediating of Psychological Distress: A Test of the Hypothesis of Functional Substitution', *The Economic and Social Review,* 23, 2:167–82.

WHELAN, C.T. (1992b), 'The Impact of Realistic and Illusory Control on Psychological Distress: A Test of the Model of Instrumental Realism', *The Economic and Social Review,* 23, 4:439–54.

WHELAN, C.T. (1992c), 'The Role of Income Life-style, Deprivation and Financial Strain in Mediating the Impact of Unemployment on Psychological Distress: Evidence from the Republic of Ireland', *Journal of Occupational and Organisational Psychology,* 65:331–44.

WHELAN, C.T. (1994), 'Social Class, Unemployment and Psychological Distress', *European Sociological Review*, 10, 1:49–61.

WHELAN, C.T. (1996). 'Marginalization, Deprivation and Fatalism in the Republic of Ireland: Class and Underclass Perspectives', *European Sociological Review*, 12, 1.

WHELAN, C.T., HANNAN, D.F. and CREIGHTON, S. (1991), *Unemployment, Poverty and Psychological Distress*, Dublin: The Economic and Social Research Institute.

WHELAN, C.T. and WHELAN, B.J. (1984), *Social Mobility in the Republic of Ireland: A Comparative Perspective*, Dublin: The Economic and Social Research Institute.

WHELAN, C.T. and WHELAN, B. (1988), *The Transition to Retirement*, Dublin: The Economic and Social Research Institute.

WHELAN, C.T., BREEN, R. and WHELAN, B.J. (1992), 'Industrialisation, Class Formation and Social Mobility in Ireland', in Goldthorpe and C.T. Whelan (eds), *The Development of Industrial Society*, Oxford: Oxford University Press.

WHELAN, C.T. and WHELAN, B.J. (1995), 'In What Sense is Poverty Multidimensional?', in G. Room (ed.), *The Measurement and Analysis of Social Exclusion*, Bristol: Policy Studies Press.

WILSON, W.J. (1987), *The Truly Disadvantaged: The Inner City, the Underclass and Public Policy*, Chicago: University of Chicago Press.

WILSON, W.J. (1991), 'Studying Inner City Social Dislocations', *American Sociological Review*, 56, 1:1–14.